MATHEMATICAL FOUNDATIONS
OF COMPUTER SCIENCE

MATHEMATICAL FOUNDATIONS OF COMPUTER SCIENCE

FORB.SC(COMPUTERSCIENCE),B.C.A,M.C.A AND ALL COMPUTER SCIENCE COURSES

PUSHPALATHA RAMESH

PARTRIDGE
A Penguin Random House Company

To order additional copies of this book, contact
Partridge India
000 800 10062 62
orders.india@partridgepublishing.com

www.partridgepublishing.com/india

Dedicated to my Husband

M.Ramesh

and my lovely Daughters

R.Vainavi

R.Vibhavi

for their love, support and guidance.

PREFACE

The Subject Mathematical Foundation of Computer Science is gaining importance in the curriculum of Engineering, especially Computer Science and Information Technology subjects. This book is the outcome of my teaching experience. This text contains six chapters.

Chapter I   Matrices which contains its types, Basic Operations in Matrix, Determinants, Properties of Determinants, Inverse of a Matrix, Rank of Matrix, Characteristics Roots (or) Eigen Values and Eigen Vectors and Cayley - Hamilton Theorem.

Chapter II   Set Theory includes, Definition, Basic Set Operations and Laws of Set Theory, Relations, Types of Relations, Representation of Relations in Matrix Form, Composition of Relations, Functions, Types of Functions and Principle of Mathematical Induction.

Chapter III   Boolean Algebra contains Definition, Karnaugh Map, Sum of Product and Product of Sum.

Chapter IV   Mathematical Logic covers Introduction, Connectives, Derived Connectives, Conditional Propositions, Conditional Statement, Bi-Conditional Statement, Order of Precedence for Logical Connectives, Converse, Inverse and Contra Positive Propositions, Tautologies and Contradictions, Equivalence of Formulae, Tautological Implications, Normal Forms, Principal Disjunctive Normal Form (PDNF), Principal Conjunctive Normal Form (PCNF), Indirect Method of Proof, Predicate Calculus, Bound and Free Variables and Inference Theory for Predicate Calculus.

Chapter V Graph Theory includes Graphs, Diagraph, Types of Graph, Definitions of Paths, Reachability and Connectedness, Matrix Representation of Graphs, Shortest Path in a Weighted Graph Algorithm, Shortest Path in a Graph without Weights, Traveling Salesman Problem, Binary Trees, Traversals of Binary Trees and Expression Trees.

Chapter VI Grammars And Language covers PSG (Phrase Structure Grammar), Types of Grammars, Productions, Derivation Tree, Left Most and Right Most Derivations, Finite State Automata (FSA), Deterministic Finite Automata (DFA), Non-Deterministic Finite-State Automata, Procedure for Converting NFA to DFA.

This edition is developed as per the syllabus of the M.C.A. It suits the needs of the B.Sc (Computer Science), B.C.A., M.C.A. and M.Sc curriculum of various universities.

Suggestions for improvements of the book shall be gratefully acknowledged.

Pushpalatha Ramesh

CONTENTS

CHAPTER - V 268-305

5. GRAPH THEORY

CHAPTER - VI 306-353

6. GRAMMARS AND LANGUAGE

CHAPTER – I

1. MATRICES

In 1848 in England, J.J. Sylvester first introduced the term "Matrix" which was Latin word, as the name for an array of numbers. Subject of Matrix was found by French Mathematicians Cayley and William Hamilton in the year 1858.

1.1 DEFINITION

MATRIX

A set of mn numbers (real or complex) arranged in the form of a rectangular array having m rows and n columns is called an m x n (m by n) matrix. We shall mostly be concerned with matrices having real numbers as entries. The horizontal arrays of a matrix are called its **rows** and the vertical arrays are called its **columns**. A matrix having m rows and n columns is said to have the **order m x n**.

A matrix A of order m x n can be represented in the following form.

$$A = \begin{bmatrix} a_{11} & a_{12} & \cdots & a_{1n} \\ a_{21} & a_{22} & \cdots & a_{2n} \\ \cdot & & & \\ \cdot & & & \\ \cdot & & & \\ a_{m1} & a_{m2} & \cdots & a_{mn} \end{bmatrix}$$

Denoted by $A=(a_{ij})_{m \times n}$ known as matrix A of **order** m x n or **size** m x n or **type** m x n.

The co-efficients a_{ij}, i = 1, 2,..., m, j = 1,..., n are known as elements of A. In a more concise manner, we also denote the matrix A by $[a_{ij}]$ by suppressing its order.

[a_{ij} is the entry at the intersection of ith row and j[th] column].

1

Let $A = \begin{bmatrix} 1 & 3 & 7 \\ 4 & 5 & 6 \end{bmatrix}$

Then $a_{11} = 1,$ $a_{12} = 3,$ $a_{13} = 7$

           $a_{21} = 4,$ $a_{22} = 5\, a_{23} = 6$

A matrix having only one column is called a **column vector** and a matrix with only one row is called **row vector**.

EQUALITY OF TWO MATRICES

Two matrices $A = [a_{ij}]$, $B = [b_{ij}]$ having the same order m x n are equal if $a_{ij} = b_{ij}$ for each i = 1, 2, ..., m and j = 1, 2, ..., n. Two matrices are said to be equal if they have the same order and their corresponding entries are equal.

1.2 TYPES OF MATRICES

VECTORS

Vectors are type of matrix having only one column or only one row.

(1) Row vector (or) Row Matrix

Any 1 x n matrix which has only one row and n columns is called a **row matrix** (or) a **row vector**. Here A is a row vector. $A = [a_{11}, a_{12}, ..., a_{1n}]$. Similarly any m x 1 matrix which has m rows and only one column is a **column matrix** or a **column vector**.

$B = \begin{bmatrix} a_{11} \\ a_{12} \\ \vdots \\ a_{m1} \end{bmatrix}$ Here B is a column vector.

Example

A matrix containing only one row (1 x n matrix) is called a row matrix. A = (1 6 9 3). A matrix containing only one column (m x 1 matrix) is called column matrix.

$$B = \begin{bmatrix} 1 \\ 0 \\ 2 \end{bmatrix}$$

Example

$A = \begin{bmatrix} a_{ij} \end{bmatrix}_{n \times n}$ for which i = j. A matrix which is not a square matrix is called a rectangular matrix.

NULL / ZERO MATRIX

In the m x n matrix, whose all elements are equal to 0 is called the **null matrix** or **zero matrix** of the type m x n it is denoted by O (read as zero)

Example

$$\begin{bmatrix} 0 & 0 & 0 & 0 & 0 \\ 0 & 0 & 0 & 0 & 0 \\ 0 & 0 & 0 & 0 & 0 \end{bmatrix}_{3 \times 5} \quad \text{and} \quad \begin{bmatrix} 0 & 0 & 0 \\ 0 & 0 & 0 \\ 0 & 0 & 0 \end{bmatrix}_{3 \times 3}$$

Zero matrixes of types 3 x 5 and 3 x 3 respectively.

Note : Order or type

m x n matrix is said to be of the type m x n it has m rows and n columns

A matrix having 4 rows and 2 columns will be the type 4 x 2.

Example

What is the type of matrix given below.

$$A = \begin{bmatrix} 3 & 2 & 1 & 4 & 5 \\ 2 & 2 & 1 & 5 & 3 \\ 2 & 2 & 5 & 6 & 7 \end{bmatrix}$$

Type of matrix is 3 x 5

UNIT MATRIX OR IDENTITY MATRIX

A square matrix each of whose diagonal elements is 1 and each of whose non-diagonal elements is equal to zero is called a **UNIT matrix or an Identity matrix** and is denoted by I.

Unit matrix of order n is denoted by I_n.

Example

$$I_4 = \begin{bmatrix} 1 & 0 & 0 & 0 \\ 0 & 1 & 0 & 0 \\ 0 & 0 & 1 & 0 \\ 0 & 0 & 0 & 1 \end{bmatrix}$$

$$I_3 = \begin{bmatrix} 1 & 0 & 0 \\ 0 & 1 & 0 \\ 0 & 0 & 1 \end{bmatrix} \qquad I_2 = \begin{bmatrix} 1 & 0 \\ 0 & 1 \end{bmatrix}$$

Thus a square matrix $A = [a_{ij}]$ is unit matrix

If $a_{ij} = 1$ when $i = j$ and $aij = 0$ when $i \neq j$

SQUARE MATRIX

A **square matrix** is an n x n matrix, (i.e) a matrix with same number of rows and columns. $A = \begin{bmatrix} a_{ij} \end{bmatrix}_{n \times n}$ for which $i = j$

Example

$$A = \begin{bmatrix} 2 & 3 \\ 4 & 2 \end{bmatrix}$$

A matrix which is not a square matrix is called a rectangular matrix. Now we consider special kinds of square matrices,

TRANSPOSE OF MATRIX

For any given matrix A, the matrix whose rows are columns of A and whose columns are rows of A is called the transpose of A and is denoted by A^T or A'. A is a m x n matrix, then A^T is a n x m matrix.

Example

$$A = \begin{pmatrix} 1 & 2 & 3 \\ 0 & 1 & 2 \end{pmatrix} \quad A^T \text{ or } A' = \begin{pmatrix} 1 & 0 \\ 2 & 1 \\ 3 & 2 \end{pmatrix}$$

SYMMETRIC MATRIX

A square matrix $A = (a_{ij})$ is a called a symmetric matrix of $a_{ij} = a_{ji}$ for all i and j.

A symmetric matrix remains unchanged if rows and columns are interchanged (i.e) called **transpose of matrix.** If the transpose of a matrix is equal to itself, that matrix is said to be **symmetric**. Two examples of symmetric matrices appear below.

$$(1)\ A = A^T \text{ (or) } A' = \begin{bmatrix} 1 & 2 \\ 2 & 3 \end{bmatrix} \qquad\qquad (2)\ B = B' = \begin{bmatrix} 5 & 6 & 7 \\ 6 & 3 & 2 \\ 7 & 2 & 1 \end{bmatrix}$$

Note that each of these matrices satisfy the defining requirement of symmetric matrix $A = A'$ and $B = B'$

DIAGONAL MATRIX

A square matrix in which all the elements other than the leading diagonal are zero called a **Diagonal matrix**.

A diagonal matrix is a special kind of symmetric matrix. It is a symmetric matrix with zeros in the off-diagonal elements.

Example

$$A = \begin{bmatrix} 1 & 0 \\ 0 & 3 \end{bmatrix} \qquad B = \begin{bmatrix} 5 & 0 & 0 \\ 0 & 3 & 0 \\ 0 & 0 & 1 \end{bmatrix}$$

SCALAR MATRIX

A **scalar matrix** is a special kind of diagonal matrix. It is a diagonal matrix with equal-valued elements along the diagonal.

Example

$$A = \begin{bmatrix} 3 & 0 \\ 0 & 3 \end{bmatrix} \qquad B = \begin{bmatrix} 5 & 0 & 0 \\ 0 & 5 & 0 \\ 0 & 0 & 5 \end{bmatrix}$$

SUB MATRIX

A **sub matrix** is obtained by deleting any number of rows and any number of columns from a given matrix A.

Example

$$A = \begin{bmatrix} 1 & 2 & 3 & 9 \\ 7 & 11 & 6 & 5 \\ 0 & 2 & 1 & 8 \end{bmatrix}$$

Sub matrix of $A = \begin{bmatrix} 1 & 2 & 3 \\ 0 & 2 & 1 \end{bmatrix}$ it is obtained by omitting second row and 4th column.

TRACE OF A

In a square matrix A, the elements a_{ij} (i = j) are called its diagonal elements and

their sum is called the trace of A denoted by trace $A = \sum\limits_{i=1}^{n} a_{ij}$

Example

$$A = \begin{bmatrix} 3 & 2 & 1 \\ 4 & 2 & 0 \\ 2 & 3 & 9 \end{bmatrix}$$

Consider the diagonal elements

Trace of A $= \sum\limits_{i=1}^{n} a_{ij}$ $= 3 + 2 + 9 = 14$

SKEW SYMMETRIC MATRIX

A square matrix A = (a_{ij}) is said to be **skew symmetric** if aij = -aji ----- (1) for

all i and j. In equ (1) put j = i. Therefore in a skew symmetric matrix a_{ii} = $-a_{ii}$.

We note that a_{ii} = 0 for all i. That is all the diagonal elements are zero in a skew

symmetric matrix.

Example

$$\begin{pmatrix} 0 & -4 & 5 \\ 4 & 0 & 7 \\ 5 & -7 & 0 \end{pmatrix}$$ is a skew symmetric matrix.

TRIANGULAR MATRIX

UPPER TRIANGULAR MATRIX

A square matrix in which all elements below the principal diagonals are zero is

called **upper triangular matrix**.

A square matric A = (a$_{ij}$) of order n is said to be upper triangular matrix a$_{ij}$ =0

for i > j such as
$$\begin{bmatrix} a_{11} & a_{12} & \cdots & a_{1n} \\ 0 & a_{22} & \cdots & a_{2n} \\ \cdots & \cdots & \cdots & \cdots \\ 0 & 0 & \cdots & a_{nn} \end{bmatrix}$$

Example

$$\begin{pmatrix} 6 & -1 & 5 \\ 0 & 4 & 3 \\ 0 & 0 & 2 \end{pmatrix}$$

LOWER TRIANGULAR MATRIX

A square matrix in which all the elements above the principal diagonals are zero is called a **lower triangular matrix**.

A square matrix A = (a$_{ij}$) is said to be lower triangular matrix if a$_{ij}$ = 0 for i < j

such as
$$\begin{pmatrix} a_{11} & 0 & \cdots & 0 \\ a_{21} & a_{22} & \cdots & 0 \\ \cdots & \cdots & \cdots & \cdots \\ a_{n1} & a_{n2} & \cdots & a_{nn} \end{pmatrix}$$

Example

$$\begin{pmatrix} 1 & 0 & 0 \\ 4 & 2 & 0 \\ -1 & 3 & 3 \end{pmatrix}$$

A square matrix A is said to be **triangular** if it is an upper or lower triangular matrix.

A square matrix of order n which is both upper and lower triangular is known as a **diagonal matrix.**

A square matrix of the form

$$A = \begin{pmatrix} a_{11} & a_{12} & 0 & 0 \\ a_{21} & a_{22} & a_{23} & 0 \\ 0 & a_{32} & a_{33} & a_{34} \\ 0 & 0 & a_{43} & a_{44} \end{pmatrix}$$ is known as a **tridiagonal matrix**.

1.3 BASIC OPERATIONS OF MATRICES

(1) EQUALITY OF MATRICES

Two matrices $A = [a_{ij}]$ and $B = [b_{ij}]$ are said to be equal if

(i) they are of the same size and

(ii) The elements in the corresponding places of the two matrices are the same.

(i.e) $a_{ij} = b_{ij}$ for each pair of subscripts i and j. If two matrices A and B are

equal, we write $A = B$, if two matrices A and B are not equal, we write $A \neq B$.

If two matrices are not of the same size, they cannot be equal.

Example 1

Are the following matrices equal ?

$$A = \begin{pmatrix} 1 & 3 & -1 \\ 2 & 4 & 2 \\ 3 & 0 & 7 \\ 1 & 0 & 9 \end{pmatrix} \qquad B = \begin{pmatrix} 1 & 3 & -1 \\ 2 & 4 & 2 \\ 3 & 0 & 7 \\ 1 & 0 & 9 \end{pmatrix}$$

Solution

The matrix A is of the type 4 x 3 and the matrix B is also of the type 4 x 3. Also

the corresponding elements of A and b are equal Hence $A = B$.

Example 2

Find the value of a, b, c and d. So that matrices A and B may be equal, where

$$A = \begin{pmatrix} a & b \\ c & d \end{pmatrix}, \quad B = \begin{pmatrix} 1 & -1 \\ 0 & 3 \end{pmatrix}$$

Solution

We see that the matrices A and B are of the same size 2 x 2. If A = B, then the corresponding elements of A and B must be equal.

∴ If a = 1, b = -1, c = 0 & d = 3 then we will have A = B.

Example 3

Are the following matrices equal ?

$$A = \begin{pmatrix} 1 & 7 & 3 \\ 2 & 4 & 0 \end{pmatrix}, \qquad B = \begin{pmatrix} 1 & 7 & 3 \\ 2 & 4 & -1 \end{pmatrix}$$

Solution

Here both the matrices A and B are of the same size. But $a_{23} = 0$, and $b_{23} = -1$. Thus $a_{23} \neq b_{23}$. Therefore A $\neq$ B.

(2) ADDITION OF MATRICES

Definition

Let A and B be two matrices of the same type m x n. Then their sum (to be denoted by A + B is defined to be the matrix of the type m x n obtained by adding the corresponding elements of A and B.

$$A = \begin{pmatrix} a_{11} & a_{12} & \cdots & a_{1n} \\ a_{21} & a_{22} & \cdots & a_{2n} \\ \vdots & & & \\ a_{m1} & a_{m2} & \cdots & a_{mn} \end{pmatrix}_{m \times n} \quad \text{and} \quad B = \begin{pmatrix} b_{11} & b_{12} & \cdots & b_{1n} \\ b_{21} & b_{22} & \cdots & b_{2n} \\ \vdots & & & \\ b_{m1} & b_{m2} & \cdots & b_{mn} \end{pmatrix}_{m \times n}$$

then

$$A + B = \begin{pmatrix} a_{11} + b_{11} & a_{12} + b_{12} & \cdots & a_{1n} + b_{1n} \\ a_{21} + b_{21} & a_{22} + b_{22} & \cdots & a_{2n} + b_{2n} \\ \vdots & & & \\ a_{m1} + b_{m1} & a_{m2} + b_{m2} & \cdots & a_{mn} + b_{mn} \end{pmatrix}_{m \times n}$$

Example

$$A = \begin{pmatrix} 3 & 2 & -1 \\ 4 & -3 & 1 \end{pmatrix}_{2\times3} \quad \text{and} \quad B = \begin{pmatrix} 1 & -2 & 7 \\ 3 & 2 & -1 \end{pmatrix}_{2\times3}$$

then $A + B = \begin{pmatrix} 3+1 & 2-2 & -1+7 \\ 4+3 & -3+2 & 1-1 \end{pmatrix} = \begin{pmatrix} 4 & 0 & 6 \\ 7 & -1 & 0 \end{pmatrix}_{2\times3}$

Note :

If two matrices A and B are of the same size they are said to be conformable for addition. If the matrices A and B are not of the same size, we cannot find their sum.

PROPERTIES OF MATRIX ADDITION

(i) Matrix Addition is Commutative :

If A and B be two m x n matrices then A + B = B + A ----- (1)

Proof

Let $A = \left(a_{ij}\right)_{mxn}$ and $B = \left(b_{ij}\right)_{mxn}$ then

$A + B = \left(a_{ij}\right)_{mxn} + \left(b_{ij}\right)_{mxn}$

$\qquad = \left(a_{ij} + b_{ij}\right)_{mxn}$

Similarly,

$B + A = \left(b_{ij}\right)_{mxn} + \left(a_{ij}\right)_{mxn}$

$\qquad = \left(b_{ij} + a_{ij}\right)_{mxn}$

Since a_{ij} and b_{ij} are numbers and addition of numbers are commutative.

$\therefore a_{ij} + b_{ij} = b_{ij} + a_{ij}$

Hence the above result (1).

(ii) Matrix Addition is Associative :

If A, B, C be three matrices each of type m x n, then $(A+B)+C = A+(B+C)$ ---

--- (1)

Proof

$$\text{Let } A = \left(a_{ij}\right)_{mxn}, \quad B = \left(b_{ij}\right)_{mxn}, \quad C = \left(C_{ij}\right)_{mxn}$$

$$\text{Then } (A+B)+C = \left(\left(a_{ij}\right)_{mxn} + \left(b_{ij}\right)_{mxn}\right) + \left(c_{ij}\right)_{mxn}$$

$$= \left(a_{ij}+b_{ij}\right)_{mxn} + \left(c_{ij}\right)_{mxn} \qquad \text{[By definition of A + B]}$$

$$= \left(\left(a_{ij}+b_{ij}\right)+c_{ij}\right)_{mxn}$$

$$= \left(a_{ij}+\left(b_{ij}+c_{ij}\right)\right)_{mxn}$$

Since a_{ij}, b_{ij}, c_{ij} are numbers and addition of numbers are associative.

$$= \left(a_{ij}\right)_{mxn} + \left(\left(b_{ij}\right)_{mxn} + \left(c_{ij}\right)_{mxn}\right)$$

$$= A + (B+C)$$

Hence the above result (1).

(iii) Distributive Law

$$K(A+B) = KA + KB$$

K is any complex number called **scalar**.

Example

Evaluate

$$2\begin{pmatrix} 1 & 2 & 3 \\ -1 & -3 & 2 \end{pmatrix} + 3\begin{pmatrix} 1 & 0 & 2 \\ 3 & 4 & 5 \end{pmatrix}$$

$$= \begin{pmatrix} 2 & 4 & 6 \\ -2 & -6 & 4 \end{pmatrix} + \begin{pmatrix} 3 & 0 & 6 \\ 9 & 12 & 15 \end{pmatrix} = \begin{pmatrix} 5 & 4 & 12 \\ 7 & 6 & 9 \end{pmatrix}$$

(iv) Existence of Additive Identity

If O be the m x n matrix each of whose elements is zero then

A + O = A = O + A for every m x n matrix

Proof

Let $A = \left(a_{ij}\right)_{mxn}$. Then

$A + O = \left(a_{ij} + o\right)_{mxn} = \left(a_{ij}\right)_{mxn} = A$

Also, $O + A = \left(o + a_{ij}\right)_{mxn} = \left(a_{ij}\right)_{mxn} = A$

(v) Existence of the Additive Inverse

Let $A = \left(a_{ij}\right)_{mxn}$. Then the negative of the matrix A is defined as the matrix $\left(-a_{ij}\right)_{mxn}$ and is denoted by - A.

- A matrix is the additive inverse of the matrix A.

$\therefore -A + A = 0$

$\therefore A + (-A) = 0$

Here O is the null matrix of the type m x n. It is identity element for matrix addition.

SUBTRACTION OF TWO MATRICES

Definition

If A and B are two m x n matrices, then we define

A − B = A + (-B)

Thus the difference A − B is obtained by subtracting from each element of A the corresponding element of B.

Example

$$A = \begin{pmatrix} a_{11} & b_{12} & c_{13} \\ a_{21} & b_{22} & c_{23} \end{pmatrix} \qquad B = \begin{pmatrix} x_{11} & y_{12} & z_{13} \\ x_{21} & y_{22} & z_{23} \end{pmatrix}$$

$$A - B = \begin{pmatrix} a_{11} - x_{11} & b_{12} - y_{12} & c_{13} - z_{13} \\ a_{21} - x_{21} & b_{22} - y_{22} & c_{23} - z_{23} \end{pmatrix}$$

Example

If $A = \begin{pmatrix} 1 & 0 \\ 2 & -1 \end{pmatrix}$, $B = \begin{pmatrix} 3 & 7 \\ 4 & 8 \end{pmatrix}$, $C = \begin{pmatrix} -1 & 1 \\ 0 & 0 \end{pmatrix}$ verify that $A + (B + C) = (A + B) + C$

Solution

We have $A + B$ $= \begin{pmatrix} 1 & 0 \\ 2 & -1 \end{pmatrix} + \begin{pmatrix} 3 & 7 \\ 4 & 8 \end{pmatrix} = \begin{pmatrix} 1+3 & 0+7 \\ 2+4 & -1+8 \end{pmatrix} = \begin{pmatrix} 4 & 7 \\ 6 & +7 \end{pmatrix}$

$\therefore (A + B) + C$ $= \begin{pmatrix} 4 & 7 \\ 6 & 7 \end{pmatrix} + \begin{pmatrix} -1 & 1 \\ 0 & 0 \end{pmatrix} = \begin{pmatrix} 3 & 8 \\ 6 & 7 \end{pmatrix}$ ------ (1)

$B + C$ $= \begin{pmatrix} 3 & 7 \\ 4 & 8 \end{pmatrix} + \begin{pmatrix} -1 & 1 \\ 0 & 0 \end{pmatrix} = \begin{pmatrix} 2 & 8 \\ 4 & 8 \end{pmatrix}$ ------ (2)

$A + (B + C)$ $= \begin{pmatrix} 1 & 0 \\ 2 & -1 \end{pmatrix} + \begin{pmatrix} 2 & 8 \\ 4 & 8 \end{pmatrix}$ $= \begin{pmatrix} 3 & 8 \\ 6 & 7 \end{pmatrix}$

From (1) & (2)

$(1) = (2)$

$\therefore (A + B) + C = A + (B + C)$

Hence the result.

2) Find the additive inverse of the matrix $A = \begin{pmatrix} 2 & 3 & -1 & 1 \\ 3 & -1 & 2 & 2 \\ 1 & 2 & 8 & 7 \end{pmatrix}$

Solution

The additive inverse of the 3 x 4 matrix A is the 3 x 4 matrix each of whose elements is the negative of the corresponding element of A. Therefore if we denote the additive inverse of A by -A.

We have

$$-A = \begin{pmatrix} -2 & -3 & 1 & -1 \\ -3 & 1 & -2 & -2 \\ -1 & -2 & -8 & -7 \end{pmatrix}$$

Obviously, $A + (-A) = -A + A = 0$

Where O is the null matrix of the type 3 x 4.

(3) If $A = \begin{pmatrix} 2 & 7 \\ 9 & 8 \end{pmatrix}$ $B = \begin{pmatrix} 1 & 2 \\ 0 & 3 \end{pmatrix}$ find $A - B$

Solution

According to our definition of $A - B$ we have

$A - B = A + (-B)$

$$= \begin{pmatrix} 2 & 7 \\ 9 & 8 \end{pmatrix} + \begin{pmatrix} -1 & -2 \\ 0 & -3 \end{pmatrix} = \begin{pmatrix} 2-1 & 7-2 \\ 9+0 & 8-3 \end{pmatrix} = \begin{pmatrix} 1 & 5 \\ 9 & 5 \end{pmatrix}$$

MATRIX MULTIPLICATION

Here multiplication of rows and columns matrices. Let us consider a row matrix A of type 1 x m and column matrix of type m x1.

(i.e) $A = [a_{11} \ a_{12} \ a_{13} \ .... \ a_{1m}]_{1 \times m}$

$$B = \begin{bmatrix} b_{11} \\ b_{21} \\ \vdots \\ b_{m1} \end{bmatrix}_{m \times 1}$$

It is to be noted that **the number of columns in A is the same as the number of rows in B**. Then the product.

Example

$$A = \begin{pmatrix} 1 & 2 & 3 \end{pmatrix}_{1 \times 3} \qquad B = \begin{bmatrix} 5 \\ 3 \\ 2 \end{bmatrix}_{3 \times 1}$$

$$AB = [1 \times 5 + 2 \times 3 + 3 \times 2] = [5 + 6 + 6] = (17)_{1 \times 1}$$

$$AB = (17)$$

Note

Type of A is $1 \times m$ and

Type of B is $m \times 1$

Then the Type of Result AB is 1×1.

Example 1

If $A = \begin{pmatrix} 2 & 3 & 4 \\ 1 & 2 & 3 \\ -1 & 1 & 2 \end{pmatrix}$, $B = \begin{pmatrix} 1 & 3 & 0 \\ -1 & 2 & 1 \\ 0 & 0 & 2 \end{pmatrix}$

Find AB and BA and show that AB ≠ BA.

Solution

We have

$$AB = \begin{pmatrix} 2 & 3 & 4 \\ 1 & 2 & 3 \\ -1 & 1 & 2 \end{pmatrix} \begin{pmatrix} 1 & 3 & 0 \\ -1 & 2 & 1 \\ 0 & 0 & 2 \end{pmatrix}$$

$$= \begin{pmatrix} 2.1+3.-1+4.0 & 2.3+3.2+4.0 & 2.0+3.1+4.2 \\ 1.1+2.-1+3.0 & 1.3+2.2+3.0 & 1.0+2.1+3.2 \\ -1.1+(-1.1)+2.0 & -1.3+1.2+2.0 & -1.0+1.1+2.2 \end{pmatrix}$$

$$= \begin{pmatrix} -1 & 12 & 11 \\ -1 & 7 & 8 \\ -2 & -1 & 5 \end{pmatrix}_{3 \times 3}$$

Similarly

$$BA = \begin{pmatrix} 5 & 9 & 13 \\ -1 & 2 & 4 \\ -2 & 2 & 4 \end{pmatrix}_{3 \times 3}$$

∴ The matrix AB is of type 3×3 and the matrix BA is also of the type 3×3.

But the corresponding elements of these matrices are not equal. Hence AB ≠ BA.

Example 2

If $A = \begin{pmatrix} -1 & 2 \\ 3 & 1 \end{pmatrix}$ $B = \begin{pmatrix} 1 & -1 \\ 3 & 4 \\ -1 & 5 \end{pmatrix}$ does AB exist ?

A is a matrix of type 2×2. While B is a matrix of type 3×2.

Here **number of rows in B is not equal to number of columns in A**.

Hence A and B are not conformable for multiplication and therefore AB does

not exist.

Exercise Problems

1) Find the product matrix of the matrices.

$$A = \begin{pmatrix} 2 & 1 & 2 & 1 \\ 1 & 1 & 1 & 1 \end{pmatrix}, \quad B = \begin{pmatrix} 2 & -1 & 0 \\ 0 & 4 & 1 \\ -2 & 1 & 0 \\ 1 & -3 & 2 \end{pmatrix} \qquad \textbf{Answer} \begin{pmatrix} 1 & 1 & 3 \\ 1 & 1 & 3 \end{pmatrix}$$

2) If $A = \begin{pmatrix} 1 & -2 & 3 \\ -4 & 2 & 5 \end{pmatrix}$, $B = \begin{pmatrix} 2 & 3 \\ 4 & 5 \\ 2 & 1 \end{pmatrix}$ Find AB and show that AB $\neq$ BA.

3) If $A = \begin{pmatrix} 1 & 0 & -2 \\ 2 & 2 & 4 \\ 0 & 0 & 2 \end{pmatrix}$, Show that A satisfies the equation $A^2 - 3A + 2\,I = 0$

Answer $A^2 = \begin{pmatrix} 1 & 0 & -6 \\ 6 & 4 & 12 \\ 0 & 0 & 0 \end{pmatrix}$

Hence $A^2 - 3A + 2\,I = 0$

$$= \begin{pmatrix} 1 & 0 & -6 \\ 6 & 4 & 12 \\ 0 & 0 & 0 \end{pmatrix} - 3 \begin{pmatrix} 1 & 0 & -2 \\ 2 & 2 & 4 \\ 0 & 0 & 0 \end{pmatrix} + 2 \begin{pmatrix} 1 & 0 & 0 \\ 0 & 1 & 0 \\ 0 & 0 & 1 \end{pmatrix} \qquad = \begin{pmatrix} 0 & 0 & 0 \\ 0 & 0 & 0 \\ 0 & 0 & 0 \end{pmatrix}$$

Example Problems

1) If $A = \begin{pmatrix} 4 & 2 \\ -1 & 1 \end{pmatrix}$, Find $(A - 2I)\ (A - 3I)$

Solution

$$A - 2I = \begin{pmatrix} 4 & 2 \\ -1 & 1 \end{pmatrix} - 2 \begin{pmatrix} 1 & 0 \\ 0 & 1 \end{pmatrix} \qquad = \begin{pmatrix} 2 & 2 \\ -1 & 1 \end{pmatrix}$$

$$A - 3I = \begin{pmatrix} 1 & 2 \\ -1 & -2 \end{pmatrix}$$

$$(A - 2I)\ (A - 3I) = 0$$

5) If $A = \begin{pmatrix} -1 & 2 \\ 2 & 3 \end{pmatrix}$, $B = \begin{pmatrix} 3 & 0 \\ 1 & 1 \end{pmatrix}$, verify that $(A + B)^2 = A^2 + AB + BA + B^2$ can this

be put in the simple form $A^2 + 2AB + B^2$?

$$A + B \qquad = \begin{pmatrix} 2 & 2 \\ 3 & 4 \end{pmatrix}$$

$$(A + B)^2 \quad = \quad \begin{pmatrix} 10 & 12 \\ 18 & 22 \end{pmatrix} \qquad \text{------ (1)}$$

$$A^2 = \begin{pmatrix} 5 & 4 \\ 4 & 13 \end{pmatrix}, \ B^2 = \begin{pmatrix} 9 & 0 \\ 4 & 1 \end{pmatrix}, \ AB = \begin{pmatrix} -1 & 2 \\ 9 & 3 \end{pmatrix}, \ BA = \begin{pmatrix} -3 & 6 \\ 1 & 5 \end{pmatrix}$$

$$\therefore A^2 + AB + BA + B^2 = \begin{pmatrix} 10 & 12 \\ 18 & 22 \end{pmatrix} \qquad \text{------- (2)}$$

From (1) and (2)

$$(A+B)^2 = A^2 + AB + BA + B^2$$

Here $AB \neq BA$

$\therefore$ The given relation cannot be put in the simple form

$$(A+B)^2 = A^2 + 2AB + B^2$$

1.4 DETERMINANTS

Consider the 2×2 matrix

$A = \begin{pmatrix} a_{11} & a_{12} \\ a_{21} & a_{22} \end{pmatrix}$. The determinant of the matrix A is the number $a_{11}.a_{22} - a_{12}.a_{21}$

and is denoted by $\det(A)$ or $|A|$. The determinant of the matrix A is also denoted by

$$|A| = \begin{vmatrix} a_{11} & a_{12} \\ a_{21} & a_{22} \end{vmatrix}$$

Consider the 3×3 matrix

$$A = \begin{pmatrix} a_{11} & a_{12} & a_{13} \\ a_{21} & a_{22} & a_{23} \\ a_{31} & a_{32} & a_{33} \end{pmatrix}$$

The determinant of the matrix A is the scalar given by

$$|A| \quad = a_{11}(a_{22}.a_{33} - a_{23}.a_{32}) - a_{12}(a_{21}.a_{33} - a_{31}.a_{23}) + a_{13}(a_{21}.a_{32} - a_{31}.a_{22})$$

This can also be written as

$$|A| = a_{11} \begin{vmatrix} a_{22} & a_{23} \\ a_{32} & a_{33} \end{vmatrix} - a_{12} \begin{vmatrix} a_{21} & a_{23} \\ a_{31} & a_{33} \end{vmatrix} + a_{13} \begin{vmatrix} a_{21} & a_{22} \\ a_{31} & a_{32} \end{vmatrix}$$

Let M_{ij} be the matrix obtained by deleting i^{th} row and j^{th} column of A.

The determinant $|M_{ij}|$ is called a **minor of the matrix A.**

The scalar $A_{ij} = (-1)^{i+j} |M_{ij}|$ - is called **the co-factor of the element a_{ij} of the matrix**. We now define the determinant of matrix A in terms of co-factors such as

$$|A| = a_{11}A_{11} + a_{12}A_{12} + a_{13}A_{13}$$

Where $\quad A_{11} = \begin{vmatrix} a_{22} & a_{23} \\ a_{32} & a_{33} \end{vmatrix}, \quad A_{12} = \begin{vmatrix} a_{21} & a_{23} \\ a_{31} & a_{33} \end{vmatrix}, \quad A_{13} = \begin{vmatrix} a_{21} & a_{22} \\ a_{31} & a_{32} \end{vmatrix}$

We can also write

$$|A| = a_{21}A_{21} + a_{22}A_{22} + a_{23}A_{23}$$

$$|A| = a_{31}A_{31} + a_{32}A_{32} + a_{33}A_{33}$$

Note

Determinants are defined only for square matrices.

- A square matrix A is said to be **singular** if its determinant is zero.

- A square matrix A is said to be **non-singular** if its determinant is not equal to zero.

Example 1

Find the determinant for the given matrix.

$$\begin{vmatrix} 1 & 3 & 2 \\ 4 & 2 & 3 \\ 2 & 1 & 9 \end{vmatrix} \begin{vmatrix} + & - & + \\ - & + & - \\ + & - & + \end{vmatrix}$$

$$= 1 \begin{vmatrix} 2 & 3 \\ 1 & 9 \end{vmatrix} - 3 \begin{vmatrix} 4 & 3 \\ 1 & 9 \end{vmatrix} + 2 \begin{vmatrix} 4 & 2 \\ 2 & 1 \end{vmatrix}$$

$$= 1(18 - 3) - 3(36 - 6) + 2(4 - 4)$$

$$= 1(15) - 3(30) + 2(0)$$

$$= 15 - 90 + 0 = -75$$

Example 2

Find the value of $\begin{vmatrix} 1 & 2 \\ 3 & 8 \end{vmatrix}$

Solution

$$\begin{vmatrix} 1 & 2 \\ 3 & 8 \end{vmatrix} = 8 - 6 = 2$$

Example 3

Find the value of $\begin{vmatrix} 1 & 2 & 3 \\ 3 & 2 & 4 \\ 1 & 3 & -1 \end{vmatrix}$

Solution

$$= 1(-2 -12) - 2(-3 - 4) + 3(9 - 2)$$

$$= 1\,(-14) - 2\,(-7) + 3\,(7) \qquad = -\cancel{14} + \cancel{14} + 21 = 21$$

MINORS AND COFACTORS

Definition : Minor

The **minor** of an element in a determinant is the determinant got by suppressing the row and column in which the element appears. The order of the minor of an element in a determinant A is one less than the order of determinant A.

The minor of the element in the ith row and j^{th} column is denoted by M_{ij}.

Definition : Cofactor

The signed minor is called **cofactor**. The cofactor of the element in the ith row, j^{th} column is denoted by c_{ij} and $c_{ij} = (-1)^{i+j}\, M_{ij}$.

Note

The expansion of 3rd order determinant when expanded in terms of minors. The sign of the cofactor of the element will be as follows.

$$\begin{vmatrix} + & - & + \\ - & + & - \\ + & - & + \end{vmatrix}$$

Example Problems

(1) Find the minors and cofactors of elements -3, 3, -4, 1 in the determinant

$$\begin{vmatrix} 2 & -1 & 2 \\ 1 & 2 & -3 \\ 3 & -1 & -4 \end{vmatrix}.$$

(i)   Minor of (-3) $= M_{23} = \begin{vmatrix} 2 & -1 \\ 3 & -1 \end{vmatrix}$

Minor of (3) $= M_{31} = \begin{vmatrix} -1 & 2 \\ 2 & -3 \end{vmatrix}$

Minor of (-4) $= M_{33} = \begin{vmatrix} 2 & -1 \\ 1 & 2 \end{vmatrix}$

Minor of (1) $= M_{21} = \begin{vmatrix} -1 & 2 \\ -1 & 4 \end{vmatrix}$

(ii)   Cofactor of (-3) $= C_{23} = (-1)^{2+3} \begin{vmatrix} 2 & -1 \\ 3 & -1 \end{vmatrix} = - \begin{vmatrix} 2 & -1 \\ 3 & -1 \end{vmatrix}$

Cofactor of (3) $= C_{31} = (-1)^{3+1} = \begin{vmatrix} -1 & 2 \\ 2 & -3 \end{vmatrix} = + \begin{vmatrix} -1 & 2 \\ 2 & -3 \end{vmatrix}$

Cofactor of (-4) $= C_{33} = (-1)^{3+3} \begin{vmatrix} 2 & -1 \\ 1 & 2 \end{vmatrix} = + \begin{vmatrix} 2 & -1 \\ 1 & 2 \end{vmatrix}$

Cofactor of (1) $= C_{21} = (-1)^{2+1} \begin{vmatrix} -1 & 2 \\ -1 & -4 \end{vmatrix} = - \begin{vmatrix} -1 & 2 \\ -1 & -4 \end{vmatrix}$

(2) Find the value of the following determinants

(i) $\begin{vmatrix} \cos\theta & -\sin\theta \\ \sin\theta & \cos\theta \end{vmatrix}$

Solution

$$= \cos^2\theta - (-\sin^2\theta) \quad = \cos^2\theta + \sin^2\theta = 1$$

(ii) $\begin{vmatrix} a+ib & c+id \\ -c+id & a-ib \end{vmatrix}$

Solution

$$= (a+ib)(a-ib) - (c+id)(-c+id)$$
$$= a^2 - i b a + i b a - i^2 b^2 + c^2 - c i d + c i d - i^2 d^2$$
$$= a^2 + c^2 - i^2 b^2 - i^2 d^2 \qquad\qquad [i^2 = -1]$$
$$= a^2 + c^2 + b^2 + d^2$$

(iii) $\begin{vmatrix} 1 & 1 & 1 \\ 3 & 2 & 1 \\ 5 & 3 & 1 \end{vmatrix}$

Solution

$$= 1\,(2-3) - 1\,(3-5) + 1\,(9-10)$$
$$= 1\,(-1) - 1\,(-2) + 1\,(-1)$$
$$= -1 + 2 - 1 \qquad = -2 + 2 = 0$$

(iv) $\begin{vmatrix} 2 & -1 & 2 \\ 1 & 2 & -3 \\ 3 & -1 & -4 \end{vmatrix}$

Solution

$$= 2\,(-8-3) - (-1)\,(-4+9) + 2\,(-1-6)$$
$$= 2\,(-11) + 1\,(5) + 2\,(-7) \qquad = -22 + 5 - 14 \qquad = -36 + 5 = -31$$

(v) $\begin{vmatrix} a & h & g \\ h & b & f \\ g & f & c \end{vmatrix}$

Solution

$$= a(bc - f^2) - h(hc - gf) + g(hf - bg)$$
$$= abc - af^2 - h^2c + gfh + ghf - bg^2$$
$$= -af^2 - bg^2 - ch^2 + 2gfh + abc$$

(vi) $\begin{vmatrix} 1 & a & b+c \\ 1 & b & c+a \\ 1 & c & a+b \end{vmatrix} = 0$ prove without expansion

Solution

$$\text{L.H.S} \quad = \begin{vmatrix} 1 & a & b+c \\ 1 & b & c+a \\ 1 & c & a+b \end{vmatrix} c_3 \leftarrow c_2 + c_3$$

$$= \begin{bmatrix} 1 & a & a+b+c \\ 1 & b & a+b+c \\ 1 & c & a+b+c \end{bmatrix}$$

$$= (a+b+c) \begin{vmatrix} 1 & a & 1 \\ 1 & b & 1 \\ 1 & c & 1 \end{vmatrix}$$

$$= (a+b+c)\left[1(b-c) - a(1-1) + 1(c-b)\right]$$

$$= (a+b+c)\left[\cancel{b} - \cancel{c} - \cancel{a} + \cancel{a} + \cancel{c} - \cancel{b}\right]$$

$$= (a+b+c)(0) = 0 = \text{R. H. S.}$$

(3) Solve for x

(i) $\begin{vmatrix} x & 6 \\ 6 & x \end{vmatrix} + \begin{vmatrix} 1 & -1 \\ -1 & 1 \end{vmatrix} = 0$

Solution

$$x^2 - 36 + 1 - 1 = 0$$
$$x^2 - 36 = 0$$
$$x^2 = 36$$
$$\therefore x = \pm 6$$

(ii) $\begin{vmatrix} x & x \\ 4 & 3x \end{vmatrix} = 0$

Solution

$$3x^2 - 4x = 0$$

$$3x\cancel{x} = 4\cancel{x}$$

$$\therefore 3x = 4$$

$$x = \frac{4}{3}$$

Put   x = 0, then

$$3x^2 - 4x = 0$$

$$\therefore x = 0, \frac{4}{3}$$

(iii) $\begin{vmatrix} x+5 & 4 \\ 0 & x-5 \end{vmatrix} = 0$

Solution

$$(x + 5)(x - 5) - 0 = 0$$

$$x^2 + \cancel{5x} - \cancel{5x} - 25 = 0$$

$x^2 - 25 = 0,\ x^2 = 25$

$\therefore\ x = \pm 5$

(iv) $\begin{vmatrix} 0 & 1 & 0 \\ x & 2 & x \\ 1 & 3 & x \end{vmatrix} = 0$

Solution

$0(2x - 3x) - 1\ (x^2 - x) + 0(3x - 2) = 0$

$0 - x^2 + x + 0 = 0$

$-x^2 + x = 0\quad$ put $x = 0$ then $-x^2 + x = 0$

$x^2 - x = 0\quad$ then $x^{\cancel{2}} = \cancel{x}\quad\quad \therefore\ x = 1$

$\therefore\ x = 0,\ 1$

DETERMINANT OF ORDER 4

$$\Delta = \begin{vmatrix} a_{11} & a_{12} & a_{13} & a_{14} \\ a_{21} & a_{22} & a_{23} & a_{24} \\ a_{31} & a_{32} & a_{33} & a_{34} \\ a_{41} & a_{42} & a_{43} & a_{44} \end{vmatrix}$$

is called a determinant of order 4 and its value is the number

$$a_{11}\begin{vmatrix} a_{22} & a_{23} & a_{24} \\ a_{32} & a_{33} & a_{34} \\ a_{42} & a_{43} & a_{44} \end{vmatrix} - a_{12}\begin{vmatrix} a_{21} & a_{23} & a_{24} \\ a_{31} & a_{33} & a_{34} \\ a_{41} & a_{43} & a_{44} \end{vmatrix} + a_{13}\begin{vmatrix} a_{21} & a_{22} & a_{24} \\ a_{31} & a_{32} & a_{34} \\ a_{41} & a_{42} & a_{44} \end{vmatrix} - a_{14}\begin{vmatrix} a_{21} & a_{22} & a_{23} \\ a_{31} & a_{32} & a_{33} \\ a_{41} & a_{42} & a_{43} \end{vmatrix}$$

Example Problems

(1) Find the value of the determinant of the matrix $A = \begin{pmatrix} a & 0 & 0 & 0 \\ 0 & b & 0 & 0 \\ 0 & 0 & c & 0 \\ 0 & 0 & 0 & d \end{pmatrix}$

Note : The value of the determinant of a diagonal is equal to the product of the elements lying along its Principal diagonal.

Solution

We have $|A|$

$$= a \begin{vmatrix} b & 0 & 0 \\ 0 & c & 0 \\ 0 & 0 & d \end{vmatrix} \text{ On expanding the determinant along the first row.}$$

$$= a\,[b(cd - 0) - 0 + 0] \qquad = a\,b\,c\,d$$

2) Find the value of the determinant of the matrix $A = \begin{bmatrix} a & h & g & f \\ 0 & b & c & e \\ 0 & 0 & d & k \\ 0 & 0 & 0 & 1 \end{bmatrix}$

Solution: We have

$$|A| = a \begin{vmatrix} b & c & e \\ 0 & d & k \\ 0 & 0 & 1 \end{vmatrix}$$

$$= a\big[b[dl - k.0]\big] \qquad = a\,b\,d\,l$$

Note : Here the given matrix is upper triangular matrix. So the value of the determinant of an upper triangular matrix ((i.e) in which all the elements below the principal diagonal are zero) is equal to the product of the elements along the principal diagonal.

Similarly the value of the determinant of a lower triangular matrix ((i.e) in which all the elements above the principal diagonal are zero) is equal to the product of the elements along the principal diagonal.

Exercise Problem

Find the value of the determinant of the matrix $A = \begin{bmatrix} 4 & 7 & 8 \\ -9 & 0 & 0 \\ 2 & 3 & 4 \end{bmatrix}$ [Ans : 36]

1.5 PROPERTIES OF DETERMINANTS

Theorem 1

The value of a determinant does not change when rows and columns are interchanged.

Proof

Let $\Delta = \begin{vmatrix} a_1 & b_1 & c_1 \\ a_2 & b_2 & c_2 \\ a_3 & b_3 & c_3 \end{vmatrix}$

be the given determinant. Expanding Δ along the first row,

We get $\Delta = a_1(b_2c_3 - c_2b_3) - b_1(a_2c_3 - c_2a_3) + c_1(a_2b_3 - b_2a_3)$ ------ (1)

Let us interchange the rows and columns of Δ we get determinant,

$\Delta_1 = \begin{vmatrix} a_1 & a_2 & a_3 \\ b_1 & b_2 & b_3 \\ c_1 & c_2 & c_3 \end{vmatrix}$

Expanding along the first row

$\Delta_1 = a_1(b_2c_3 - b_3c_2) - a_2(b_1c_3 - b_3c_1) + a_3(b_1c_2 - b_2c_1)$

$= a_1b_2c_3 - a_1b_3c_2 - a_2b_1c_3 + a_2b_3c_1 + a_3b_1c_2 - a_3b_2c_1$

$= a_1(b_2c_3 - b_3c_2) - b_1(a_2c_3 - a_3c_2) + c_1(a_2b_3 - a_3b_2)$ ----- (2)

From (1) and (2) we get $\Delta = \Delta_1$

Thus the value of the determinant does not change if its rows be changed into columns and columns into rows.

Theorem 2

If two rows or columns of determinant are interchanged the determinant changes in sign but its numerical value is unaltered.

Proof

$$\text{Let } \Delta = \begin{vmatrix} a_1 & b_1 & c_1 \\ a_2 & b_2 & c_2 \\ a_3 & b_3 & c_3 \end{vmatrix}$$

$$= a_1(b_2c_3 - b_3c_2) - b_1(a_2c_3 - c_2a_3) + c_1(a_2b_3 - b_2a_3) \qquad \text{----- (1)}$$

Let Δ_1 be the determinant obtained from Δ by interchanging its 1st and 2nd columns. (i.e)

$$\Delta_1 = \begin{vmatrix} b_1 & a_1 & c_1 \\ b_2 & a_2 & c_2 \\ b_3 & a_3 & c_3 \end{vmatrix}$$

Expanding Δ_1 along the first row, we get

$$= b_1(a_2c_3 - c_2a_3) - a_1(b_2c_3 - c_2b_3) + c_1(b_2a_3 - a_2b_3)$$

$$= b_1a_2c_3 - b_1c_2a_3 - a_1b_2c_3 + a_1c_2b_3 + c_1b_2a_3 - c_1a_2b_3$$

$$= a_1(-b_2c_3 + c_2b_3) - b_1(c_2a_3 - a_2c_3) + c_1(b_2a_3 - a_2b_3)$$

$$\quad - \{a_1(b_2c_3 - b_3c_2) - b_1(a_2c_3 - a_3c_2) + c_1(a_2b_3 - a_3b_2)\}$$

$$= -\Delta \text{ from (1)}$$

Corollary : If any row (or column) of a determinant passed over n parallel rows or columns, the resulting determinant $\Delta_1 = (-1)^n \Delta$.

Theorem 3

If two rows or columns of a determinant are identical, then the value of the determinant is zero.

$$\text{Let } \Delta = \begin{vmatrix} a_1 & b_1 & c_1 \\ a_1 & b_1 & c_1 \\ a_3 & b_3 & c_3 \end{vmatrix} \qquad \text{------ (1)}$$

be the given determinant. Here first row R_1 = second row R_2

Let Δ_1 be the determinant obtained from Δ by interchanging its 1st and 2nd rows.

So that

$$\Delta_1 = \begin{vmatrix} a_1 & b_1 & c_1 \\ a_2 & b_1 & c_1 \\ a_3 & b_3 & c_3 \end{vmatrix} \quad (R_1 \Leftrightarrow R_2) \text{ ------ (2)}$$

But by theorem (2), the value of a determinant changes in sign if its any two rows (or) columns are interchanged.

$$\therefore \Delta_1 = -\Delta \qquad \text{------ (3)}$$

From (1) and (2) we have $\Delta = \Delta_1$

From (3) $\Delta_1 = -\Delta$

$$\therefore \Delta = -\Delta$$

$$\Delta + \Delta = 0$$

$$2\Delta = 0$$

$$\therefore \Delta = 0$$

Hence a determinant vanishes if it has two identical rows or columns.

Theorem 4

If every element in a row or a column of a determinant is multiplied by the same constant k, (k≠0), then the value of the determinant is multiplied by the constant k.

Proof

$$\text{Let } \Delta = \begin{vmatrix} a_1 & b_1 & c_1 \\ a_2 & b_2 & c_2 \\ a_3 & b_3 & c_3 \end{vmatrix}$$

$$= a_1(b_2 c_3 - b_3 c_2) - b_1(a_2 c_3 - a_3 c_2) + c_1(a_2 b_3 - a_3 b_2) \quad \ldots\ldots\ldots\ldots(1)$$

Let Δ_1 be the determinant obtained from Δ by multiplying every element of its

first row by a constant k, (k ≠ 0), so that

$$\Delta = \begin{vmatrix} \alpha + a_1 & \beta + b_1 & \gamma + c_1 \\ a_2 & b_2 & c_2 \\ a_3 & b_3 & c_3 \end{vmatrix}$$

Expanding Δ_1 along the first row, we get

$$\Delta \quad = ka_1(b_2 c_3 - b_3 c_2) - kb_1(a_2 c_3 - a_3 c_2) + kc_1(a_2 b_3 - a_3 b_2)$$

$$= k\{a_1(b_2 c_3 - b_3 c_2) - b_1(a_2 c_3 - a_3 c_2) + c_1(a_2 b_3 - a_3 b_2)\}$$

$$= k\Delta \quad [\text{ from (1)}]$$

Hence, the theorem.

Theorem 5

If every element in any row or column can be expressed as the sum of two quantities, then the given determinant can be expressed as the sum of two determinants of the same order.

Proof

$$\text{Let } \Delta = \begin{vmatrix} a_1 & b_1 & c_1 \\ a_2 & b_2 & c_2 \\ a_3 & b_3 & c_3 \end{vmatrix}$$

and suppose that each element of the first row can be expressed as follows :

$$a_1 = \alpha + \lambda, \qquad b_1 = \beta + \mu, \qquad c_1 = \gamma + v,$$

$$\text{Then } \Delta = \begin{vmatrix} \alpha + \lambda & \beta + \mu & \gamma + v \\ a_2 & b_2 & c_2 \\ a_3 & b_3 & c_3 \end{vmatrix}$$

Expanding Δ along the first row, we have

$$\Delta \quad = (\alpha + \lambda)(b_2 c_3 - b_3 c_2) - (\beta + \mu)(a_2 c_3 - a_3 c_2) + (\gamma + v)(a_2 b_3 - a_3 b_2)$$

$$= \alpha(b_2 c_3 - b_3 c_2) - \beta(a_2 c_3 - a_3 c_2) + \gamma(a_2 b_3 - a_3 b_2)$$

$$+ \lambda(b_2 c_3 - b_3 c_2) - \mu(a_2 c_3 - a_3 c_2) + v(a_2 b_3 - a_3 b_2)$$

$$= \begin{vmatrix} \alpha & \beta & \gamma \\ a_2 & b_2 & c_2 \\ a_3 & b_3 & c_3 \end{vmatrix} + \begin{vmatrix} \lambda & \mu & v \\ a_2 & b_2 & c_2 \\ a_3 & b_3 & c_3 \end{vmatrix}$$

$$= \Delta_1 + \Delta_2$$

Where

$$\Delta_1 = \begin{vmatrix} \alpha & \beta & \gamma \\ a_2 & b_2 & c_2 \\ a_3 & b_3 & c_3 \end{vmatrix} \qquad \Delta_2 = \begin{vmatrix} \lambda & \mu & v \\ a_2 & b_2 & c_2 \\ a_3 & b_3 & c_3 \end{vmatrix}$$

Hence the theorem.

Theorem 6

A determinant is unaltered when to each element of any row or column are added those of several other rows or columns multiplied respectively by constant factors.

Proof

Let $\Delta = \begin{vmatrix} a_1 & b_1 & c_1 \\ a_2 & b_2 & c_2 \\ a_3 & b_3 & c_3 \end{vmatrix}$

Let Δ_1 be a determinant obtained when the elements of first column of Δ are added those of second column and third column multiplied respectively by m and n.

$$\Delta_1 = \begin{vmatrix} a_1 + mb_1 + nc_1 & b_1 & c_1 \\ a_2 + mb_2 + nc_2 & b_2 & c_2 \\ a_3 + mb_3 + nc_3 & b_3 & c_3 \end{vmatrix} \qquad [C_1 \rightarrow C_1 + mC_2 + nC_3]$$

$$= \begin{vmatrix} a_1 & b_1 & c_1 \\ a_2 & b_2 & c_2 \\ a_3 & b_3 & c_3 \end{vmatrix} + \begin{vmatrix} mb_1 & b_1 & c_1 \\ mb_2 & b_2 & c_2 \\ mb_3 & b_3 & c_3 \end{vmatrix} + \begin{vmatrix} nc_1 & b_1 & c_1 \\ nc_2 & b_2 & c_2 \\ nc_3 & b_3 & c_3 \end{vmatrix} \qquad \text{[by theorem 5]}$$

$$= \begin{vmatrix} a_1 & b_1 & c_1 \\ a_2 & b_2 & c_2 \\ a_3 & b_3 & c_3 \end{vmatrix} + m\begin{vmatrix} b_1 & b_1 & c_1 \\ b_2 & b_2 & c_2 \\ b_3 & b_3 & c_3 \end{vmatrix} + n\begin{vmatrix} c_1 & b_1 & c_1 \\ c_2 & b_2 & c_2 \\ c_3 & b_3 & c_3 \end{vmatrix} \qquad \text{[by theorem 4]}$$

$$= \begin{vmatrix} a_1 & b_1 & c_1 \\ a_2 & b_2 & c_2 \\ a_3 & b_3 & c_3 \end{vmatrix} + m(0) + n(0) \qquad \text{[by theorem 3]}$$

$$= \begin{vmatrix} a_1 & b_1 & c_1 \\ a_2 & b_2 & c_2 \\ a_3 & b_3 & c_3 \end{vmatrix} = \Delta$$

Hence the theorem.

Theorem 7

In any determinant, if the elements of any two (or column) are multiplied by the co-factors of the corresponding elements of any other row (or column) the sum of these products will be equal to zero.

Proof

Now let us consider the 3rd order determinant

$$\Delta = \begin{vmatrix} a_1 & b_1 & c_1 \\ a_2 & b_2 & c_2 \\ a_3 & b_3 & c_3 \end{vmatrix}$$

$$= a_1 \begin{vmatrix} b_2 & c_2 \\ b_3 & c_3 \end{vmatrix} - b_1 \begin{vmatrix} a_2 & c_2 \\ a_3 & c_3 \end{vmatrix} + c_1 \begin{vmatrix} a_2 & b_2 \\ a_3 & b_3 \end{vmatrix}$$

$$= a_1 A_1 + b_1 B_1 + c_1 C_1$$

Where A_1, B_1, C_1 are the co-factors of the elements a_1, b_1, c_1 respectively.

If now we substitute a_2, b_2, c_2 respectively in the place of a_1, b_1, c_1 we get $a_2 A_1 + b_2 B_1 + c_2 C_1$, which then becomes the value of a determinant in which the 1st row is a_2, b_2, c_2 which is the same as the 2nd row of the same determinant. But the value of such a determinant is which the 2nd and 1st row are identical is equal to zero.

$$\therefore a_1 A_1 + b_1 B_1 + c_1 C_1 = 0$$

Note

i.   A similar argument holds good for columns

ii. $\Delta = a_1 A_1 + b_1 B_1 + c_1 C_1 = a_2 A_2 + b_2 B_2 + c_2 C_2$

     $= a_3 A_3 + b_3 B_3 + c_3 C_3 = a_1 A_1 + a_2 A_2 + a_3 A_3$

     $= b_1 B_1 + b_2 B_2 + b_3 B_3 = c_1 C_1 + c_2 C_2 + c_3 C_3$

iii. $a_1 A_2 + b_1 B_2 + c_1 C_2 = a_1 A_3 + b_1 B_3 + c_1 C_3 = a_1 B_1 + a_2 B_2 + a_3 B_3 = 0$

Example Problems

1. Show that
$$\begin{vmatrix} 1 & a & a^2 \\ 1 & b & b^2 \\ 1 & c & c^2 \end{vmatrix} = (a-b)(b-c)(c-a)$$

Solution

$$\Delta = \begin{vmatrix} 1 & a & a^2 \\ 1 & b & b^2 \\ 1 & c & c^2 \end{vmatrix}$$

$$\Delta = \begin{vmatrix} 1 & a & a^2 \\ 0 & b-a & b^2-c^2 \\ 0 & c-a & c^2-a^2 \end{vmatrix} \qquad \begin{array}{l} R_2 \to R_2 - R_1 \\ R_3 \to R_3 - R_1 \end{array}$$

On expanding the determinant along the first column

$$= 1 \begin{vmatrix} b-a & b^2-a^2 \\ c-a & c^2-a^2 \end{vmatrix}$$

$$= 1 \begin{vmatrix} b-a & (b-a)(b+a) \\ c-a & (c-a)(c+a) \end{vmatrix}$$

Taking out (b-a) common from the first row and (c-a) from the second row.

$$= (b-a)(c-a) \begin{vmatrix} 1 & b+a \\ 1 & c+a \end{vmatrix}$$

$$= (b-a)(c-a)\{(c+a)-(b+a)\}$$

$$= (b-a)(c-a)\{c+a-b-a\}$$

$$= (b-a)(c-a)(c-b)$$

$$= -(a-b) \times (c-a) \times -(b-c) \qquad = (a-b)(b-c)(c-a)$$

2. Evaluate $\Delta = \begin{vmatrix} a-b & m-n & x-y \\ b-c & n-p & y-z \\ c-a & p-m & z-x \end{vmatrix}$

Solution

Applying $R_1 \rightarrow R_1 + R_2 + R_3$

$$\Delta = \begin{vmatrix} a-b & m-n & x-y \\ b-c & n-p & y-z \\ c-a & p-m & z-x \end{vmatrix}$$

$$\Delta = \begin{vmatrix} 0 & 0 & 0 \\ b-c & n-p & y-z \\ c-a & p-m & z-x \end{vmatrix} = 0$$

3. Show that $\begin{vmatrix} 1 & \omega & \omega^2 \\ \omega & \omega^2 & 1 \\ \omega^2 & 1 & \omega \end{vmatrix}$

Where ω is a cube root of unity since symbol ω is a cube root of unity $1+\omega+\omega^2 = 0$.

Solution

$$\Delta = \begin{vmatrix} 1 & \omega & \omega^2 \\ \omega & \omega^2 & 1 \\ \omega^2 & 1 & \omega \end{vmatrix} \qquad \text{Applying} \qquad C_1 \rightarrow C_1 + C_2 + C_3$$

$$\Delta = \begin{vmatrix} 1+\omega+\omega^2 & \omega & \omega^2 \\ \omega+\omega^2+1 & \omega^2 & 1 \\ \omega^2+1+\omega & 1 & \omega \end{vmatrix} \qquad [\because 1+\omega+\omega^2 = 0]$$

$$= \begin{vmatrix} 0 & \omega & \omega^2 \\ 0 & \omega^2 & 1 \\ 0 & 1 & \omega \end{vmatrix} \qquad [\text{expanding by } 1^{st} \text{ row}]$$

$$= \because 0(\omega^3-1)-\omega(0-0)+\omega^2(0-0) \qquad = 0$$

4. Evaluate $\Delta = \begin{vmatrix} a & b & c \\ b & c & a \\ c & a & b \end{vmatrix}$

Solution

Applying $\quad C_1 \rightarrow C_1 + C_2 + C_3$

$$\Delta = \begin{vmatrix} a+b+c & b & c \\ a+b+c & c & a \\ a+b+c & a & b \end{vmatrix}$$

Taking out $(a + b + c)$ common from the first column

$$= (a+b+c)\begin{vmatrix} 1 & b & c \\ 1 & c & a \\ 1 & a & b \end{vmatrix}$$

$$= (a+b+c)\begin{vmatrix} 1 & b & c \\ 0 & c-b & a-c \\ 0 & a-b & b-a \end{vmatrix} \quad \begin{matrix} R_2 \rightarrow R_2 - R_1 \\ R_3 \rightarrow R_3 - R_1 \end{matrix}$$

$$= (a+b+c)\{(c-b)(b-c)-(a-b)(a-c)\}$$

$$= (a+b+c)(bc+ac+ab-a^2-b^2-c^2)$$

$$= -(a+b+c)(a^2+b^2+c^2-bc-ac-ab)$$

$$= -(a^3+b^3+c^3-3abc)$$

5. Prove that $\begin{vmatrix} x & a & a & a \\ a & x & a & a \\ a & a & x & a \\ a & a & a & x \end{vmatrix} = (x+3a)(x-a)^3$

Solution

Let Δ $=\begin{vmatrix} x & a & a & a \\ a & x & a & a \\ a & a & x & a \\ a & a & a & x \end{vmatrix}$

Applying $C_1 \rightarrow C_1 + C_2 + C_3 + C_4$ and taking x+3a common from the first

column, we get

$$\Delta = (x+3a)\begin{vmatrix} 1 & a & a & a \\ 1 & x & a & a \\ 1 & a & x & a \\ 1 & a & a & x \end{vmatrix}$$

$$= (x+3a)\begin{vmatrix} 1 & a & a & a \\ 0 & x-a & 0 & 0 \\ 0 & 0 & x-a & 0 \\ 0 & 0 & 0 & x-a \end{vmatrix} \begin{matrix} R_2 \rightarrow R_2 - R_1 \\ R_3 \rightarrow R_3 - R_1 \\ R_4 \rightarrow R_4 - R_1 \end{matrix}$$

On expanding the determinant along the first column

$$= (x+3a)1\begin{vmatrix} x-a & 0 & 0 \\ 0 & x-a & 0 \\ 0 & 0 & x-a \end{vmatrix}$$

$$= (x+3a)(x-a)\begin{vmatrix} x-a & 0 \\ 0 & x-a \end{vmatrix} \quad \text{expanding along the first column}$$

$$= (x+3a)(x-a)^3, \quad \text{Hence the result.}$$

6. Prove that $\begin{vmatrix} 1+a & b & c & d \\ a & 1+b & c & d \\ a & b & 1+c & d \\ a & b & c & 1+d \end{vmatrix} = 1+a+b+c+d$

Solution

Let $\Delta = \begin{vmatrix} 1+a & b & c & d \\ a & 1+b & c & d \\ a & b & 1+c & d \\ a & b & c & 1+d \end{vmatrix}$.

Applying $C_1 \to C_1 + C_2 + C_3$ and taking $1+a+b+c+d$ common from the

first column

$$\Delta \equiv (1+a+b+c+d) \begin{vmatrix} 1 & b & c & d \\ 1 & 1+b & c & d \\ 1 & b & 1+c & d \\ 1 & b & c & 1+d \end{vmatrix}$$

$$= (1+a+b+c+d) \begin{vmatrix} 1 & b & c & d \\ 0 & 1 & 0 & 0 \\ 0 & 0 & 1 & 0 \\ 0 & 0 & 0 & 1 \end{vmatrix} \begin{matrix} \\ R_2 \to R_2 - R_1 \\ R_3 \to R_3 - R_1 \\ R_4 \to R_4 - R_1 \end{matrix}$$

Expanding along the first column

$$= (1+a+b+c+d) \begin{vmatrix} 1 & 0 & 0 \\ 0 & 1 & 0 \\ 0 & 0 & 1 \end{vmatrix}$$

$$= (1+a+b+c+d).1\,(1-0)$$

$$= (1+a+b+c+d).1 \ = 1+a+b+c+d$$

Hence the Result.

7. Prove that $\Delta \equiv \begin{vmatrix} 1+a & 1 & 1 & 1 \\ 1 & 1+b & 1 & 1 \\ 1 & 1 & 1+c & 1 \\ 1 & 1 & 1 & 1+d \end{vmatrix} = abcd\left(1+\dfrac{1}{a}+\dfrac{1}{b}+\dfrac{1}{c}+\dfrac{1}{d}\right)$

Solution

Taking out a, b, c, d common from the first, second and third and fourth column respectively

$$\Delta = abcd \begin{vmatrix} \dfrac{1}{a}+1 & \dfrac{1}{b} & \dfrac{1}{c} & \dfrac{1}{d} \\ \dfrac{1}{a} & \dfrac{1}{b}+1 & \dfrac{1}{c} & \dfrac{1}{d} \\ \dfrac{1}{a} & \dfrac{1}{b} & \dfrac{1}{c}+1 & \dfrac{1}{d} \\ \dfrac{1}{a} & \dfrac{1}{b} & \dfrac{1}{c} & \dfrac{1}{d}+1 \end{vmatrix} \qquad \text{Applying } C_1 \rightarrow C_1+C_2+C_3+C_4$$

$$= abcd \begin{vmatrix} 1+\dfrac{1}{a}+\dfrac{1}{b}+\dfrac{1}{c}+\dfrac{1}{d} & \dfrac{1}{b} & \dfrac{1}{c} & \dfrac{1}{d} \\ 1+\dfrac{1}{a}+\dfrac{1}{b}+\dfrac{1}{c}+\dfrac{1}{d} & \dfrac{1}{b}+1 & \dfrac{1}{c} & \dfrac{1}{d} \\ 1+\dfrac{1}{a}+\dfrac{1}{b}+\dfrac{1}{c}+\dfrac{1}{d} & \dfrac{1}{b} & \dfrac{1}{c}+1 & \dfrac{1}{d} \\ 1+\dfrac{1}{a}+\dfrac{1}{b}+\dfrac{1}{c}+\dfrac{1}{d} & \dfrac{1}{b} & \dfrac{1}{c} & \dfrac{1}{d}+1 \end{vmatrix}$$

$$= abcd\left(1+\dfrac{1}{a}+\dfrac{1}{b}+\dfrac{1}{c}+\dfrac{1}{d}\right) \begin{vmatrix} 1 & \dfrac{1}{b} & \dfrac{1}{c} & \dfrac{1}{d} \\ 1 & \dfrac{1}{b}+1 & \dfrac{1}{c} & \dfrac{1}{d} \\ 1 & \dfrac{1}{b} & \dfrac{1}{c}+1 & \dfrac{1}{d} \\ 1 & \dfrac{1}{b} & \dfrac{1}{c} & \dfrac{1}{d}+1 \end{vmatrix}$$

$$= abcd\left(1+\frac{1}{a}+\frac{1}{b}+\frac{1}{c}+\frac{1}{d}\right)\begin{vmatrix} 1 & \dfrac{1}{b} & \dfrac{1}{c} & \dfrac{1}{d} \\ 0 & 1 & 0 & 0 \\ 0 & 0 & 1 & 0 \\ 0 & 0 & 0 & 1 \end{vmatrix}$$

$$\begin{aligned} R_2 &\to R_2 - R_1 \\ R_3 &\to R_3 - R_1 \\ R_4 &\to R_4 - R_1 \end{aligned}$$

$$= abcd\left(1+\frac{1}{a}+\frac{1}{b}+\frac{1}{c}+\frac{1}{d}\right)\begin{vmatrix} 1 & 0 & 0 \\ 0 & 1 & 0 \\ 0 & 0 & 1 \end{vmatrix}$$

$$= abcd\left(1+\frac{1}{a}+\frac{1}{b}+\frac{1}{c}+\frac{1}{d}\right)1(1-0)$$

$$= abcd\left(1+\frac{1}{a}+\frac{1}{b}+\frac{1}{c}+\frac{1}{d}\right)$$

Hence the Result.

8. Prove that $\Delta = \begin{vmatrix} a^2+1 & ab & ac \\ ab & b^2+1 & bc \\ ac & bc & c^2+1 \end{vmatrix} = 1+a^2+b^2+c^2$

Solution

Multiplying the 1st, 2nd and 3rd columns by a, b and c respectively, we get

$$\Delta = \frac{1}{abc}\begin{vmatrix} a(a^2+1) & ab^2 & ac^2 \\ a^2b & b(b^2+1) & bc^2 \\ a^2c & b^2c & c(c^2+1) \end{vmatrix}$$

Taking out a, b, c common from the first, second and third rows respectively

$$= \frac{abc}{abc}\begin{vmatrix} a^2+1 & b^2 & c^2 \\ a^2 & b^2+1 & c^2 \\ a^2 & b^2 & c^2+1 \end{vmatrix}$$

$$= \begin{vmatrix} 1+a^2+b^2+c^2 & b^2 & c^2 \\ 1+a^2+b^2+c^2 & b^2+1 & c^2 \\ 1+a^2+b^2+c^2 & b^2 & c^2+1 \end{vmatrix} \qquad \text{Applying } C_1 \rightarrow C_1 + C_2 + C_3$$

$$= (1+a^2+b^2+c^2) \begin{vmatrix} 1 & b^2 & c^2 \\ 1 & b^2+1 & c^2 \\ 1 & b^2 & c^2+1 \end{vmatrix}$$

$$= (1+a^2+b^2+c^2) \begin{vmatrix} 1 & b^2 & c^2 \\ 0 & 1 & 0 \\ 0 & 0 & 1 \end{vmatrix} \quad \begin{matrix} R_2 \rightarrow R_2 - R_1 \\ R_3 \rightarrow R_3 - R_1 \end{matrix}$$

Expanding by first column

$$= (1+a^2+b^2+c^2) \begin{vmatrix} 1 & 0 \\ 0 & 1 \end{vmatrix}$$

$$= (1+a^2+b^2+c^2)$$

Hence the Result.

9. Show that $\Delta \equiv \begin{vmatrix} 1 & 1 & 1 & 1 \\ \alpha & \beta & \gamma & \delta \\ \beta+\gamma & \gamma+\delta & \delta+\alpha & \alpha+\beta \\ \delta & \alpha & \beta & \gamma \end{vmatrix} = 0$

Solution

Applying $R_2 \rightarrow R_2 + R_3 + R_4$

$$\Delta = \begin{vmatrix} 1 & 1 & 1 & 1 \\ \alpha+\beta+\gamma+\delta & \alpha+\beta+\gamma+\delta & \alpha+\beta+\gamma+\delta & \alpha+\beta+\gamma+\delta \\ \beta+\gamma & \gamma+\delta & \delta+\alpha & \alpha+\beta \\ \delta & \alpha & \beta & \gamma \end{vmatrix}$$

$$\Delta = (\alpha + \beta + \gamma + \delta) \begin{vmatrix} 1 & 1 & 1 & 1 \\ 1 & 1 & 1 & 1 \\ \beta + \gamma & \gamma + \delta & \delta + \alpha & \alpha + \beta \\ \delta & \alpha & \beta & \gamma \end{vmatrix}$$

$\Delta = (\alpha + \beta + \gamma + \delta) \cdot 0$ [∵ Since the first two rows are identical]

   $= 0$

Hence the Result.

10. Prove that $\begin{vmatrix} a - b - c & 2a & 2a \\ 2b & b - c - a & 2b \\ 2a & 2c & c - a - b \end{vmatrix} = (a + b + c)^3$

Solution

Let us denote the given determinant by Δ.

Applying $R_1 \rightarrow R_1 + R_2 + R_3$

$$\Delta = \begin{vmatrix} a + b + c & a + b + c & a + b + c \\ 2b & b - c - a & 2b \\ 2c & 2c & c - a - b \end{vmatrix}$$

Taking (a+b+c) common from the first row.

$$= (a + b + c) \begin{vmatrix} 1 & 1 & 1 \\ 2b & b - c - a & 2b \\ 2c & 2c & c - a - b \end{vmatrix}$$

$$= (a + b + c) \begin{vmatrix} 1 & 1 & 1 \\ 2b & -b - c - a & 0 \\ 2c & 0 & -c - a - b \end{vmatrix} \quad \begin{matrix} C_2 \rightarrow C_2 - C_1 \\ C_3 \rightarrow C_3 - C_1 \end{matrix}$$

$= (a+b+c) \cdot 1 \, (b+c+a)$

$= (a+b+c)^3$

Hence the Result.

11. Prove that
$$\begin{vmatrix} a+b+2c & a & b \\ c & b+c+2a & b \\ c & a & c+a+2b \end{vmatrix} = 2(a+b+c)^3$$

Solution

Let us denote the given determinant by Δ.

Applying $C_1 \to C_1 + C_2 + C_3$

$$\Delta = \begin{vmatrix} 2a+2b+2c & a & b \\ 2a+2b+2c & b+c+2a & b \\ 2a+2b+2c & a & c+a+2b \end{vmatrix}$$

$$= 2(a+b+c)\begin{vmatrix} 1 & a & b \\ 1 & b+c+a & 0 \\ 0 & 0 & c+a+b \end{vmatrix} \quad \begin{matrix} R_2 \to R_2 - R_1 \\ R_3 \to R_3 - R_1 \end{matrix}$$

Expanding with respect to first column

$$= 2(a+b+c)\begin{vmatrix} b+c+a & 0 \\ 0 & c+a+b \end{vmatrix}$$

$$= 2(a+b+c)\,[(b+c+a)(c+a+b)]$$

$$= 2(a+b+c)^3$$

Hence the Result.

12. Evaluate
$$\begin{vmatrix} y+z & x & y \\ z+x & z & x \\ x+y & y & z \end{vmatrix}$$

Solution

Let us denote the given determinant by Δ

$$\therefore \ \Delta = \begin{vmatrix} y+z & x & y \\ z+x & z & x \\ x+y & y & z \end{vmatrix}$$

Applying $R_1 \rightarrow R_1 + R_2 + R_3$

$$\Delta = \begin{vmatrix} 2x + 2y + 2z & x + y + z & x + y + z \\ z + x & z & x \\ x + y & y & z \end{vmatrix}$$

$$= (x + y + z) \begin{vmatrix} 2 & 1 & 1 \\ z + x & z & x \\ x + y & y & z \end{vmatrix}$$

$$= (x + y + z) \begin{vmatrix} 0 & 1 & 1 \\ 0 & z & x \\ x - z & y & z \end{vmatrix} \quad C_1 \rightarrow C_1 - C_2 - C_3$$

$$= (x + y + z)(x - z) \begin{vmatrix} 1 & 1 \\ z & x \end{vmatrix}$$

Expanding with respect to the first column

$$= (x + y + z)(x - z)(x - z)$$

$$= (x + y + z)(x - z)^2$$

13. Evaluate $\begin{vmatrix} b + c & a + b & a \\ c + a & b + c & b \\ a + b & c + a & c \end{vmatrix}$

Solution

Let us denote the given determinant by Δ

$$\therefore \Delta = \begin{vmatrix} b + c & a + b & a \\ c + a & b + c & b \\ a + b & c + a & c \end{vmatrix}$$

Applying $C_1 \rightarrow C_1 + C_3$

$$\Delta = \begin{vmatrix} a+b+c & a+b & a \\ a+b+c & b+c & b \\ a+b+c & c+a & c \end{vmatrix}$$

$$= (a+b+c) \begin{vmatrix} 1 & a+b & a \\ 1 & b+c & b \\ 1 & c+a & c \end{vmatrix}$$

$$= (a+b+c) \begin{vmatrix} 1 & a+b & a \\ 0 & c-a & b-a \\ 0 & c-b & c-a \end{vmatrix} \qquad \begin{matrix} R_2 \to R_2 - R_1 \\ R_3 \to R_3 - R_1 \end{matrix}$$

$$= (a+b+c) \begin{vmatrix} c-a & b-a \\ c-b & c-a \end{vmatrix}$$

Expanding with respect to the first column

$$= (a+b+c)[(c-a)^2 - (c-b)(b-a)]$$

$$= (a+b+c)[c^2 + a^2 - 2ac - (cb - ca - b^2 + ab)]$$

$$= (a+b+c)[a^2 + b^2 + c^2 - bc - ca - ab] \quad = a^3 + b^3 + c^3 - 3abc$$

14. Prove that $\begin{vmatrix} 1 & bc & a(b+c) \\ 1 & ca & b(c+a) \\ 1 & ab & c(a+b) \end{vmatrix} = 0$

Solution

Let $\Delta = \begin{vmatrix} 1 & bc & a(b+c) \\ 1 & ca & b(c+a) \\ 1 & ab & c(a+b) \end{vmatrix}$

Applying $C_2 \to C_2 + C_3$

$$\Delta = \begin{vmatrix} 1 & bc + ab + ac & a(b+c) \\ 1 & ca + bc + ab & b(c+a) \\ 1 & ab + ca + cb & c(a+b) \end{vmatrix}$$

$$= (bc + ab + ac) \begin{vmatrix} 1 & 1 & a(b+c) \\ 1 & 1 & b(c+a) \\ 1 & 1 & c(a+b) \end{vmatrix}$$

$= (bc + ab + ac) \times 0$, since the first two columns are identical

$= 0$

Hence the Result.

15. Prove that $\begin{vmatrix} 1 & bc+ad & b^2c^2 + a^2d^2 \\ 1 & ca+bd & c^2a^2 + b^2d^2 \\ 1 & ab+cd & a^2b^2 + c^2d^2 \end{vmatrix} = (a-b)(a-c)(a-d)\ (b-c)(b-d)(c-d)$

Solution

Let $\Delta = \begin{vmatrix} 1 & bc+ad & b^2c^2 + a^2d^2 \\ 1 & ca+bd & c^2a^2 + b^2d^2 \\ 1 & ab+cd & a^2b^2 + c^2d^2 \end{vmatrix}$

$\Delta = \begin{vmatrix} 1 & bc+ad & b^2c^2 + a^2d^2 \\ 0 & (a-b)(c-d) & (a^2-b^2)(c^2-d^2) \\ 0 & (a-c)(b-d) & (a^2-c^2)(b^2-d^2) \end{vmatrix} \begin{matrix} \\ R_2 \rightarrow R_2 - R_1 \\ R_3 \rightarrow R_3 - R_1 \end{matrix}$

$= \begin{vmatrix} (a-b)(c-d) & (a-b)(a+b)(c-d)(c+d) \\ (a-c)(b-d) & (a-c)(a+c)(b-d)(b+d) \end{vmatrix}$

$= (a-b)(c-d)(a-c)(b-d) \begin{vmatrix} 1 & (a+b)(c+d) \\ 1 & (a+c)(b+d) \end{vmatrix}$

$= (a-b)(c-d)(a-c)(b-d)[(a+c)(b+d) - (a+b)(c+d)]$

$= (a-b)(c-d)(a-c)(b-d)[ab + ad\!\!\!/ + cb\!\!\!/ + cd - ac - ad\!\!\!/ - bc\!\!\!/ - bd]$

$= (a-b)(c-d)(a-c)(b-d)[ab + cd - ac - bd]$

$= (a-b)(c-d)(a-c)(b-d)(b-c)(a-d)$

$= (a-b)(a-c)(a-d)(b-c)(b-d)(c-d)$

Note : $ab + cd - ac - bd$

$= b(a - d) - c(a - d)$

$= (a - d)(b - c)$

Hence the Result.

16. Prove that $\begin{vmatrix} -a^2 & ab & ac \\ ab & -b^2 & bc \\ ac & bc & -c^2 \end{vmatrix} = 4a^2b^2c^2$

Solution

Let Δ $= \begin{vmatrix} -a^2 & ab & ac \\ ab & -b^2 & bc \\ ac & bc & -c^2 \end{vmatrix}$

Taking out a, b, c common from the first, second and third columns respectively,

Δ $= abc \begin{vmatrix} -a & a & a \\ b & -b & b \\ c & c & -c \end{vmatrix}$

Taking out a, b, c common from the first, second and third rows respectively, we get

$= a^2b^2c^2 \begin{vmatrix} -1 & 1 & 1 \\ 1 & -1 & 1 \\ 1 & 1 & -1 \end{vmatrix}$

$= a^2b^2c^2 \begin{vmatrix} -1 & 1 & 1 \\ 0 & 0 & 2 \\ 0 & 2 & 0 \end{vmatrix}$ $R_2 \rightarrow R_2 + R_1$
                                                $R_3 \rightarrow R_3 + R_1$

$= a^2b^2c^2 \{(-1)(-4)\}$

$= 4a^2b^2c^2$

Hence the Result.

17. Prove that $\begin{vmatrix} a^2 & bc & ac+c^2 \\ a+b & b^2 & ac \\ ab & b^2+bc & c^2 \end{vmatrix} = 4a^2b^2c^2$

Solution

Taking out a, b, c common from the first, second and third column respectively,

then

$$\Delta = abc \begin{vmatrix} a & c & a+c \\ a+b & b & a \\ b & b+c & c \end{vmatrix}$$

$$= abc \begin{vmatrix} 0 & 2c & 2c \\ a+b & b & a \\ b & b+c & c \end{vmatrix} \quad R_1 \to R_1 + R_3 - R_2$$

$$= abc \begin{vmatrix} 0 & 0 & 2c \\ a+b & b-a & a \\ b & b & c \end{vmatrix} \quad C_2 \to C_2 - C_3$$

Expanding the determinant along the first row

$$= abc \cdot 2c \, [b(a+b) - b(b-a)]$$

$$= abc \cdot 2c \left[ab + \cancel{b^2} - \cancel{b^2} + ab \right]$$

$$= abc \cdot 2c \, [2ab]$$

$$= abc \cdot 4abc$$

$$= 4a^2b^2c^2$$

Hence the Result.

18. Prove that $\begin{vmatrix} a & c & a+c \\ a+b & b & a \\ b & b+c & c \end{vmatrix} = 4abc$

Solution

$$\text{Let } \Delta \quad = \begin{vmatrix} 0 & 2c & 2c \\ a+b & b & a \\ b & b+c & c \end{vmatrix} \quad R_1 \to R_1 + R_3 - R_2$$

$$= \begin{vmatrix} 0 & 0 & 2c \\ a+b & b-a & a \\ b & b & c \end{vmatrix} \quad C_2 \to C_2 - C_3$$

Expanding the determinant along the first row

$$= 2c\,[b(a + b) - b(b - a)]$$

$$= 2c\left[ab + \cancel{b^2} - \cancel{b^2} + ab \right]$$

$$= 2c\,(2ab) \quad = 4abc$$

Hence the Result.

19) Prove that $\begin{vmatrix} 1+a_1 & a_2 & a_3 & a_4 \\ a_1 & 1+a_2 & a_3 & a_4 \\ a_1 & a_2 & 1+a_3 & a_4 \\ a_1 & a_2 & a_3 & 1+a_4 \end{vmatrix} = 1+a_1+a_2+a_3+a_4$

Solution

$$\begin{vmatrix} 1+a_1+a_2+a_3+a_4 & a_2 & a_3 & a_4 \\ 1+a_1+a_2+a_3+a_4 & 1+a_2 & a_3 & a_4 \\ 1+a_1+a_2+a_3+a_4 & a_2 & 1+a_3 & a_4 \\ 1+a_1+a_2+a_3+a_4 & a_2 & a_3 & 1+a_4 \end{vmatrix} \quad C_1 \to C_1 + C_2 + C_3 + C_4$$

$$= (1+a_1+a_2+a_3+a_4) \begin{vmatrix} 1 & a_2 & a_3 & a_4 \\ 1 & 1+a_2 & a_3 & a_4 \\ 1 & a_2 & 1+a_3 & a_4 \\ 1 & a_2 & a_3 & 1+a_4 \end{vmatrix}$$

$$= (1+a_1+a_2+a_3+a_4) \begin{vmatrix} 1 & a_2 & a_3 & a_4 \\ 0 & 1 & 0 & 0 \\ 0 & 0 & 1 & 0 \\ 0 & 0 & 0 & 1 \end{vmatrix} \begin{matrix} \\ R_2 \rightarrow R_2 - R_1 \\ R_3 \rightarrow R_3 - R_1 \\ R_4 \rightarrow R_4 - R_1 \end{matrix}$$

$$= (1 + a_1 + a_2 + a_3 + a_4) \ 1[1(1\text{-}0)] - a_2[0] + a_3[0] - a_4[0]]$$

$$= (1 + a_1 + a_2 + a_3 + a_4) \ 1(1)$$

$$= 1 + a_1 + a_2 + a_3 + a_4$$

Hence the Result.

20) Prove that $\begin{vmatrix} 1 & a & a^2 - bc \\ 1 & b & b^2 - ca \\ 1 & c & c^2 - ab \end{vmatrix} = 0$

Solution

$$\text{LHS} = \begin{vmatrix} 1 & a & a^2 - bc \\ 1 & b & b^2 - ca \\ 1 & c & c^2 - ab \end{vmatrix}$$

$$D = \begin{vmatrix} 1 & a & a^2 \\ 1 & b & b^2 \\ 1 & c & c^2 \end{vmatrix} - \begin{vmatrix} 1 & a & bc \\ 1 & b & ca \\ 1 & c & ab \end{vmatrix}$$

$$D = \Delta_1 - \Delta_2$$

$$\Delta_2 \quad = \quad \begin{vmatrix} 1 & a & bc \\ 1 & b & ca \\ 1 & c & ab \end{vmatrix}$$

1st row is multiplied by a/a

2nd row is multiplied by b/b

and 3rd row is multiplied by c/c

$$= \begin{vmatrix} \dfrac{a}{a} & \dfrac{a^2}{a} & \dfrac{abc}{a} \\ \dfrac{b}{b} & \dfrac{b^2}{b} & \dfrac{abc}{b} \\ \dfrac{c}{c} & \dfrac{c^2}{c} & \dfrac{abc}{c} \end{vmatrix}$$

Taking out $\dfrac{1}{a}, \dfrac{1}{b}, \dfrac{1}{c}$ from $1^{st}, 2^{nd}, 3^{rd}$ rows respectively,

$$= \dfrac{1}{abc} \begin{vmatrix} a & a^2 & abc \\ b & b^2 & abc \\ c & c^2 & abc \end{vmatrix}$$

Taking out abc from 3rd column as common.

$$= \dfrac{abc}{abc} \begin{vmatrix} a & a^2 & 1 \\ b & b^2 & 1 \\ c & c^2 & 1 \end{vmatrix}$$

Interchange 3rd and 2nd column

$$= - \begin{vmatrix} a & 1 & a^2 \\ b & 1 & b^2 \\ c & 1 & c^2 \end{vmatrix}$$

According to Theorem 2, if two rows (or) columns of determinant are interchanged, the determinant changes in sign.

= Again interchange 1st and 2nd column.

$$\Delta_2 = -x - \begin{vmatrix} 1 & a & a^2 \\ 1 & b & b^2 \\ 1 & c & c^2 \end{vmatrix} = \begin{vmatrix} 1 & a & a^2 \\ 1 & b & b^2 \\ 1 & c & c^2 \end{vmatrix}$$

$$\therefore \ D = \Delta_1 - \Delta_2$$

$$= \begin{vmatrix} 1 & a & a^2 \\ 1 & b & b^2 \\ 1 & c & c^2 \end{vmatrix} - \begin{vmatrix} 1 & a & a^2 \\ 1 & b & b^2 \\ 1 & c & c^2 \end{vmatrix} = 0$$

Hence the Result.

21) Solve $\begin{vmatrix} x+1 & 0 & x+2 \\ 0 & x+2 & x+3 \\ 0 & 0 & x+3 \end{vmatrix} = 0$

Solution

Expanding the determinant along the first column, we get

$(x+1) [(x+2)(x+3) - 0] = 0 \Rightarrow \quad (x+1)(x+2)(x+3) = 0$

$\therefore x = -1, -2, -3$

22) Prove that $\begin{vmatrix} 2a+b & a & b \\ 2b+c & b & c \\ 2c+a & c & a \end{vmatrix} = 0$

Solution

Now $\begin{vmatrix} 2a+b & a & b \\ 2b+c & b & c \\ 2c+a & c & a \end{vmatrix} \quad = \begin{vmatrix} a & a & b \\ b & b & c \\ c & c & a \end{vmatrix} \qquad C_1 \rightarrow C_1 - (C_2 + C_3)$

$= 0 \qquad\qquad [\because C_1 = C_2]$

Hence the Result.

23) Show that $\begin{vmatrix} x+a & x+2a & x+3a \\ x+2a & x+3a & x+4a \\ x+4a & x+5a & x+6a \end{vmatrix} = 0$

Solution

Now consider $\begin{vmatrix} x+a & x+2a & x+3a \\ x+2a & x+3a & x+4a \\ x+4a & x+5a & x+6a \end{vmatrix}$

$$= \begin{vmatrix} x+a & a & 2a \\ x+2a & a & 2a \\ x+4a & a & 2a \end{vmatrix} \quad \begin{aligned} C_2 &\to C_2 - C_1 \\ C_3 &\to C_3 - C_1 \end{aligned}$$

[2nd and 3rd column are proportional]

$$= 0$$

Hence the Result.

24) Prove that $\begin{vmatrix} 1+a & 1 & 1 \\ 1 & 1+b & 1 \\ 1 & 1 & 1+c \end{vmatrix} = abc\left(1 + \dfrac{1}{a} + \dfrac{1}{b} + \dfrac{1}{c}\right)$

Solution

Taking out a, b, c common from 1st, 2nd and 3rd columns respectively

$$\begin{vmatrix} 1+a & 1 & 1 \\ 1 & 1+b & 1 \\ 1 & 1 & 1+c \end{vmatrix} = abc \begin{vmatrix} \dfrac{1}{a}+1 & \dfrac{1}{b} & \dfrac{1}{c} \\ \dfrac{1}{a} & \dfrac{1}{b}+1 & \dfrac{1}{c} \\ \dfrac{1}{a} & \dfrac{1}{b} & \dfrac{1}{c}+1 \end{vmatrix}$$

$$= \quad abc \begin{vmatrix} 1+\dfrac{1}{a}+\dfrac{1}{b}+\dfrac{1}{c} & \dfrac{1}{b} & \dfrac{1}{c} \\ 1+\dfrac{1}{a}+\dfrac{1}{b}+\dfrac{1}{c} & \dfrac{1}{b}+1 & \dfrac{1}{c} \\ 1+\dfrac{1}{a}+\dfrac{1}{b}+\dfrac{1}{c} & \dfrac{1}{b} & 1+\dfrac{1}{c} \end{vmatrix} \qquad C_1 \rightarrow C_1 + C_2 + C_3$$

$$= \quad abc\left(1+\dfrac{1}{a}+\dfrac{1}{b}+\dfrac{1}{c}\right) \begin{vmatrix} 1 & \dfrac{1}{b} & \dfrac{1}{c} \\ 1 & 1+\dfrac{1}{b} & \dfrac{1}{c} \\ 1 & \dfrac{1}{b} & 1+\dfrac{1}{c} \end{vmatrix}$$

$$= \quad abc\left(1+\dfrac{1}{a}+\dfrac{1}{b}+\dfrac{1}{c}\right) \begin{vmatrix} 1 & \dfrac{1}{b} & \dfrac{1}{c} \\ 0 & 1 & 0 \\ 0 & 0 & 1 \end{vmatrix} \qquad \begin{matrix} R_2 \rightarrow R_2 - R_1 \\ R_3 \rightarrow R_3 - R_2 \end{matrix}$$

$$= \quad abc\left(1+\dfrac{1}{a}+\dfrac{1}{b}+\dfrac{1}{c}\right)\{1(1)\} \qquad \text{(expanding along the first column)}$$

$$= \quad abc\left(1+\dfrac{1}{a}+\dfrac{1}{b}+\dfrac{1}{c}\right)$$

Hence the Result.

Exercise Problems

1. $\begin{vmatrix} 0 & c & b \\ c & 0 & a \\ b & a & 0 \end{vmatrix}$ is equal to

   (i) 0   (ii) 2abc   (iii) abc   (iv) – abc

2. If $\begin{vmatrix} 1 & 3 & 5 \\ m & 5 & 7 \\ 3 & 9 & 1 \end{vmatrix}$ = 0 then the value of m is

   (i) 0   (ii) 1   (iii) 2   (iv) 3

3. If $\begin{vmatrix} 1 & 2 & 3 \\ 3 & 1 & 2 \\ 2 & 3 & 1 \end{vmatrix}$ = A then, If $\begin{vmatrix} 3 & 1 & 2 \\ 1 & 2 & 3 \\ 2 & 3 & 1 \end{vmatrix}$ is equal to

   (i) -A   (ii) A   (iii) 2A   (iv) -2A

4. The solution of $\begin{vmatrix} x & 2 \\ 1 & 1 \end{vmatrix}$ is

   (i) 0   (ii) 1   (iii) -1   (iv) 2

5. If $\begin{vmatrix} 1 & a & a^2 \\ 1 & b & b^2 \\ 1 & c & c^2 \end{vmatrix}$ = (a – b) (b – c) (c – a), then the value of $\begin{vmatrix} 1 & 5 & 25 \\ 1 & 8 & 64 \\ 1 & 11 & 121 \end{vmatrix}$ is

   (i) 34   (ii) 44   (iii) 54   (iv) 64

6. The value of $\begin{vmatrix} 1 & 1 & 1 \\ a & b & c \\ 2a & 2b & 2c \end{vmatrix}$ is equal to

   (i) 0   (ii) 1   (iii) 2 abc   (iv) abc

7. The value of $\begin{vmatrix} 1 & a & b+c \\ 1 & b & c+a \\ 1 & c & a+b \end{vmatrix}$ is equal to

   (i) a +b + c   (ii) abc   (iii) 1   (iv) 0

8. The value of $\begin{vmatrix} a-b & b-c & c-a \\ b-c & c-a & a-b \\ c-a & a-b & b-c \end{vmatrix}$ is equal to

    (i) abc   (ii) - abc   (iii) (a+b+c)   (iv) 0

9. Prove that $\begin{vmatrix} 1 & bc & a(b+c) \\ 1 & ca & b(c+a) \\ 1 & ab & c(a+b) \end{vmatrix} = 0$

10. Prove that $\begin{vmatrix} b^2c^2 & bc & b+c \\ c^2a^2 & ca & c+a \\ a^2b^2 & ab & a+b \end{vmatrix} = 0$

11. Prove that $\begin{vmatrix} \dfrac{1}{a} & a^2 & bc \\ \dfrac{1}{b} & b^2 & ca \\ \dfrac{1}{c} & c^2 & ab \end{vmatrix} = 0$

12. Prove that $\begin{vmatrix} a-b-c & 2a & 2a \\ 2b & b-c-a & 2b \\ 2c & 2c & c-a-b \end{vmatrix} = (a+b+c)^3$

13. Prove that $\begin{vmatrix} a+b+2c & a & b \\ c & b+c+2a & b \\ c & a & c+a+2b \end{vmatrix} = 2(a+b+c)^3$

14. Prove that $\begin{vmatrix} a & b & c \\ a-b & b-c & c-a \\ b+c & c+a & a+b \end{vmatrix} = a^3 + b^3 + c^3 - 3abc$

15. Prove that $\begin{vmatrix} 1+a & 1 & 1 \\ 1 & 1+a & 1 \\ 1 & 1 & 1+a \end{vmatrix} = a^2(a+3)$

ADJOINT OF A SQUARE MATRIX (OR) ADJUGATE

Let A be any square matrix to find an adjoint of A

Step 1

Replace each element of A by its co-factor value

Step 2

Take the transpose of A.

(i.e.) The Adjoint or Adjugate matrix of a square matrix A is the transpose of the matrix formed by cofactors of elements of determinant |A|.

$$\text{Let } A = \begin{pmatrix} a_{11} & a_{12} & a_{13} \\ a_{21} & a_{22} & a_{23} \\ a_{31} & a_{32} & a_{33} \end{pmatrix} \text{ be 3 x 3 square matrix.}$$

Let A_{ij} denote the cofactor of the element a_{ij} in the determinant |A|.

The matrix formed by cofactors of elements of determinant |A| is

$$\begin{pmatrix} A_{11} & A_{12} & A_{13} \\ A_{21} & A_{22} & A_{23} \\ A_{31} & A_{32} & A_{33} \end{pmatrix}.$$

$$\therefore \text{ adj } A = \begin{pmatrix} A_{11} & A_{12} & A_{13} \\ A_{21} & A_{22} & A_{23} \\ A_{31} & A_{32} & A_{33} \end{pmatrix}^{T}$$

Example Problems

1) Find adjoint A of $A = \begin{pmatrix} 1 & 2 \\ -3 & 0 \end{pmatrix}$

Solution

Let A_{ij} denote the cofactor of a_{ij} in |A|

A_{11} = cofactor of a_{11} = $(-1)^{1+1} (0)$ = 0

A_{12} = cofactor of a_{12} = $(-1)^{1+2}(-3) = 3$

A_{21} = cofactor of a_{21} = $(-1)^{2+1}(2) = -2$

A_{22} = cofactor of a_{22} = $(-1)^{2+2}(1) = 1$

$$\therefore \text{ Adj A} = \begin{pmatrix} A_{11} & A_{12} \\ A_{21} & A_{22} \end{pmatrix}^{T} = \begin{pmatrix} 0 & 3 \\ -2 & 1 \end{pmatrix}^{T}$$

$$\therefore \text{ Adj A} = \begin{pmatrix} 0 & -2 \\ 3 & 1 \end{pmatrix}$$

2) Find adjoint A of A = $\begin{pmatrix} 0 & 1 & 2 \\ 1 & 2 & 3 \\ 3 & 1 & 1 \end{pmatrix}$

Solution

Let A_{ij} denote the cofactor of a_{ij} in $|A|$.

A_{11} = Cofactor of $a_{11}(0) = (-1)^{1+1}\begin{vmatrix} 2 & 3 \\ 1 & 1 \end{vmatrix}$

$$= + (2 - 3) = -1$$

A_{12} = Cofactor of $a_{12}[1] = (-1)^{1+2}\begin{vmatrix} 1 & 3 \\ 3 & 1 \end{vmatrix}$

$$= -(1 - 9) = 8$$

A_{13} = Cofactor of $a_{13}[2] = (-1)^{1+3}\begin{vmatrix} 1 & 2 \\ 3 & 1 \end{vmatrix}$

$$= (1 - 6) = -5$$

A_{21} = Cofactor of $a_{21}[1] = (-1)^{2+1}\begin{vmatrix} 1 & 2 \\ 1 & 1 \end{vmatrix}$

$$= -(1 - 2) = 1$$

A_{22} $= $ Cofactor of a_{22} $[2] = (-1)^{2+2} \begin{vmatrix} 0 & 2 \\ 3 & 1 \end{vmatrix}$

$$= (0 - 6) = -6$$

A_{23} $= $ Cofactor of a_{23} $[3] = (-1)^{2+3} \begin{vmatrix} 0 & 1 \\ 3 & 1 \end{vmatrix}$

$$= -1 (0 - 3) = 3$$

A_{31} $= $ Cofactor of a_{31} $[3] = (-1)^{3+1} \begin{vmatrix} 1 & 2 \\ 2 & 3 \end{vmatrix}$

$$= (3 - 4) = -1$$

A_{32} $= $ Cofactor of a_{32} $[1] = (-1)^{3+2} \begin{vmatrix} 0 & 2 \\ 1 & 3 \end{vmatrix}$

$$= - (0 - 2) = -2$$

A_{33} $= $ Cofactor of a_{33} $[1] = (-1)^{3+3} \begin{vmatrix} 0 & 1 \\ 1 & 2 \end{vmatrix}$

$$= (0 - 1) = -1$$

Cofactor of A $= \begin{pmatrix} -1 & 8 & -5 \\ 1 & -6 & 3 \\ -1 & 2 & -1 \end{pmatrix}$

Transpose of co-factor of A is $A^{T} = \begin{pmatrix} -1 & 1 & -1 \\ 8 & -6 & 2 \\ -5 & 3 & -1 \end{pmatrix} = $ adj of A

$\therefore$ Adj of A $= \begin{pmatrix} -1 & 1 & -1 \\ 8 & -6 & 2 \\ -5 & 3 & -1 \end{pmatrix}$

1.6 INVERSE OF A MATRIX

Method to Find the Inverse of Square Matrix A

Step (1) :   Evaluate the value of $|A|$ (only if $|A| \neq 0$ we can find A^{-1})

(i.e.) if determinant value is not equal to 0 then inverse exist, otherwise

we cannot find inverse.

Step (2) :   Find adjoint of matrix A.

$$adj\ A = \begin{bmatrix} A_{11} & A_{12} & A_{13} \\ A_{21} & A_{22} & A_{23} \\ A_{31} & A_{32} & A_{33} \end{bmatrix}^{T}$$

Step (3) :   By formula write down $A^{-1} = \dfrac{1}{|A|}(adj\ A)$

Step (4) :   Finally check $A^{-1} \cdot A = I$ (or)

$$A \cdot A^{-1} = I$$

(I is a unit matrix of order same as that of A)

Example Problems

1) Find A^{-1} when $A = \begin{pmatrix} 5 & -2 \\ 3 & 4 \end{pmatrix}$

Solution

Step (1)   : Find Determinant of A.

$$|A| = \begin{vmatrix} 5 & -2 \\ 3 & 4 \end{vmatrix}$$

$$= 20 - (-6) = 20 + 6 = 26 \neq 0$$

Note :   If $|A| = 0$, A is called as singular matrix.

If $|A| \neq 0$, A is called as non-singular matrix.

Therefore A is a non-singular matrix and A^{-1} exists.

Step (2)   : Find Adjoint of Matrix A.

Let A_{ij} denote the cofactor of a_{ij} in $|A|$.

A_{11} = cofactor of 5 = +4 = 4

A_{12} = cofactor of -2 = -3   = -3

A_{21} = cofactor of 3   = -(-2)= 2

A_{22} = cofactor of 4 = +5 = 5

$$\therefore \text{ adj } A = \begin{pmatrix} A_{11} & A_{12} \\ A_{21} & A_{22} \end{pmatrix}^T = \begin{pmatrix} 4 & -3 \\ 2 & 5 \end{pmatrix}^T = \begin{pmatrix} 4 & 2 \\ -3 & 5 \end{pmatrix}$$

Step (3)   : Find A^{-1}

$$A^{-1} = \frac{1}{|A|} \text{adj.A}$$

$$= \frac{1}{26} \begin{pmatrix} 4 & 2 \\ -3 & 5 \end{pmatrix}$$

$$A^{-1} = \begin{pmatrix} \frac{4}{26} & \frac{2}{26} \\ \frac{-3}{26} & \frac{5}{26} \end{pmatrix}$$

2) Find the inverse of the matrix $\begin{pmatrix} 1 & 1 & 1 \\ 1 & 2 & 3 \\ 1 & 4 & 9 \end{pmatrix}$.

Solution

Step (1)   : Find Determinant of A.

$$\text{Let } A = \begin{bmatrix} 1 & 1 & 1 \\ 1 & 2 & 3 \\ 1 & 4 & 9 \end{bmatrix}$$

$|A|$ $= 1(18 - 12) - 1(9 - 3) + 1(4 - 2)$

$= 6 - 6 + 2 = 2 \neq 0$ $\therefore A^{-1}$ exists.

Step (2)   : Find Adjoint of Matrix A.

Let A_{ij} denote the cofactor of a_{ij} in $|A|$.

$$A_{11} = +\begin{vmatrix} 2 & 3 \\ 4 & 9 \end{vmatrix} \qquad = 18 - 12 \qquad = 6$$

$$A_{12} = -\begin{vmatrix} 1 & 3 \\ 1 & 9 \end{vmatrix} \qquad = -(9 - 3) \qquad = -6$$

$$A_{13} = +\begin{vmatrix} 1 & 2 \\ 1 & 4 \end{vmatrix} \qquad = 4 - 2 \qquad = 2$$

$$A_{21} = -\begin{vmatrix} 1 & 1 \\ 4 & 9 \end{vmatrix} \qquad = -(9 - 4) \qquad = -5$$

$$A_{22} = +\begin{vmatrix} 1 & 1 \\ 1 & 9 \end{vmatrix} \qquad = (9 - 1) \qquad = 8$$

$$A_{23} = -\begin{vmatrix} 1 & 1 \\ 1 & 4 \end{vmatrix} \qquad = -(4 - 1) \qquad = -3$$

$$A_{31} = +\begin{vmatrix} 1 & 1 \\ 2 & 3 \end{vmatrix} \qquad = 3 - 2 \qquad = 1$$

$$A_{32} = -\begin{vmatrix} 1 & 1 \\ 1 & 3 \end{vmatrix} \qquad = -(3 - 1) \qquad = -2$$

$$A_{33} = +\begin{vmatrix} 1 & 1 \\ 1 & 2 \end{vmatrix} \qquad = 2 - 1 \qquad = 1$$

$$\therefore \ \text{adj } A = \begin{bmatrix} A_{11} & A_{12} & A_{13} \\ A_{21} & A_{22} & A_{23} \\ A_{31} & A_{32} & A_{33} \end{bmatrix}^{T} = \begin{bmatrix} 6 & -6 & 2 \\ -5 & 8 & -3 \\ 1 & -2 & 1 \end{bmatrix}^{T}$$

$$\text{adj } A = \begin{bmatrix} 6 & -5 & 1 \\ -6 & 8 & -2 \\ 2 & -3 & 1 \end{bmatrix}$$

Step (3)   : Find A^{-1}

$$A^{-1} = \frac{1}{|A|} adj.A$$

$$A^{-1} = \frac{1}{2}\begin{bmatrix} 6 & -5 & 1 \\ -6 & 8 & -2 \\ 2 & -3 & 1 \end{bmatrix} = \begin{bmatrix} 3 & \dfrac{-5}{2} & \dfrac{1}{2} \\ -3 & 4 & -1 \\ 1 & \dfrac{-3}{2} & \dfrac{1}{2} \end{bmatrix}$$

Exercise Problem

1) Find the inverse of $\begin{bmatrix} 3 & 5 & 7 \\ 2 & -3 & 1 \\ 1 & 1 & 2 \end{bmatrix}$

Answer : $\dfrac{1}{-1}\begin{bmatrix} -7 & -3 & 26 \\ -3 & -1 & 11 \\ 5 & 2 & -19 \end{bmatrix}$

$$\therefore \ A^{-1} = \begin{bmatrix} 7 & 3 & -26 \\ 3 & 1 & -11 \\ -5 & -2 & 19 \end{bmatrix}$$

Note : $A^{-1} \cdot A = I$

1.7 RANK OF A MATRIX

A matrix A is said to be of rank r if at least one minor of A of order r is non-zero. While all minors of order (r+1) are zero.

The rank r of a matrix A is denoted symbolically by

Rank $(A) = r$ (or) $\rho(A) = r$

(i.e.) The rank of A is the order of its highest non-zero minor.

Example Problems

1) Find the Rank of the given matrix $A = \begin{pmatrix} 1 & 2 & 3 \\ 4 & 5 & 6 \\ 3 & 2 & 1 \end{pmatrix}$

Solution

$$|A| = 1(5-12) - 2(4-18) + 3(8-15)$$

$$= 1(-7) - 2(-14) + 3(-7)$$

$$= -7 + 28 - 21$$

$$= 28 - 28 = 0$$

Consider 2 x 2 order

$$\begin{vmatrix} 5 & 6 \\ 2 & 1 \end{vmatrix} = (5-12) = -7 \neq 0$$

$$\therefore \text{ Rank } \rho(A) = 2$$

2) Find the Rank of the given matrix $A = \begin{pmatrix} 1 & 1 & 2 \\ 2 & 0 & 1 \\ 0 & 1 & 1 \end{pmatrix}$

Solution

$$= 1(0-1) - 1(2-0) + 2(2-0)$$

$$= 1(-1) - 1(2) + 4$$

$$= -1 - 2 + 4$$

$$= 1 \neq 0$$

$$\rho(A) = 3$$

3) Find the Rank of the given matrix $\begin{pmatrix} 1 & 0 & 1 & 0 \\ 2 & 1 & 1 & 1 \\ 1 & 1 & 0 & 1 \end{pmatrix}$

Solution

Let A denotes the given matrix

It is a 3 x 4 matrix, therefore the rank cannot exceed 3.

Consider 1st square matrix of order 3.

$\begin{vmatrix} 1 & 0 & 1 \\ 2 & 1 & 1 \\ 1 & 1 & 0 \end{vmatrix}$ $= 1(0-1) - 0(0-1) + 1(2-1) = -1 + 1 = 0$

$\begin{vmatrix} 0 & 1 & 0 \\ 1 & 1 & 1 \\ 1 & 0 & 1 \end{vmatrix}$ $= 0 - 1(1-1) + 0 = 0$

$\begin{vmatrix} 1 & 1 & 0 \\ 2 & 1 & 1 \\ 1 & 0 & 1 \end{vmatrix}$ $= 1(1-0) - 1(2-1) + 0 = 1 - 1 = 0$

$\begin{vmatrix} 1 & 0 & 0 \\ 2 & 1 & 1 \\ 1 & 1 & 1 \end{vmatrix}$ $= 1(1-1) + 0 + 0 = 0$

$\therefore$ Each of the four determinants of four square sub matrices of order 3 is zero.

But the submatrix of order 2 is $\begin{bmatrix} 1 & 0 \\ 2 & 1 \end{bmatrix} = (1-0) = 1$

is non zero hence $\rho(A) = 2$

4) Find the Rank of the given matrix $\begin{pmatrix} 0 & 2 & 3 \\ 0 & 4 & 6 \\ 0 & 6 & 9 \end{pmatrix}$

Solution

Let A be the given matrix

$|A| = 0 - 2\,(0) + 3\,(0) = 0$

So given matrix is singular, therefore the rank is less than 3. Also each of the nine minors of order 2 is zero.

Hence the rank is less than 2.

Since, it is a non-zero matrix, then the rank is 1.

1.8 CHARACTERISTICS ROOTS (OR)

EIGEN VALUES AND EIGEN VECTORS

For a square matrix $A = [a_{ij}]$ of order 2.

The characteristic equations of A is

$$\lambda^2 - a_1\lambda + a_2 = 0$$

Here

a_1 = Sum of its leading diagonals

a_2 = Determinant of $A = |A|$

For a square matrix $A = [a_{ij}]$ of order 3. The characteristic equation of A is

$$\lambda^3 - a_1\lambda^2 + a_2\lambda - a_3 = 0$$

Where

1. a_1 = Sum of its leading diagonals

2. a_2 = Sum of the minors of its leading diagonals

3. a_3 = Determinant of $A = |A|$

Example Problems

1) Find Eigen values and Eigen vectors of the given matrix $\begin{pmatrix} 2 & 2 & 1 \\ 1 & 3 & 1 \\ 1 & 2 & 2 \end{pmatrix}$.

Solution

a_1 = Sum of its leading diagonals

= 2 + 3 + 2 = 7

a_2 $= \begin{vmatrix} 3 & 1 \\ 2 & 2 \end{vmatrix} + \begin{vmatrix} 2 & 1 \\ 1 & 2 \end{vmatrix} + \begin{vmatrix} 2 & 2 \\ 1 & 3 \end{vmatrix}$

= (6 - 2) + (4 − 1) + (6 − 2)

= 4 + 3 + 4   = 11

a_3 = 2 (6 − 2) − 2 (2 − 1) + 1 (2 − 3)

= 2 (4) − 2 (1) + 1 (−1)

= 8 − 2 − 1   = 8 − 3 = 5

The characteristics equation of A is

$$\lambda^3 - 7\lambda^2 + 11\lambda - 5 = 0$$

Factorization

$$
\begin{array}{c|cccc}
1 & 1 & -7 & 11 & -5 \\
  & 0 & 1 & -6 & 5 \\
\hline
  & 1 & -6 & 5 & 0
\end{array}
$$

$$\lambda^2 - 6\lambda + 5 = 0$$
$$(\lambda - 1)(\lambda - 5) = 0$$
$$\lambda = 1, \ \lambda = 5$$

+5
/ \
-1 -5

The Eigen values are 1, 1, 5

Let us find an Eigen vector corresponding to these Eigen values.

Eigen Vectors

$$|A - \lambda I| X = 0$$

Case 1 : $\lambda = 1$

$$\begin{pmatrix} 2-\lambda & 2 & 1 \\ 1 & 3-\lambda & 1 \\ 1 & 2 & 2-\lambda \end{pmatrix} \begin{pmatrix} x_1 \\ x_2 \\ x_3 \end{pmatrix} = 0$$

$$\begin{pmatrix} 2-1 & 2 & 1 \\ 1 & 3-1 & 1 \\ 1 & 2 & 2-1 \end{pmatrix} \begin{pmatrix} x_1 \\ x_2 \\ x_3 \end{pmatrix} = 0$$

$$\begin{pmatrix} 1 & 2 & 1 \\ 1 & 2 & 1 \\ 1 & 2 & 1 \end{pmatrix} \begin{pmatrix} x_1 \\ x_2 \\ x_3 \end{pmatrix} = 0$$

$$x_1 + 2x_2 + x_3 = 0 \quad ----- (1)$$

$$x_1 + 2x_2 + x_3 = 0 \quad ----- (2)$$

$$x_1 + 2x_2 + x_3 = 0 \quad ----- (3)$$

From the last 2 of these equations, we have

x_3	x_1	x_2
1	2	1	1
1	2	1	1

Note : 1st Column is repeated in 4th Column

$$\frac{x_1}{2-2} = \frac{x_2}{1-1} = \frac{x_3}{2-2}$$

$$\frac{x_1}{0} = \frac{x_2}{0} = \frac{x_3}{0}$$

We get one Eigen Vector (0, 0, 0) corresponding to the Eigen value $\lambda = 1$

$$\therefore \ x_1 = \begin{pmatrix} 0 \\ 0 \\ 0 \end{pmatrix} \quad \& \quad x_2 = \begin{pmatrix} 0 \\ 0 \\ 0 \end{pmatrix}$$

Case 2   : $\lambda = 5$

$$\begin{pmatrix} 2-5 & 2 & 1 \\ 1 & 3-5 & 1 \\ 1 & 2 & 2-5 \end{pmatrix} \begin{pmatrix} x_1 \\ x_2 \\ x_3 \end{pmatrix} = 0$$

$$\begin{pmatrix} -3 & 2 & 1 \\ 1 & -2 & 1 \\ 1 & 2 & -3 \end{pmatrix} \begin{pmatrix} x_1 \\ x_2 \\ x_3 \end{pmatrix} = 0$$

$-3x_1 + 2x_2 + x_3 = 0$ ----- (1)

$x_1 - 2x_2 + x_3 = 0$ ----- (2)

$x_1 + x_2 - 3x_3 = 0$ ----- (3)

Take (1) and (2) equations, we have

	x_3	x_1		x_2
	-3	2	1	-3
	1	-2	1	1

Note : 1st Column is repeated in 4th Column

$$\therefore \frac{x_1}{2+2} = \frac{x_2}{1-(-3)} = \frac{x_3}{6-2}$$

$$\frac{x_1}{4} = \frac{x_2}{4} = \frac{x_3}{4}$$

The Corresponding Eigen Vector for $\lambda = 5$ is $\begin{pmatrix}4\\4\\4\end{pmatrix} = 4\begin{pmatrix}1\\1\\1\end{pmatrix}$

$\therefore x_3 = \begin{pmatrix}1\\1\\1\end{pmatrix}$

The Eigen Vectors for the corresponding Eigen values $\lambda = 1, 1, 5$ are

$$x_1 = \begin{pmatrix}0\\0\\0\end{pmatrix} \quad x_2 = \begin{pmatrix}0\\0\\0\end{pmatrix} \quad x_3 = \begin{pmatrix}1\\1\\1\end{pmatrix}$$

2) Find Eigen values and Eigen Vectors for the given matrix $\begin{pmatrix}1&1&3\\1&5&1\\3&1&1\end{pmatrix}$

Solution

$\begin{pmatrix}1&1&3\\1&5&1\\3&1&1\end{pmatrix}$

$a_1 \quad = 1+5+1 = 7$

$a_2 \quad = \begin{vmatrix}5&1\\1&1\end{vmatrix} + \begin{vmatrix}1&3\\3&1\end{vmatrix} + \begin{vmatrix}1&1\\1&5\end{vmatrix}$

$\quad = (5-1) + (1-9) + (5-1)$

$\quad = 4-8+4 = 8-8 = 0$

$$a_3 \quad = \quad 1\begin{vmatrix} 5 & 1 \\ 1 & 1 \end{vmatrix} - 1\begin{vmatrix} 1 & 1 \\ 3 & 1 \end{vmatrix} + 3\begin{vmatrix} 1 & 5 \\ 3 & 1 \end{vmatrix}$$

$$= \quad 1\,(5-1) - 1\,(1-3) + 3\,(1-15)$$

$$= \quad 1\,(4) - 1\,(-2) + 3\,(-14)$$

$$= \quad 4 + 2 - 42$$

$$\therefore \ a_3 \ = \quad 6 - 42 \ = -36$$

$\therefore$ Characteristic Equation of A is

$$\lambda^3 - 7\lambda^2 + 0\lambda - (-36) = 0$$

$$\lambda^3 - 7\lambda^2 + 0\lambda + 36 = 0$$

Factorization

$$\begin{array}{r|rrrr} 3 & 1 & -7 & 0 & 36 \\ & 0 & 3 & 12 & -36 \\ \hline & 1 & -4 & -12 & 0 \end{array}$$

$$\lambda^2 - 4\lambda - 12 = 0 \qquad\qquad -12$$

$$(\lambda + 2)(\lambda - 6) = 0 \qquad\qquad -6 \quad 2$$

$$\therefore \quad \lambda = -2, \qquad \lambda = 6$$

$\therefore$ The Eigen Values are 3, -2, 6

Let us find an Eigen vector corresponding to these Eigen values.

Eigen Vectors

$$| A - \lambda I | X = 0$$

Case 1   : when $\lambda = 3$

$$\begin{pmatrix} 1-\lambda & 1 & 3 \\ 1 & 5-\lambda & 1 \\ 3 & 1 & 1-\lambda \end{pmatrix} \begin{pmatrix} x_1 \\ x_2 \\ x_3 \end{pmatrix} = 0$$

$$\begin{pmatrix} 1-3 & 1 & 3 \\ 1 & 5-3 & 1 \\ 3 & 1 & 1-3 \end{pmatrix} \begin{pmatrix} x_1 \\ x_2 \\ x_3 \end{pmatrix} = 0$$

$$\begin{pmatrix} -2 & 1 & 3 \\ 1 & 2 & 1 \\ 3 & 1 & -2 \end{pmatrix} \begin{pmatrix} x_1 \\ x_2 \\ x_3 \end{pmatrix} = 0$$

$$-2x_1 + x_2 + 3x_3 = 0 \qquad \text{----- (1)}$$

$$x_1 + 2x_2 + x_3 = 0 \qquad \text{----- (2)}$$

$$3x_1 + x_2 - 2x_3 = 0 \qquad \text{----- (3)}$$

From (1) and (2)

Note : 1st Column is repeated in 4th Column

$$\frac{x_1}{1-6} = \frac{x_2}{3-(-2)} = \frac{x_3}{-4-1}$$

$$\frac{x_1}{-5} = \frac{x_2}{3+2} = \frac{x_3}{-5}$$

Eigen Vector Corresponding to the Eigen value $\lambda = 3$ is $\begin{pmatrix} -5 \\ 5 \\ -5 \end{pmatrix} = 5 \begin{pmatrix} -1 \\ 1 \\ -1 \end{pmatrix}$

$\therefore x_1 = \begin{pmatrix} -1 \\ 1 \\ -1 \end{pmatrix}$

Case 2 $: \lambda = -2$

$$\begin{pmatrix} 1-\lambda & 1 & 3 \\ 1 & 5-\lambda & 1 \\ 3 & 1 & 1-\lambda \end{pmatrix} \begin{pmatrix} x_1 \\ x_2 \\ x_3 \end{pmatrix} = 0$$

$$\begin{pmatrix} 1-(-2) & 1 & 3 \\ 1 & 5-(-2) & 1 \\ 3 & 1 & 1-(-2) \end{pmatrix} \begin{pmatrix} x_1 \\ x_2 \\ x_3 \end{pmatrix} = 0$$

$$\begin{pmatrix} 3 & 1 & 3 \\ 1 & 7 & 1 \\ 3 & 1 & 3 \end{pmatrix} \begin{pmatrix} x_1 \\ x_2 \\ x_3 \end{pmatrix} = 0$$

$3x_1 + x_2 + 3x_3 = 0$ ------ (1)

$x_1 + 7x_2 + x_3 = 0$ ------ (2)

$3x_1 + x_2 + 3x_3 = 0$ ------ (3)

Take (2) and (3) equations

	x_3	x_1	x_2
1	7	1	1
3	1	3	3

Note : 1st Column is repeated in 4th Column

$$\frac{x_1}{21-1} = \frac{x_2}{3-3} = \frac{x_3}{1-21}$$

$$\frac{x_1}{20} = \frac{x_2}{0} = \frac{x_3}{-20}$$

$\therefore$ The Eigen Vector Corresponding to the Eigen value $\lambda = -2$ is $\begin{pmatrix} 20 \\ 0 \\ -20 \end{pmatrix} = 20 \begin{pmatrix} 1 \\ 0 \\ -1 \end{pmatrix}$

$\therefore X_2 = \begin{pmatrix} 1 \\ 0 \\ -1 \end{pmatrix}$

Case 3 : $\lambda = 6$

$$\begin{pmatrix} 1-6 & 1 & 3 \\ 1 & 5-6 & 1 \\ 3 & 1 & 1-6 \end{pmatrix} \begin{pmatrix} x_1 \\ x_2 \\ x_3 \end{pmatrix} = 0$$

$$\begin{pmatrix} -5 & 1 & 3 \\ 1 & -1 & 1 \\ 3 & 1 & -5 \end{pmatrix} \begin{pmatrix} x_1 \\ x_2 \\ x_3 \end{pmatrix} = 0$$

$$-5x_1 + x_2 + 3x_3 = 0 \quad ----- (1)$$

$$x_1 - x_2 + x_3 = 0 \quad ----- (2)$$

$$3x_1 + x_2 - 5x_3 = 0 \quad ----- (3)$$

Take equations (1) and (2)

	X_3	X_1	X_2
	-5	1 $\quad$ 3	-5
	1	-1 $\quad$ 1	1

Note : 1st Column is repeated in 4th Column

$$\frac{x_1}{1-(-3)} = \frac{x_2}{3-(-5)} = \frac{x_3}{5-1}$$

$$\frac{x_1}{4} = \frac{x_2}{8} = \frac{x_3}{4}$$

$\therefore$ The Eigen Vector Corresponding to the Eigen Value $\lambda = 6$ is $\begin{pmatrix} 4 \\ 8 \\ 4 \end{pmatrix} = 4 \begin{pmatrix} 1 \\ 2 \\ 1 \end{pmatrix}$

$$x_3 = \begin{pmatrix} 1 \\ 2 \\ 1 \end{pmatrix}$$

The Eigen Vectors for the corresponding Eigen values $\lambda = 3, -2, 6$ are

$\therefore \quad x_1 = \begin{pmatrix} -1 \\ 1 \\ -1 \end{pmatrix} \qquad x_2 = \begin{pmatrix} 1 \\ 0 \\ -1 \end{pmatrix} \qquad x_3 = \begin{pmatrix} 1 \\ 2 \\ 1 \end{pmatrix}$

3) Determine the Eigen values (or) characteristics roots and Eigen Vectors (or)

Characteristic vector of the matrix, $A = \begin{bmatrix} 5 & 4 \\ 1 & 2 \end{bmatrix}$

Solution

The characteristic equation of A is

$a_1 \qquad$ = sum of its leading diagonal.

$\qquad = 5 + 2 = 7$

$a_2 \qquad$ = Determinant of $A = \begin{vmatrix} 5 & 4 \\ 1 & 2 \end{vmatrix} = 10 - 4 = 6$

$\therefore$ The characteristic equation of A is

$\lambda^2 - a_1\lambda + a_2 = 0 \qquad\qquad\qquad 6$

$\lambda^2 - 7\lambda + 6 = 0 \qquad\qquad\qquad -1 \qquad -6$

$(\lambda - 1)(\lambda - 6)$

$\lambda = 1, \lambda = 6$

The Eigen Values are 1, 6

Let us find an Eigen vector corresponding to these Eigen values.

Eigen Vectors

Case 1 $: \lambda = 1$

$$\begin{pmatrix} 5-\lambda & 4 \\ 1 & 2-\lambda \end{pmatrix} \begin{pmatrix} x_1 \\ x_2 \end{pmatrix} = 0$$

$$\begin{pmatrix} 5-1 & 4 \\ 1 & 2-1 \end{pmatrix} \begin{pmatrix} x_1 \\ x_2 \end{pmatrix} = 0$$

$$\begin{pmatrix} 4 & 4 \\ 1 & 1 \end{pmatrix} \begin{pmatrix} x_1 \\ x_2 \end{pmatrix} = 0$$

$$\left. \begin{aligned} 4x_1 + 4x_2 &= 0 \quad \text{----- (1)} \\ x_1 + x_2 &= 0 \quad \text{----- (2)} \end{aligned} \right\} \quad \begin{aligned} &\text{Take any one of the equation to find} \\ &\text{Eigen Vector} \end{aligned}$$

Here we Take Equation (2), then we have

Then $x_1 = 4$. Put this value in equation $x_1 + x_2 = 0$, then $4 + x_2 = 0$

$\therefore$ $x_2 = -4$

$$\therefore \ x_1 = \begin{pmatrix} 4 \\ -4 \end{pmatrix} = 4 \begin{pmatrix} 1 \\ -1 \end{pmatrix}$$

Suppose we have take equation 1, then we have

Then $x_1 = 1$ and $x_2 = -1$

$\therefore$ we have Eigen Vector $x_1 = \begin{pmatrix} 1 \\ -1 \end{pmatrix}$

$\therefore x_1 = \begin{pmatrix} 1 \\ -1 \end{pmatrix}$ is an Eigen Vector of A corresponding to the Eigen Value 1.

Case 2 $: \lambda = 6$

$\begin{pmatrix} 5-6 & 4 \\ 1 & 2-6 \end{pmatrix} \begin{pmatrix} x_1 \\ x_2 \end{pmatrix} = 0$

$\begin{pmatrix} -1 & 4 \\ 1 & -4 \end{pmatrix} \begin{pmatrix} x_1 \\ x_2 \end{pmatrix} = 0$

$-x_1 + 4x_2 = 0$ ----- (1)

$x_1 - 4x_2 = 0$ ----- (2)

Take Equation (1) then we have

Then

$x_1 = -4$, put this value in equation (1) then we get

$-(-4) + 4x_2 = 0$

$4 + 4x_2 = 0$

$4x_2 = -4$

$x_2 = -1$

$\therefore x_2 = \begin{pmatrix} -4 \\ -1 \end{pmatrix} = -1 \begin{pmatrix} 4 \\ 1 \end{pmatrix} = \begin{pmatrix} 4 \\ 1 \end{pmatrix}$

Take equation (2)

$$\begin{pmatrix} -1 & 4 \\ 1 & -4 \end{pmatrix}$$

$x_1 = +4$ and $x_2 = -(-1)$

$$x_2 = \begin{pmatrix} 4 \\ 1 \end{pmatrix}$$

$\therefore$ The Eigen Vectors for the corresponding Eigen Values $\lambda = 1, 6$ are

$$x_1 = \begin{pmatrix} 1 \\ -1 \end{pmatrix}$$

$$x_2 = \begin{pmatrix} 4 \\ 1 \end{pmatrix}$$

4. Determine the characteristic roots of the matrix $A = \begin{bmatrix} 0 & 1 & 2 \\ 1 & 0 & -1 \\ 2 & -1 & 0 \end{bmatrix}$

Solution

$$\text{Let } A = \begin{bmatrix} 0 & 1 & 2 \\ 1 & 0 & -1 \\ 2 & -1 & 0 \end{bmatrix}$$

a_1 = sum of its leading diagonal = $0 + 0 + 0 = 0$

$a_1 = 0$

a_2 = sum of the minor of its leading diagonal

$$a_2 = \begin{vmatrix} 0 & -1 \\ -1 & 0 \end{vmatrix} + \begin{vmatrix} 0 & 2 \\ 2 & 0 \end{vmatrix} + \begin{vmatrix} 0 & 1 \\ 1 & 0 \end{vmatrix}$$

$$= (0\text{-}1) + (0\text{-}4) + (0\text{-}1)$$

$$= -1 - 4 - 1$$

$$a_2 = -6$$

$a_3 \quad = |A|$

$\quad = 0(0-1) -1 (0+2) + 2(-1-0)$

$\quad = 0 - 1(2) + 2(-1) \quad = -2 -2$

$a_3 \quad = -4$

$\therefore$ The characteristic equation is

$\lambda^3 - a_1\lambda^2 + a_2\lambda - a_3 = 0$

$\lambda^3 - 0\lambda^2 - 6\lambda - (-4) = 0$

$\lambda^3 - 6\lambda + 4 = 0$

$(\lambda - 2)(\lambda^2 + 2\lambda - 2) = 0$

$\lambda^2 + 2\lambda - 2 = 0$

The formula for roots of the quadratic equation is

$$x = -b \pm \frac{\sqrt{b^2 - 4ac}}{2a} \qquad \text{here} \quad x = \lambda$$

$a = 1, b = 2, c = -2$

$$\lambda \quad = -2 \pm \frac{\sqrt{2^2 - 4(1)(-2)}}{2 \times 1}$$

$$= -2 \pm \frac{\sqrt{4+8}}{2} \qquad = \frac{-2}{2} \pm \frac{\sqrt{12}}{2} \qquad = -1 \pm \frac{\sqrt{12}}{2}$$

$$= -1 \pm \frac{\sqrt{4 \times 3}}{2} \qquad = -1 \pm \frac{2\sqrt{3}}{2}$$

$\lambda \quad = -1 \pm \sqrt{3}$ from equ. (1) $\lambda = 2$ & $-1 \pm \sqrt{3}$

$\therefore \lambda = 2, -1 \pm \sqrt{3}$

5. Verify that the matrices

$$A = \begin{bmatrix} 0 & h & g \\ h & 0 & f \\ g & f & 0 \end{bmatrix}, \; B = \begin{bmatrix} 0 & f & h \\ f & 0 & g \\ h & g & 0 \end{bmatrix}, \; C = \begin{bmatrix} 0 & g & f \\ g & 0 & h \\ f & h & 0 \end{bmatrix}$$

Have the same characteristics equation, $\lambda^3 - (f^2 + g^2 + h^2)\lambda - 2fgh = 0$

Solution

The characteristic equation of the matrix A is

$|A - \lambda I| X = 0$

$|A - \lambda I| = 0$

$$\begin{bmatrix} 0 & h & g \\ h & 0 & f \\ g & f & 0 \end{bmatrix} - \lambda \begin{bmatrix} 1 & 0 & 0 \\ 0 & 1 & 0 \\ 0 & 0 & 1 \end{bmatrix} = 0$$

$$\begin{bmatrix} 0 & h & g \\ h & 0 & f \\ g & f & 0 \end{bmatrix} - \begin{bmatrix} \lambda & 0 & 0 \\ 0 & \lambda & 0 \\ 0 & 0 & \lambda \end{bmatrix} = 0$$

$$\begin{bmatrix} 0-\lambda & h & g \\ h & 0-\lambda & f \\ g & f & 0-\lambda \end{bmatrix} = 0$$

$(0-\lambda)[(0-\lambda)(0-\lambda) - f^2] - h[h(0-\lambda) - fg] + g[hf - g(0-\lambda)] = 0$

$(0-\lambda)[0 - 0 - 0 + \lambda^2 - f^2] - h[0 - h\lambda - fg] + g[hf - 0 + g\lambda] = 0$

$-\lambda^3 + \lambda f^2 + h^2\lambda + fgh + fgh + g^2\lambda = 0$

$-\lambda^3 + \lambda(f^2 + h^2 + g^2) + 2fgh = 0$

$\lambda^3 - \lambda(f^2 + h^2 + g^2) - 2fgh = 0$

1.9 CAYLEY-HAMILTON THEOREM

This theorem is an interesting one that provides an alternative method for finding the inverse of a matrix A, also any positive integral power of A can be expressed using this theorem as a linear combination of those of lower degree.

Statement of Theorem

Every square matrix satisfies its own characteristics equation.

This means that if

$$C_0\lambda^n + C_1\lambda^{n-1} + \ldots\ldots\ldots + C_{n-1}\lambda + C_n = 0$$

is the characteristic equation of a square matrix A of order N, then

$$C_0A^n + C_1A^{n-1} + \ldots\ldots\ldots + C_{n-1}A + C_nI = 0 \quad \text{----- (1)}$$

Note

When λ is replaced by A in the characteristic equation, the constant term C_n should be replaced by C_nI to get the result of Caylay Hamilton theorem, where I is the unit matrix of order n. Also 'O' in the right hand side of (1) is a null matrix of order n.

Example Problems

(1) Find the characteristics of the matrix

$$A = \begin{pmatrix} 1 & 0 & 3 \\ 2 & 1 & -1 \\ 1 & -1 & 1 \end{pmatrix}$$ then verify the matrix for a characteristic equation also calculate A^{-1}.

Solution

Let A be the given matrix. The characteristic equation of A is

$$\lambda^3 - 9\lambda^2 + a_2\lambda - a_3 = 0$$

$$a_1 \quad = 1 + 1 + 1 = 3$$

a_2 = $\begin{vmatrix} 1 & 1 \\ -1 & 1 \end{vmatrix} + \begin{vmatrix} 1 & 3 \\ 1 & 1 \end{vmatrix} + \begin{vmatrix} 1 & 0 \\ 2 & 1 \end{vmatrix}$

= $(1-(-1)) + (1-3) + (1-0)$

= $0-2+1$ $=-1$

a_3 = determinant of A

= $1(1-1) - 0(2+1) + 3(-2-1)$

= -9

Let the characteristic equation is $\lambda^3 - a_1\lambda^2 + a_2\lambda - a_3 = 0$

$\lambda^3 - 3\lambda^2 - 1\lambda + 9 = 0$

Let $\lambda = A$ and constant value is multiplied with I, then the equation becomes

$A^3 - 3A^2 - A + 9I = 0$

A^2 = $\begin{pmatrix} 1 & 0 & 3 \\ 2 & 1 & -1 \\ 1 & -1 & 1 \end{pmatrix} \begin{pmatrix} 1 & 0 & 3 \\ 2 & 1 & -1 \\ 1 & -1 & 1 \end{pmatrix}$

= $\begin{pmatrix} 1+0+3 & 0+0+(-3) & 3+0+3 \\ 2+2-1 & 0+1+1 & 6-1-1 \\ 1-2+1 & 0-1-1 & 3+1+1 \end{pmatrix}$

= $\begin{pmatrix} 4 & -3 & 6 \\ 3 & 2 & 4 \\ 0 & -2 & 5 \end{pmatrix}$

$A^3 = A^2 - A$

= $\begin{pmatrix} 4 & -3 & 6 \\ 3 & 2 & 4 \\ 0 & -2 & 5 \end{pmatrix} \begin{pmatrix} 1 & 0 & 3 \\ 2 & 1 & -1 \\ 1 & -1 & 1 \end{pmatrix}$

$$= \begin{pmatrix} 4+(-6)+6 & 0-3-6 & 12+3+6 \\ 3+4+4 & 0+2-4 & 9-2+4 \\ 0-4+5 & 0-2-5 & 0+2+5 \end{pmatrix}$$

$$= \begin{pmatrix} 4 & -9 & 21 \\ 11 & -2 & 11 \\ 1 & -7 & 7 \end{pmatrix}$$

Consider L.H.S. equation $A^3 - 3A^2 - A + 9I$. Here I is an identity matrix.

$$= \begin{pmatrix} 4 & -9 & 21 \\ 11 & -2 & 11 \\ 1 & -7 & 7 \end{pmatrix} - 3\begin{pmatrix} 4 & -3 & 6 \\ 3 & 2 & 4 \\ 0 & -2 & 5 \end{pmatrix} - \begin{pmatrix} 1 & 0 & 3 \\ 2 & 1 & -1 \\ 1 & -1 & 1 \end{pmatrix} + \begin{pmatrix} 9 & 0 & 0 \\ 0 & 9 & 0 \\ 0 & 0 & 9 \end{pmatrix}$$

$$= \begin{pmatrix} 4 & -9 & 21 \\ 11 & -2 & 11 \\ 1 & -7 & 7 \end{pmatrix} - \begin{pmatrix} 12 & -9 & 18 \\ 9 & 6 & 12 \\ 0 & -6 & 15 \end{pmatrix} - \begin{pmatrix} 1 & 0 & 3 \\ 2 & 1 & -1 \\ 1 & -1 & 1 \end{pmatrix} + \begin{pmatrix} 9 & 0 & 0 \\ 0 & 9 & 0 \\ 0 & 0 & 9 \end{pmatrix}$$

$$= \begin{pmatrix} 4-12-1+9 & -9+9-0-0 & 21-18-3+0 \\ 11-9-2+0 & -2-6-1+9 & 11-12+1+0 \\ 1-0-1+0 & -7+6+1+0 & 7-15-1+9 \end{pmatrix}$$

$$= \begin{pmatrix} 13-13 & 0 & 21-21 \\ 11-11 & -9+9 & 12-12 \\ 0 & -7+7 & 16-16 \end{pmatrix} = \begin{pmatrix} 0 & 0 & 0 \\ 0 & 0 & 0 \\ 0 & 0 & 0 \end{pmatrix} = 0 = \text{R.H.S}$$

Thus A satisfies its characteristics equation

$$A^3 - 3A^2 - A + 9I = 0$$

Divided by A

$$A^2 - 3A - \frac{A}{A} + \frac{9A.A^{-1}}{A} = 0$$

Note : $I = A.A^{-1}$, $\therefore A^{-1} = \dfrac{1}{A}$

Substitute this value in I then we get $A \cdot \dfrac{1}{A} = I$

$$A^2 - 3A - I + 9.A^{-1} \qquad = 0$$

$$9A^{-1} = -A^2 + 3A + I$$

$$\therefore A^{-1} = \frac{1}{9}\left[-A^2 + 3A + I\right]$$

$$= \frac{1}{9}\left[-\begin{pmatrix} 4 & -3 & 6 \\ 3 & 2 & 4 \\ 0 & -2 & 5 \end{pmatrix} + 3\begin{pmatrix} 1 & 0 & 3 \\ 2 & 1 & -1 \\ 1 & -1 & 1 \end{pmatrix} + \begin{pmatrix} 1 & 0 & 0 \\ 0 & 1 & 0 \\ 0 & 0 & 1 \end{pmatrix}\right]$$

$$= \frac{1}{9}\begin{pmatrix} -4+3+1 & 3+0+0 & -6+9+0 \\ -3+6+0 & -2+3+1 & -4-3+0 \\ 0+3+0 & 2-3+0 & -5+3+1 \end{pmatrix}$$

$$= \frac{1}{9}\begin{pmatrix} 0 & 3 & 3 \\ 3 & 2 & -7 \\ 3 & -1 & -1 \end{pmatrix} = A^{-1}$$

2) Verify Cayley Hamilton Theorem for the matrix $A = \begin{pmatrix} 7 & 2 & -2 \\ -6 & -1 & 2 \\ 6 & 2 & -1 \end{pmatrix}$ and also find A^{-1}.

Solution

$$a_1 = 7 - 1 - 1 = 5$$

$$a_2 \quad = \quad \begin{vmatrix} -1 & 2 \\ 2 & -1 \end{vmatrix} + \begin{vmatrix} 7 & -2 \\ 6 & -1 \end{vmatrix} + \begin{vmatrix} 7 & 2 \\ -6 & -1 \end{vmatrix}$$

$$a_2 \quad = \quad (1-4) + (-7+12) + (-7+12)$$

$$= \quad -3 + 5 + 5 = 7$$

$$a_3 \quad = \quad 7(1-4) - 2(6-12) - 2(-12+6)$$

$$= \quad 7(-3) + 12 - 2(-6)$$

$$= \quad -21 + 12 + 12 = 3$$

Let the characteristic equation is

$$\lambda^3 - a_1\lambda^2 + a_2\lambda - a_3 = 0$$

$$\lambda^3 - 5\lambda^2 + 7\lambda - 3 = 0$$

Let $\lambda = A$

$$\therefore A^3 - 5A^2 + 7A - 3I \quad = 0$$

$$A^2 \quad = \begin{pmatrix} 7 & 2 & -2 \\ -6 & -1 & 2 \\ 6 & 2 & -1 \end{pmatrix} \begin{pmatrix} 7 & 2 & -2 \\ -6 & -1 & 2 \\ 6 & 2 & -1 \end{pmatrix} = \begin{pmatrix} 25 & 8 & -8 \\ -24 & -7 & 8 \\ 24 & 8 & -7 \end{pmatrix}$$

$$A^2.A \quad = \begin{pmatrix} 25 & 8 & -8 \\ -24 & -7 & 8 \\ 24 & 8 & -7 \end{pmatrix} \begin{pmatrix} 7 & 2 & -2 \\ -6 & -1 & 2 \\ 6 & 2 & -1 \end{pmatrix} = \begin{pmatrix} 79 & 26 & 26 \\ -78 & -25 & 26 \\ 78 & 26 & -25 \end{pmatrix}$$

$$A^3 - 5A^2 + 7A - 3I = 0$$

$$= \begin{bmatrix} 0 & 0 & 0 \\ 0 & 0 & 0 \\ 0 & 0 & 0 \end{bmatrix} = \text{R.H.S.}$$

Thus A satisfies its characteristics equation

$$A^3 - 5A^2 + 7A - 3I \ = 0$$

Divide the above equation by A

$$A^2 - 5A + 7I - 3.A^{-1} = 0$$

$$A^{-1} = \frac{1}{3}\left[A^2 - 5A + 7I\right]$$

$$A^{-1} = \frac{1}{3}\begin{pmatrix} -3 & -2 & 2 \\ 6 & 5 & -2 \\ -6 & -2 & -5 \end{pmatrix}$$

CHAPTER – II

2. SET THEORY

Symbolic Notation Meaning

$\in$	- belongs to
$\notin$	- does not belong to
"	" Vertical Line (or)	- x is to be read as 'such that'
ϕ	$\rightarrow$ Phi (null set)
$A \subseteq B$	$\rightarrow$ A is contained in B (or) A is a subset of B
$A \supseteq B$	$\rightarrow$ A contains B (or) A is a superset of B
$A \nsubseteq B$	$\rightarrow$ A is not a subset of B (or) A is not contained in B
$A \nsupseteq B$	$\rightarrow$ A is not a superset of B (or) A does not contain B
$A \subset B$	$\rightarrow$ A is a proper subset of B

Symbols in Use

$\Rightarrow$	- Implies
$\Leftarrow$	- Is implied by
$\rightleftarrows$	- Implies and is implied by
: (or) /	- such that
$\exists$	- There exists
$\in$	- Belongs to
$\notin$	- Not belongs to
$\subset$	- Proper Subset

$\supseteq$	- Contains
$\cup$	- Union
$\subseteq$	- is a subset of
$\cap$	- Intersection
Iff	- If and only if
$\wedge$	- and
$\vee$	- or
$\sim$	- Negation of
$\ni$	- Such that
$\forall$	- for all
$\supset$	- Contains

2.1 DEFINITION

Set

Set is a well defined collection of objects.

The objects can be anything people, alphabet, numbers etc.

The objects are known as elements (or) members of the set.

Member

Any object belonging to a set is called member (or) an element of that set.

Notations

Capital letters A, B, C, D, U, ... are used to denote the **sets**. Small letter a, b, c, d, X denote the **elements**.

If an object x is a member of set A, we write $x \in A$. it is read 'x is a element of A' (or) x belongs to A if there is another object y which is not a member of set A, we write $y \notin A$, it is read as 'y is not an element of A' or y is not belongs to A.

Describing Methods

There are two methods of describing a set. They are called **tabular form (or) Roster method (or) enumeration and set-builder form (or) verbal description (or) set selection method.**

Under the first method (Roster Method)

The elements are listed within braces {} and separated by commas.

Examples

(1) A set of vowels : A = {a, e, i, o, u}

(2) A set of prime-ministers :

P = {Nehru, Shastri, Indira, Manmohansingh}

(3) A set of natural numbers

N = {1, 2, 3, ... }

(4) A = {1, 2, ..., 9} set A consist of +ve integers less than 10.

Under the Second Method (Verbal Description)

The letter x is chosen to represent an orbitrary element whose property is spelled out and all elements which posses the property constitute the set.

x as well as the property is written within braces.

those 3 examples are given under this form as

1. A = {x : x is a vowel in English alphabets}

2. P = {x : x is an Indian Prime-Minister}

3. N = {x / x is a natural number}

4. A = {x / x is a positive integer less than 10}

To read the third statement as "N is the set of all x such that x is a natural number. By that it is meant N is the set of all natural numbers".

Symbol either : or / is used

Example

    A = {Mon, Tues, Wed, ….., Friday}

    A = {x / x ∈ week days of school}

    A = {x / 7 < x < 10, x ∈ N}

    The set contains natural nos. greater than 7 and less than 10.

    A = {8, 9}

TYPES OF SETS

I. Finite Set

    If there are a specific number of elements in a set, the set is a **Finite Set**.

    In particular, a set which contains only one element is called a **Singleton Set**.

    {0}, {a}

Examples

1. A set of vowels, A = {a, e, i, o, u}, it is a finite set.

2. A = {1, 2, 3, ….. , 10000}, it is a finite set.

3. There are 5 elements in a set, it is a finite set.

4. 10,000 elements this is a finite set.

II. Infinite Set

If there are countless number of elements in a set, the set is an **Infinite Set**.

Example

A set of natural numbers

$N = \{1, 2, 3, \ldots\ldots\}$ is an infinite set.

III. Cardinal Number of Set

The number of elements in a set is the **Cardinal Number** of the set

Example

Let $A = \{1, 2, 3, 4, 5\}$

$n(A) = 5$

IV. The Empty Set, NULL or VOID set

A set which has no member at all is called the **empty or the null or the void set**. It is denoted by the Greek letter ϕ(read as phi)

Examples

(1) $\{\ \}$

(2) $\{x / x$ is an unmarried Indian Prime Minister$\}$

$\{0\} \to$ is not a null set but $\{\}$ is a null set.

$\{\phi\} \to$ is not a null set but ϕ is a null set.

V. Equal Set (or) Equality of Sets

Two sets A and B are said to be **equal** if every element of A is an element of B and every element of B is an element of A.

Equality can be written in symbolic form $A = B \Leftrightarrow (x \in A \Leftrightarrow x \in B)$

Here ⇔ This symbol stands for 'implies' or 'is implied by' or 'if and only if' or iff. If two sets A and B are not equal. We shall write as A ≠ B. The above statement given in the definition of equality of sets is known as **axiom of extension**.

Examples

Consider the following sets

1. A = {1, 3, 5, 7}, B = {7, 3, 1, 5}.

The two sets are equal (ie) A = B, as according to our definition every elements which belongs to set A also belongs to set B and vice versa.

[From the above we conclude that a set does not change if we change the order in which its elements are tabulated] (i.e) order of the elements is immaterial.

2. A = {2, 4, 5, 9}, B = {2, 9, 5, 4, 9, 2}.

The two sets A and B are equal (i.e) A = B as according to our definition every elements of A is also an element of B and vice versa.

[From the above we conclude that a set does not change if one or more of its elements are repeated] (i.e) Repetition of any member does not alter the set.

3. If A = {2, 4, 6}, B = {2, 4, 5, 7}.

Here A ≠ B because the element 6 of A does not belong to B and similarly elements 5, 7 of B do not belong to A.

VI. Subset and Superset

If every element of a set A is also an element of another set B. A is called a **subset** of set B.

It is denoted by A⊆B and is read as 'A is a subset of B' or 'A is contained in B'.

In that context, B is called **Superset** of A. In symbols B⊇A and it is read as, 'B

is a superset of A' (or) 'B contains A'.

Example 1

A = {1, 2, 3} and   B={1, 2, 5, 3, 7}, Then A⊆B, so A is a subset of a set B.

Example 2

A = {1, 2, 3, 4} and B = {1, 2, 5, 3, 7},

A ⊄ B, Here A is not a subset of B.

VII. Proper Subset

Set A is called **proper subset** of superset B if every element of A is an element

of B and at least one element of B is not an element of A. In symbols A⊂B and it is

read as 'A is a proper subset of superset B'.

Example 1

A={4, 0, 2, 7} and B={4, 0, 2, 7, 9}, so A⊂B, A is the proper subset of B.

Example 2

A={-4, 0, 2, 7} and B={0, -4, 2, 7}, it is a subset but not a proper subset. It is

an improper subset.

VIII. Improper Set

A is said to be an **improper subset** of B A ⊆ B and A = B.

Example

A={-4, 0, 2, 7} and B={0, -4, 2, 7}, it is an improper subset.

From this Theorem

(i)   Any set is a subset of itself.

(ii)   The null set is a subset of every set.

(iii)   If A is a subset of B. B is a subset of C, then A is a subset of C.

IX. Universal Set

The set which is superset of all sets under consideration is called **universal set** and it is denoted by '$\cup$' or $\in$.

X. Complement of a Set

The set of all those elements of the universal set $\cup$, which are not the elements of A, is the **complement of A**, it is denoted by A' or A^C.

Example

If $\cup = \{1, 2, 3, 4, 5, 6, 7, 8, 9\}, A = \{1, 2\}, B = \{1, 2, 3, 4, 5\}$ and $C = \{7, 8, 9\}$

Then $A' = \{3, 4, 5, 6, 7, 8, 9\}$

$B' = \{6, 7, 8, 9\}$

$C' = \{1, 2, 3, 4, 5, 6\}$

XI. Difference of Sets

The **difference of sets** A and B is the set of elements of A which are not elements of B. In symbols it is A - B and it is read as 'A difference B' (or) 'A minus B'.

Example

If   A = {Book, Pen, Pencil}

and   B = {Purse, Notebook, Pen, Pencil}   then   A – B = {Book}

XII. Power Set

Let A be the given set, a collection of family of all subsets of A is called the powerset of A.

The power set of A is denoted as P(A).

Example 1

If A = {x, y} → then its subsets are

Then P(A) = {{x}, {y}, {x, y}, {}}   Here {} (or) ϕ is null set

Here n(P(A)) = 4 = 2^2.

Generally n(A) = m

Then n(P(A)) = 2^m.

Example 2

If A = {a, b, c}

P(A) = {{a}, {b}, {c}, {a, b}, {b, c}, {c, a}, {a, b, c}, ϕ}

= {A, {a, b}, {b, c}, {c, a}, {a, b, c}, ϕ}   Here ϕ is a null set

n(A) = 3

$\therefore$ n(P(A)) = 2^3 = 2 x 2 x 2 = 8 elements

Example 3

Power set of null set ϕ has only one element

i) if A = ϕ then P(A) = {ϕ}

ii) If A = {a} then its subsets are ϕ, {a}.

$\therefore$ P(A) = {ϕ,{a}} = {ϕ, A}

XIII. Disjoint Sets

Two sets A and B are said to be **disjoint sets** if no element of A is in B and no element of B is in A.

Example

A = {1, 2, 3}, B = {5, 7, 9}. So A and B are disjoint sets they have no common element.

$A \cap B = \phi$.

XIV. Family of Set

If the elements of a set are set themselves, then such a set is called the **family of sets**.

Example

If A = {a, b} then set {ϕ, {a}, {b}, {a, b}} is the family of sets whose elements are subsets of the set A.

XV. Equivalent Set

If the elements of one set can be put into one-to-one correspondence with the elements of another set, then the two sets are called **equivalent sets**. The symbol ~ or ≡ is used to denote equivalent sets.

Example

A = {a, b, c, d}, B = {1, 2, 3, 4}, A ≠ B but elements of A can be put one-to-one correspondence with those of B, so we write A = B.

XVI. Standard Sets

The sets given below are some **standard sets** which are frequently used in Algebra.

(i) N = The set of natural numbers

{x : x is a natural number}

(ii) Z or I = The set of integers

{x : x is an integers}

(iii) Q = The set of rational numbers

{x : x is rational}

(iv) R = The set of real numbers

{x : x is a real number}

VENN DIAGRAM

Diagrams which represent sets are called Venn Diagrams. They are named after the English logician John Venn. A rectangle represents the Universal set U and circles inside the rectangle represent the sets under consideration.

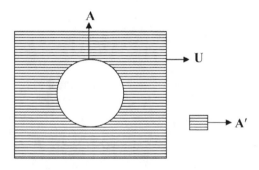

Set A and its complement A'

2.2 BASIC SET OPERATIONS AND LAWS OF SET THEORY

1) Union of Two Sets

If A and B be two non-empty sets then the set of all elements belonging to either in A or in B or in both A and B is defined as the UNION of A and B and is denoted by $A \cup B$ (Read as A union B)

Thus

$$A \cup B = \{x \mid x \in A \text{ or } x \in B\}$$

Example

1) If $A = \{2, 4, 6, 8\}$

$B = \{1, 2\}$

$A \cup B = \{1, 2, 4, 6, 8\}$

2) If $X = \{a, b, c\}, Y = \{b, c, d, n\}$

$X \cup Y = \{a, b, c, d, n\}$

Venn Diagram

The union of set can be easily understood by means of geometrical illustrations called Venn Diagrams.

A and B are two sets and U is the Universal Set.

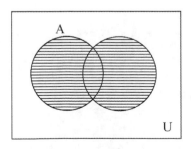

A∪B Shaded

Example

If $A = \{x : x \in I, 0 < x < 7\}$ and $B = \{y : y \in I, 8 < y < 12\}$ then

$A \cup B = \{Z : Z \in I, 0 < Z < 7 ; 8 < Z < 12\}$, $\therefore$ $A \cup B = \{1, 2, 3, 4, 5, 6, 9, 10, 11\}$

2) Intersection of two sets

If A and B are two non-empty sets then the set of all elements belonging to A

and B is defined as the intersection of A and B which is denoted by $A \cap B$ (read as A

'intersection' B) symbolically, $A \cap B = \{x : x \in A \text{ and } x \in B\}$.

To find the intersection of two sets means, finding elements common to

A and B.

Venn Diagram

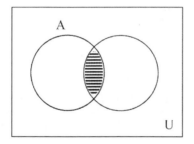

$A \cap B$ Shaded

Examples

(i) $A = \{a, e, b, c, \}$ $B = \{a, b, d, g\}$ $A \cap B = \{a, b\}$

(ii) If $A = \{x : x \in I, 0 < x < 5\}$ and $B = \{y : y \in I, 4 \leq y < 7\}$

    then $A \cap B = \{Z : Z \in I, 4 \leq Z < 5\} = \{4\}$.

(iii) $X = \{1, 2, 3\}$ $Y = \{4, 5, 6\}$ then $X \cap Y = \phi$

3) Disjoint Sets (Disjoint or Mutually Exclusive)

Two sets A and B are **disjoint** if A∩B is φ. That is they have no element in common (i.e) their intersection is a null set. Symbolically, A∩B = φ

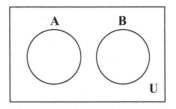

Disjoint sets of A and B is φ

Example

If A = {1, 2, 3, 4} B = {5, 6, 7} then A∩B = φ

(1) PROPERTIES OF UNION OF SETS

(i) The union of sets is Commutative

If A and B are two sets, then A∪B = B∪A

Proof :

For proving A∪B = B∪A

We shall prove A∪B ⊆ B∪A and B∪A ⊆ A∪B.

Let x be an arbitrary elements of A∪B then

$$x \in A \cup B \qquad \Leftrightarrow x \in A \text{ or } x \in B$$

$$\Leftrightarrow x \in B \text{ or } x \in A \qquad \textbf{Note :} \Leftrightarrow \text{ implies (or) implied by}$$

$$\Leftrightarrow x \in B \cup A$$

$$\therefore A \cup B \subseteq B \cup A \qquad \qquad ----- (1)$$

Again, let $y \in B \cup A$ then

$$y \in B \cup A \quad \Leftrightarrow y \in B \text{ or } y \in A$$

$$\Leftrightarrow y \in A \text{ or } y \in B$$

$$\Leftrightarrow y \in A \cup B$$

$$\therefore B \cup A \subseteq A \cup B \qquad \text{------ (2)}$$

From equation (1) and (2) we have

$$A \cup B = B \cup A$$

(ii) The union of sets is associative

If A, B and C are any three sets, then

$$A \cup (B \cup C) = (A \cup B) \cup C$$

Proof :

Let x be an arbitrary element of set $A \cup (B \cup C)$, then

$$x \in A \cup (B \cup C) \quad \Leftrightarrow \quad x \in A \text{ (or) } x \in (B \cup C)$$

$$\Leftrightarrow \quad x \in A \text{ (or) } (x \in B \text{ or } x \in C)$$

$$\Leftrightarrow \quad (x \in A \text{ or } x \in B) \text{ or } x \in C$$

$$\Leftrightarrow \quad x \in (A \cup B) \text{ or } x \in C$$

$$\Leftrightarrow \quad x \in (A \cup B) \cup C$$

$$\Leftrightarrow \quad (A \cup B) \cup C$$

$$\therefore A \cup (B \cup C) = (A \cup B) \cup C$$

(iii) The union of sets is idempotent

If A is any set, then $A \cup A = A$

Proof :

Let x be an arbitrary element of the set $A \cup A$. then

$x \in A \cup A$ $\quad \Leftrightarrow \quad$ $x \in A$ or $x \in A$

$\quad\quad\quad\quad \Leftrightarrow \quad$ $x \in A$

$A \cup A = A$

(iv) If A and B are any sets, then $A \subseteq A \cup B$ and $B \subseteq A \cup B$.

Proof :

Let x be an arbitrary element of the set A. Then

$x \in A$ $\quad\quad \Leftrightarrow \quad$ $x \in A$ or $x \in B$

$\quad\quad\quad\quad \Leftrightarrow \quad$ $x \in A \cup B$

$\therefore A \subseteq A \cup B$, similarly it can be proved that $B \subseteq A \cup B$.

(v) If A is any set, then $A \cup \phi = A$, where ϕ is the null set.

Proof :

Let x be an arbitrary element of the set $A \cup \phi$, then

$x \in A \cup \phi$ $\quad \Leftrightarrow \quad$ $x \in A$ or $x \in \phi$

$\quad\quad\quad\quad \Leftrightarrow \quad$ $x \in A$ [by definition of null set $x \notin \phi$]

$\therefore A \cup \phi = A$.

(vi) If A is any subset of the universal set $\cup$, then $A \cup \cup = \cup$.

Proof :

We know that every set is a subset of the universal set.

Consequently, $A \cup \cup \subseteq \cup$, also

By property (iv), $\cup \subseteq A \cup \cup$

Thus $\cup = A \cup \cup$.

(vii) If $A \subseteq B$, then $A \cup B = B$, and if $B \subseteq A$ then $A \cup B = A$

Proof :

From property (iv), we have

$$B \subseteq A \cup B \qquad\qquad \text{------ (1)}$$

Now let $x \in A \cup B \quad \Rightarrow \quad x \in A$ or $x \in B$

$$\Rightarrow \quad x \in B, \text{ as } A \subseteq B$$

$$\therefore A \cup B \subseteq B \qquad\qquad \text{------- (2)}$$

From (1) and (2) we have $A \cup B = B$, $\|$ ^{ly} it can be proved that if $B \subseteq A$, then

$A \cup B = A$.

(2) Properties of Intersection of Sets

(i) The intersection of set is commutative

If A and B are two sets then $A \cap B = B \cap A$

Proof :

Let $x \in A \cap B$

$$\Leftrightarrow x \in A \text{ and } x \in B$$

$$\Leftrightarrow x \in B \text{ and } x \in A$$

$\Leftrightarrow x \in B \cap A$

Hence $A \cap B = B \cap A$

(ii) The intersection of set is associative

If A, B and C are any 3 sets, then

$A \cap (B \cap C) = (A \cap B) \cap C$

Proof :

Let x be an arbitrary element of $A \cap (B \cap C)$ then

$x \in A \cap (B \cap C)$ $\qquad \Leftrightarrow \qquad x \in A$ and $x \in (B \cap C)$

$\qquad\qquad\qquad\qquad \Leftrightarrow \qquad x \in A$ and $x \in B$ and $x \in C$

$\qquad\qquad\qquad\qquad \Leftrightarrow \qquad (x \in A$ and $x \in B)$ and $x \in C$

$\qquad\qquad\qquad\qquad \Leftrightarrow \qquad x \in (A \cap B) \cap C$

Hence $(A \cap B) \cap C = A \cap (B \cap C)$

(iii) The Intersection of sets is Idempotent

If A is any set, then $A \cap A = A$

Proof :

Let x be an arbitrary element of the set $A \cap A$. Then

$x \in A \cap A$ $\qquad \Leftrightarrow \qquad x \in A$ and $x \in A$

$\qquad\qquad\qquad \Leftrightarrow \qquad x \in A$

Hence $A \cap A = A$

(iv) If A and B are any two sets. Then

$A \cap B \subseteq A$ and $A \cap B \subseteq B$

Proof :

Let $x \in A \cap B$ then

$x \in A \cap B \qquad \Leftrightarrow \qquad x \in A$ and $x \in B$

$\qquad \qquad \Leftrightarrow \qquad x \in A$ as $A \cap B \subseteq A$

$\therefore A \cap B \subseteq A$. similarly, it can be proved that $A \cap B \subseteq B$

(v) If A is any set, then $A \cap \phi = \phi$, where ϕ is the null set.

Proof :

We know that the empty set is the subset of every set. Consequently

$\phi \subseteq A \cap \phi$

Again by property (iv), $A \cap \phi \subseteq \phi$, thus $\phi \subseteq A \cap \phi$ and $A \cap \phi \subseteq \phi \Leftrightarrow A \cap \phi = \phi$

(vi) If A is any subset of the universal set $\cup$, then $A \cap \cup = A$

Proof :

As in property (iv), we can show that $A \cap \cup \subseteq A$ $\qquad$ ------ (1)

Let $x \in A \qquad \Rightarrow x \in A$ and $x \in \cup$ (Since $A \subseteq \cup$)

$\qquad \qquad \Rightarrow x \in A \cap \cup$

$A \subseteq A \cap \cup$ $\qquad \qquad$ ------- (2)

From (1) and (2) we have $A = A \cap \cup$.

DIFFERENCE OF TWO SETS

If A and B are two sets then the difference of A and B denoted by A – B is the set of elements which belongs to A but not belong to B. The difference of A and B is read as A difference B or simply A minus B. it is also denoted by A~B.

Symbolically

A – B = {x : x∈A and x∉B} and similarly B – A = {x : x∈B and x∉A}

Venn Diagram

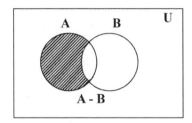

Difference of sets A and B, A – B is shaded.

Example

If A = {0, 2, 4, 9} and B = {0, 3, 6, 8, 9} then

A – B = {2, 4} and B – A = {3, 6, 8}

Obviously A – B ≠ B – A

Properties of Difference of Two Sets

(i) A – A = ϕ

Proof :

Let x ∈ A – A ⇒ x∈A and x∉A. But there is no element satisfying both these conditions.

Hence, no element belongs to A – A, i.e., A – A = ϕ.

(ii) A – ϕ = A

Proof :

Let $x \in A - \phi \Rightarrow x \in A$ and $x \notin \phi$.

This simply means that $x \in A$, since there is no element belonging to ϕ.

Conversely, $x \in A \Leftrightarrow x \in A - \phi$. That is $A - \phi = A$.

(iii) A – B ⊆ A

Proof :

Let $x \in A - B$ $\Leftrightarrow x \in A$ and $x \notin B$

$\Leftrightarrow x \in A$

$\therefore A - B \subseteq A$

(iv) A – B, A∩B and B-A are mutually disjoint.

Proof :

To prove $(A-B) \cap (A \cap B) = \phi$,

Let $x \in (A-B) \cap (A \cap B)$

$\Leftrightarrow x \in (A-B)$ and $x \in (A \cap B)$

$\Leftrightarrow (x \in A$ and $x \notin B)$ and $(x \in A$ and $x \in B)$

$\Leftrightarrow x \in A$ and $x \in \phi$

(Since there is no element satisfying both $x \in B$ and $x \notin B$)

According to theorem (i) so $B - B = \phi$ (i.e) $x \in B - x \notin B = \phi$.

$\Leftrightarrow x \in (A \cap \phi)$

$\Leftrightarrow x \in \phi$

Similarly it can be proved that

$(B - A) \cap (A \cap B) = \phi$

Now to prove that $(A - B) \cap (B - A) = \phi$, let

$$x \in (A - B) \cap (B - A) \qquad \Leftrightarrow x \in (A\text{-}B) \text{ and } x \in (B\text{-}A)$$

$$\Leftrightarrow (x \in A \text{ and } x \notin B) \text{ and}$$

$$(x \in B \text{ and } x \notin A)$$

[Since there is no element satisfying both $x \in A$ and $x \notin A$ (or) $x \in B$ and $x \notin B$]

$$\Leftrightarrow x \in \phi$$

From the above discussion it is clear that $(A\text{-}B)$, $(B\text{-}A)$ and $(A \cap B)$ are disjoint

sets.

(v) $(A\text{-}B) \cap B = \phi$

Proof :

To prove $(A\text{-}B) \cap B = \phi$, let

$$x \in (A\text{-}B) \cap B \qquad \Leftrightarrow x \in (A\text{-}B) \text{ and } x \in B$$

$$\Leftrightarrow (x \in A \text{ and } x \notin B) \text{ and } x \in B$$

$$\Leftrightarrow x \in A \text{ and } x \in \phi$$

Since there is no element satisfying both $x \in B$ and $x \notin B$ $(B\text{-}B = \phi)$

$$\Leftrightarrow x \in (A \cap \phi) \qquad [\therefore \text{ We Know the theorem (iii) in}$$

$$\text{properties of intersection } A \cap \phi = \phi]$$

$$\Leftrightarrow x \in \phi$$

(vi) To prove $(A - B) \cup A = A$.

Proof :

Let $x \in (A - B) \cup A \Leftrightarrow (x \in A \text{ and } x \notin B) \text{ or } x \in A$

$$\Leftrightarrow x \in A \text{ and } x \notin B$$

$$\Leftrightarrow x \in A$$

Hence $(A - B) \cup A = A$

COMPLEMENT OF A SET

Let A be any set, the complement of A is the set of elements that belong to the universal set but donot belong to A. thus U is the universal set the complement of A is the set U - A is denoted by A', A^C, $\overline{A}$ or $-A$ symbolically

$$A^C \quad = U - A \quad\quad = \{x : x \in U \text{ and } x \notin A\}$$

$$= \{x : x \notin A\}$$

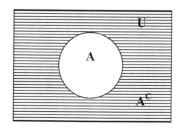

Complement of set A (Shaded Area)

Example

If $N = \{1, 2, 3, 4, \ldots\ldots\}$ is the universal set and let $A = \{1, 3, 5, 7, \ldots\ldots\}$ then $A^C = N - A = \{2, 4, 6, 8, \ldots\ldots\}$

Properties of Complement of Set

(i) $A \cup A^C = U$

Proof

Since every set is a subset of the universal set, we have

$$A \cup A^C \subseteq U \quad\quad\quad\quad ------ (1)$$

Now let $x \in U \quad \Rightarrow x \in A$ (or) $x \in A^C$

$\Rightarrow x \in A \cup A^C \qquad\qquad [A + A^C = U,\ so\ A \cup A^C = U]$

$\therefore U \subseteq A \cup A^C \qquad\qquad$ ------- (2)

From (1) and (2) we have $A \cup A^C = U$

(ii) $A \cap A^C = \phi$

Proof :

Let $x \in A \cap A^C \qquad\qquad \Leftrightarrow x \in A$ and $x \in A^C$

$\Rightarrow x \in \phi$

Since there is no element x satisfying both $x \in A$ and $x \in A^C$. Therefore $A \cap A^C = \phi$.

(iii) $U^C = \phi$

Proof :

Let $x \in U^C \Rightarrow x \notin U$ since there is no such element which does not belong to the universal set, therefore $U^C = \phi$.

(iv) $\phi^C = U$

Proof :

Let $\phi^C \qquad = \{x : x \in \cup$ and $x \notin \phi\}$

$= \{x : x \in \cup\} = \cup$

Which is a universal truth. Hence ϕ^C is the set consisting of all possible elements in the universal set. Hence $\phi^C = \cup$.

(vi) $(A^C)^C = A$

Proof :

Let $x \in (A^C)^C \Leftrightarrow x \notin (A^C) \Leftrightarrow x \in A$

Hence $A = (A^C)^C$

(vi) $(A - B) = A \cap B^C$

Proof :

Let $x \in (A\text{-}B)$ $\qquad \Leftrightarrow x \in A$ and $x \notin B$

$\qquad\qquad\qquad\qquad \Leftrightarrow x \in A$ and $x \notin B^C$

$\qquad\qquad\qquad\qquad \Leftrightarrow x \in A \cap B^C$

Hence $A - B = A \cap B^C$

(vii) If $A \subseteq B$, then $A \cup (B - A) = B$

Proof :

Given $A \subseteq B$

Then to prove $A \cup (B\text{-}A) = B$, let

$x \in A \cup (B\text{-}A)$ $\qquad \Leftrightarrow x \in A$ or $x \in (B\text{-}A)$

$\qquad\qquad\qquad\qquad \Leftrightarrow x \in A$ or $x \in B \cap A^C$ $\qquad$ [by Property (vi)]

$\qquad\qquad\qquad\qquad \Leftrightarrow x \in A$ or $(x \in B$ and $x \in A^C)$

$\qquad\qquad\qquad\qquad \Leftrightarrow (x \in A$ or $x \in B)$ and $(x \in A$ or $x \in A^C)$

$\qquad\qquad\qquad\qquad \Leftrightarrow x \in A \cup B$ and $x \in \cup$ $\quad [\therefore A \cup A^C = \cup]$

$\qquad\qquad\qquad\qquad \Leftrightarrow x \in (A \cup B)$ $\qquad$ [Since $A \subseteq A \cup B = B$]

$\qquad\qquad\qquad\qquad \Leftrightarrow x \in B$ $\qquad\qquad$ Hence $A \cup (B\text{-}A) = B$

Distributive Laws

(1) Union is distributive over intersection

If A, B and C are any three sets, then

$$A \cup (B \cap C) \quad = \quad (A \cup B) \cap (A \cup C)$$

Proof :

Let x be an arbitrary element of $A \cup (B \cap C)$, then

$x \in A \cup (B \cap C) \qquad \Leftrightarrow \qquad x \in A \text{ or } x \in (B \cap C)$

$\qquad\qquad\qquad\qquad\qquad \Leftrightarrow \qquad x \in A \text{ or } (x \in B \text{ and } x \in C)$

$\qquad\qquad\qquad\qquad\qquad \Leftrightarrow \qquad (x \in A \text{ or } x \in B) \text{ and } (x \in A \text{ or } x \in C)$

$\qquad\qquad\qquad\qquad\qquad \Leftrightarrow x \in (A \cup B) \text{ and } x \in (A \cup C)$

$\qquad\qquad\qquad\qquad\qquad \Leftrightarrow x \in (A \cup B) \cap (A \cup C)$

Hence, $\qquad A \cup (B \cap C) \Leftrightarrow (A \cup B) \cap (A \cup C)$

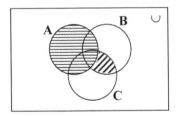

(a) $A \cup (B \cap C)$ Shaded Area

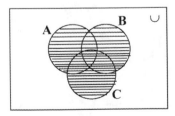

$(A \cup B) \cap (A \cup C)$

Cross Hatche Area.

(2) Intersection is Distributive Over Union

   If A, B and C are any three sets then $A \cap (B \cup C) = (A \cap B) \cup (A \cap C)$

Proof

   Let x be an arbitrary element of $A \cap (B \cup C)$, then

$x \in A \cap (B \cup C)$	$\Leftrightarrow$	$x \in A$ and $x \in (B \cup C)$
	$\Leftrightarrow$	$x \in A$ and $(x \in B$ or $x \in C)$
	$\Leftrightarrow$	$(x \in A$ and $x \in B)$ or $(x \in A$ and $x \in C)$
	$\Leftrightarrow$	$x \in (A \cap B)$ or $x \in (A \cap C)$
	$\Leftrightarrow$	$x \in (A \cap B) \cup (A \cap C)$

   Hence, $A \cap (B \cap C) = (A \cap B) \cup (A \cap C)$

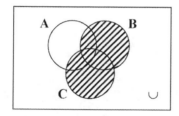

Cross Hatche Area.

(b) $(A \cap B) \cup (A \cap C)$

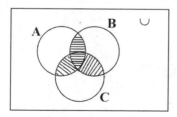

Symmetric Difference of Sets

Let A and B be two nonempty sets. Then the Symmetric Difference of A and B,

denoted by A $\oplus$ B or A Δ B, is the set of elements which either belong to A or B but

not t both.

$$A \oplus B \qquad = (A \cup B) - (B \cap A)$$

$$= (A\text{-}B) \cup (B\text{-}A)$$

$$= \{x : x \in A \ \text{or} \ x \in B\}$$

For Example let

A = {1, 2, 3}, B = {3, 4, 5} then

$$A \oplus B \qquad = \qquad (A \cup B) - (B \cap A)$$

$$= \qquad \{1, 2, 3, 4, 5\} - \{3\}$$

$$= \qquad \{1, 2, 4, 5\}$$

A $\oplus$ B shaded

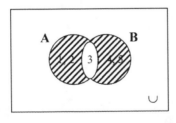

LAWS OF THE ALGEBRA OF OPERATIONS

(1) Idempotent Law

    (a) $A \cup A = A$ (b) $A \cap A = A$

(2) Commutative Law

    (a) $A \cup B = B \cup A$ (b) $A \cap B = B \cap A$

(3) Associative Law

(a) $A \cup (B \cup C) = (A \cap B) \cup C$ (b) $A \cap (B \cap C) = (A \cap B) \cap C$

(4) Identity Laws

(a) (i) $A \cup \phi = A$ (ii) $A \cup \cap = A$

(b) (i) $A \cup \cup = \cup$ (ii) $A \cap \phi = \phi$

(5) Distributive Law

(a) $A \cup (B \cap C) = (A \cup B) \cap (A \cup C)$

(b) $A \cap (B \cup C) = (A \cap B) \cup (A \cap C)$

(6) Complement Law

(a) (i) $A \cup A^C = \cup$ (ii) $A \cap A^C = \phi$

(b) (i) $U^C = \phi$ (ii) $\phi^C = \cup$

(c) (i) $A - A = \phi, A - \phi = A, A - B = A \cap B^C$

(7) Absorption Law

(a) $A \cup (A \cap B) = A$ (b) $A \cap (A \cup B) = A$

(8) Involution Law

(a) $(A')' = A$

(9) Demorgan's Law

(a) $(A \cup B)^C = A^C \cap B^C$

(b) $(A \cap B)^C = A^C \cap B^C$

(a) Complement of the union of two sets is the intersection of their complements.

$$(A \cup B)^C = A^C \cap B^C$$

Proof

Let x be any element of set (a) $(A \cup B)^C$

Then

$$x \in (a) (A \cup B)^C \quad \Leftrightarrow \quad (x \in \cup) \text{ and } (x \notin (A \cup B))$$

$$\Leftrightarrow \quad (x \in \cup) \text{ and } (x \notin A \text{ or } x \notin A)$$

$$\Leftrightarrow \quad (x \in \cup \text{ and or but } x \notin A) \text{ and}$$

$$(x \in \cup \text{ and or but } x \notin B)$$

$$\Leftrightarrow \quad x \in A^C \text{ and } x \in B^C$$

$$\Leftrightarrow \quad x \in A^C \cap B^C$$

$$\text{Hence } (A \cup B)^C \quad = \quad A^C \cap B^C \qquad\qquad (1)$$

(b) Complement of the intersection of two sets is the union of their complements.

$$(\text{i.e.}) (A \cap B)^C \quad = \quad A^C \cup B^C \quad (\text{or}) \quad (A \cap B)' \quad = \quad A' \cup B'$$

Proof

Let x be any arbitrary element of the set $(A \cap B)^C$ then

$$x \in (A \cap B)^C \quad \Rightarrow \quad x \notin (A \cap B)$$

$$\Rightarrow \quad x \notin A \text{ and } x \notin B$$

$$\Rightarrow \quad x \in A' \text{ or } x \in B'$$

$$\Rightarrow \quad x \in (A' \cup B')$$

$$(A \cap B)^C \quad \Rightarrow \quad A^C \cup B^C$$

(a) $A - (B \cup C)$ $=$ $(A - B) \cap (A - C)$

Proof

Let x be any arbitrary element of $A - (B \cup C)$ then

$x \in A - (B \cup C)$ $\Leftrightarrow$ $x \in A$ and $x \notin (B \cup C)$

$\Leftrightarrow$ $x \in A$ and $(x \notin$ or $x \notin C)$

$\Leftrightarrow$ $(x \in A$ but $x \notin B)$ and $(x \in A$ but $x \notin C)$

$\Leftrightarrow$ $x \in (A - B)$ and $x \in (A - C)$

$\Leftrightarrow$ $x \in (A - B) \cap (A - C)$

Hence $A - (B \cup C) = (A - B) \cap (A - C)$

(b) $A - (B \cap C)$ $=$ $(A - B) \cup (A - C)$

Proof

Let x be an arbitrary element of $A - (B \cap C)$ then

$x \in A - (B \cap C)$ $\Leftrightarrow$ $x \in A$ and $x \notin (B \cap C)$

$\Leftrightarrow$ $x \in A$ and $(x \notin$ or $x \notin C)$

$\Leftrightarrow$ $(x \in A$ but $x \notin B)$ and $(x \in A$ but $x \notin C)$

$\Leftrightarrow$ $x \in (A - B)$ and $x \in (A - C)$

$\Leftrightarrow$ $x \in (A - B) \cup (A - C)$

Hence $A - (B \cap C) = (A - B) \cup (A - C)$

(1) Given $A = \{1, 2, 4, 5\}$, $B = \{2, 3, 5, 6\}$, $C = \{4, 5, 6, 7\}$ verify

$$A \cup (B \cap C) = (A \cup B) \cap (A \cup C)$$

Proof

$$(B \cap C) \qquad = \{1, 2, 4, 5, 6\} \qquad\qquad (1)$$

$$A \cup (B \cap C) = \{1, 2, 3, 4, 5, 6\}$$

$$(A \cup B) \qquad = \{1, 2, 3, 4, 5, 6\}$$

$$(A \cup C) \qquad = \{1, 2, 3, 4, 5, 6, 7\}$$

$$(A \cup B) \cap (A \cup C) = \{1, 2, 3, 4, 5, 6\} \qquad\qquad (2)$$

From (1) & (2)

$$\therefore A \cup (B \cap C) = (A \cup B) \cap (A \cup C)$$

Consider the sets A, B, C given above

$$(B \cup C) \qquad\qquad = \{2, 3, 4, 5, 6, 7\}$$

$$A \cap (B \cup C) \qquad = \{2, 4\}$$

$$(A \cap B) \qquad\qquad = \{2\}$$

$$(A \cap C) \qquad\qquad = \{4\}$$

$$(A \cap B) \cup (A \cap C) \ = \{2, 4\}$$

From (1) and (2)

$$A \cap (B \cup C) = (A \cap B) \cup (A \cap C)$$

(2) Given $A = \{2, 5, 6\}$, $B = \{3, 4, 2\}$, $C = \{1, 3, 4\}$ find $(A - B)$ and $(B - A)$ show that $A - B \neq B - A$ and $A - C = A$

Proof

$A - B$ = {the elements in A but not in B}

$A - B$ = $\{5, 6\}$ (1)

$B - A$ = $\{3, 4\}$ (2)

From (1) & (2)

$A - B \neq B - A$

$A - C = \{2, 5, 6\} = A$

(3) Given $A = \{x : x$ is an integer and $1 \leq x \leq 5\}$, $B = \{3, 4, 5, 17\}$, $C = \{1, 2, 3\}$, $A = \{1, 2, , 3, 4, 5\}$ find $A \cap B, A \cap C, A \cup B$ and $A \cup C$

Solution

$A \cap B = \{1, 2, 3, 4, 5\} \cap \{3, 4, 5, 17\} = \{3, 4, 5\}$

$A \cap C = \{1, 2, 3\}$, $A \cup B = \{1, 2, 3, 4, 5, 17\}$, $A \cup B = \{1, 2, 3, 4, 5\}$

(3) If $A_1 = \{1, 2\}$, $A_2 = \{2, 3\}$, $A_3 = \{1, 2, 3, 6\}$ find $\bigcup\limits_{i=1}^{3} A_i$ & $\bigcap\limits_{i=1}^{3} A_i$

Solution

$\bigcup\limits_{i=1}^{3} A_i$ = $A_1 \cup A_2 \cup A_3$

$A_1 \cup A_2$ = $\{1, 2, 3\}$

$A_1 \cup A_2 \cup A_3 =$ $\{1, 2, 3, 6\}$

$\bigcap\limits_{i=1}^{3} A_i$ = $A_1 \cap A_2 \cap A_3$

$$A_1 \cap A_2 \qquad = \qquad \{2\}$$

$$(A_1 \cap A_2) \cap A_3 \quad = \qquad \{2\}$$

From (1) & (2)

$$\therefore (A_1 \cup A_2 \cup A_3) \cap (A_1 \cap A_2 \cap A_3)$$

$$\{1, 2, 3, 6\} \cap (A_1 \cap A_2 \cap A_3)$$

$$\{1, 2, 3, 6\} \cap \{2\} = \{2\}$$

$$\therefore \bigcup_{i=1}^{3} A_i \text{ and } \bigcap_{i=1}^{3} A_i = \{2\}$$

INCLUSION AND EXCLUSION PRINCIPLE

(1) If A and B are disjoint finite sets

Then $A \cup B$ is finite and

    (i) $n(A \cup B) = n(A) + n(B)$

    (ii) $n(A \cap B) = n(\phi) = 0$

[Two sets A and B are disjoint (no element is in common) $(A \cap B) = \phi$]

(2) Suppose A and B are finite sets, then $A \cup B$ and $A \cap B$ are finite and

$n(A \cup B) = n(A) + n(B) - n(A \cap B)$, thus $n(A \cap B) = n(A) + n(B) - n(A \cup B)$

(3) Suppose A, B and C are finite sets. Then $A \cup B \cup C$ is finite and

$n(A \cup B \cup C) = n(A) + n(B) + n(c) - n(A \cap B) - n(A \cap C) - n(B \cap C) + n(A \cap B \cap C)$

Example

A computer company must hire 20 programmers to handle system programming jobs and 30 programmers for applications programming. Of these hired, 5 are expected to perform jobs of both types. How many programmers must be hired ?

Solution

Let A be the set of syste4ms programmers hired and B be the set of application programmers hired.

Given

$n(A) = 20$, $n(B) = 30$ and $n(A \cap B) = 5$. The number of programmers that must be hired is $n(A \cup B)$, but $n(A \cup B) = n(A) + n(B) - n(A \cap B)$.

$= 20 + 30 - 5 = 45$.

So, the company must hire 45 programmers.

ORDERED PAIR AND CARTESIAN PRODUCT

Ordered Pair

A ordered pair is a pair of objects whose components occur in a special order. It is written by listing the two components in the specific order, separating them by a comma and enclosing the pair in parenthesis. In the ordered pair (a, b), a is called the first components and b, the second component.

Cartesian Product

Let A and B be sets. Cartesian products of A and B, denoted by A x B, is defined as

$A \times B = \{(a, b) : a \in A \text{ and } b \in B\}$

that the A X B is the set of all possible ordered pairs whose first component

comes from A and second component comes from B.

Example 1

   If A = {a, b} and B = {1}

Then   A X B = {(a,1), (b,1)}

     B X A = {(1,a), (1,b)}

And   A X A = {(a,a), (a,b), (b,a), (b,b)}

Note

1) The Cartesian product

     A X B ≠ B X A   unless A = B

2) In A X B, the elements of A will appear as the first component of the ordered pairs.

   In B X A, the elements of B will appear as the first component of the ordered

pairs

3) If $n(A) = m$, $n(B) = n$, then $n(A \times B) = mn$.

4) If either A or B is infinite and the other is empty then A X B = ϕ.

5) If either A or B infinite and other is not empty then A X B is infinite. If A and B are

finite sets then $n(A \times B) = n(A) \cdot n(B)$

Example 2

$$\prod_{i=1}^{3} A_i \quad = \quad A_1 \times A_2 \times A_3 = \{(a_1, a_2, a_3)\}:$$

$$a_1 \in A_1, a_2 \in A_2, a_3 \in A_3$$

$$\prod_{i=1}^{n} A_i \quad = \quad A_1 \times A_2 \times A_3 \ldots \ldots A_n$$

$$= \quad \{(a_1, a_2, \ldots \ldots, a_n): a_i \in A_i \text{ for all } i\}$$

Example 3

Let A = {1, 4}, B = {2, 3}, C = {3, 5}

Prove that A X B ≠ B X A. Also find (A X B) ∩ (A X C)

A X B   = {(1, 2), (1, 3), (4, 2), (4, 3)}

B X A   = {(2, 1), (2, 4), (3, 1), (3, 4)}

So A X B ≠ B X A

Now A X C = {(1, 3), (1, 5), (4, 3), (4, 5)}

Then (A X B) ∩ (A X C) = {(1, 3), (4, 3)}

Example 4

Let A = {a, b}, B = {p, q} and c = {q, r} find

a) A X (B ∪ C)   b) (A X B) ∪ (A X C)

c) A X (B ∩ C)   d) (A X B) ∩ (A X C)

Solution

First we compute B ∪ C = {p, q, r}

Then

a)   A X (B ∪ C) = {(a, p), (a, q), (a, r), (b, p), (b, q), (b, r)}

b)   (A X B)   = {(a, p), (a, q), (b, p), (b, q)}

        (A X C)   = {(a, q), (a, r), (b, q), (b, r)}

Then (A X B) ∪ (A X C) = {(a, p), (a, q), (b, p), (b, q), (a, r), (b, r)}

c) (B ∩ C) = {q} therefore

        A X (B ∩ C) = {a, b} x {q}   = {(a, q), (b, q)}

d) (A X B) ∩ (A X C)   = {(a, q), (b, q)}

2.3 RELATIONS

Relations involving two elements are binary or dyadic relations.

BINARY RELATION

Definition

Let A and B be two non-empty sets. The binary relation R from the set A to the set B is defined to be a subset of the Cartesian Product A X B. Symbolically, $R : A \rightarrow B$ if and only if $R \subseteq A X B$ and $(a, b) \in R$ where $a \in A$ and $b \in B$.

R is a set of ordered pairs (a, b) where $a \in A$ and $b \in B$. Every such ordered pair is written as a R b and read as a is related to b by R'. Thus $(a, b) \in R \Leftrightarrow a R b$.

If $(a, b) \notin R$ then a is not related to b by R and is written as $a \not{R} b$.

Consider the Cartesian product

$A X B = \{(x, y) : x \in A \text{ and } y \in B\}$

If $A = \{1, 2, 5\}$ and $B = \{2, 4\}$ then

$A X B = \{(1, 2), (1, 4), (2, 2), (2, 4), (5, 2), (5, 4)\}$

If we take the **relationship x < y** then some ordered pairs are related and some or not.

The subset of A X B whose elements are related is the Relation R and is given by $R = \{(1, 2), (1, 4), (2, 4)\}$

* If R is a relation from a set A to itself (A), that is if R is a subset of $A^2 = A X A$, then we say R is relation on A.

Example

Let $A = \{a, b\}$, $A^2 = A X A = \{aa, ab, ba, bb\}$

DOMAIN AND RANGE OF A RELATION

The domain D of a relation R from A to B is set of all those first elements of the ordered pairs (x, y) which belong to R.

(i.e.)

$$D = \{x : x \in A, (x, y) \in R\}$$

Evidently (D is the subset of A) $D \subseteq A$.

RANGE (OR) CODOMAIN

The range E of a relation R from A to B is the set of all those second elements of the ordered pairs (x, y) which belong to R.

(i.e.)

$$E = \{y : y \in B \ (x, y) \in R\} \text{ evidently } E \subseteq B$$

Example 1

Let A = {2, 3, 4} and B = {3, 4, 5} list the elements of each relation R defined below and the domain and range,

a) a ∈ A is related to b ∈ B, that is, a R b if and only if a < b.

b) a ∈ A is related to b ∈ B, that is, a R b if a and b are both odd numbers.

Solution

a) 2 ∈ A is less than 3 ∈ B, that is 2 R 3. similarly 2 R 4, 2 R 5, 3 R 4, 3 R 5, 4 R 5

($\because a < b$)

Therefore   R = {(2, 3), (2, 4), (2, 5), (3, 4), (3, 5), (4, 5)}

           Dom (R)   = {2, 3, 4}

           And Range (R) = {3, 4, 5}

b) Since $3 \in A$ is related to $3 \in B$ are both odd then 3R3, similarly 3R5.

Therefore   R = {(3, 3), (3, 5)}

Dom (R) = {3}

Ran (R) = {3, 5}

Example 2

Let   S = {1, 2, 3, 4}

T = {1, 2, 3, 4}

List the elements of each relation R defined below and the domain and Range.

a) R = {(x, y) | (x = y)} is a relation in S X T

b) R = {(x, y) | x < y} is a relation in S X T

Solution

S X T   = {(1, 1), (1, 2), (1, 3), (1, 4), (2, 1), (2, 2), (2, 3), (2, 4), (3, 1),

(3, 2), (3, 3), (3, 4), (4, 1), (4, 2), (4, 3), (4, 4)}

No. of elements of S = m = 4 elements

No. of elements of T = n = 4 elements

∴ S X T = m X n = 4 x 4 = 16 elements

a) R = {(x, y) | (x = y)} is a relation in S X T

The set   R = {(1, 1), (2, 2), (3,3), (4, 4)}

Dom (R) = {1, 2, 3, 4}

Ran (R) = {1, 2, 3, 4}

Dom (R) = Ran (R)

Similarly

b) R = {(x, y) | x < y} is a relation in S X T

R = {(1, 2), (1, 3), (1, 4), (2, 3), (2, 4), (3, 4)}

Hence

> Dom (R) = {1, 2, 3}
>
> Ran (R) = {2, 3, 4}

SET OPERATIONS ON RELATIONS

Let R and S be two relation, then few relations are defined as

1) Intersection of R and S

    $x\,(R \cap S)\,y = x\,R\,y \;\wedge\; x\,S\,y$ $\wedge \rightarrow$ AND

2) Union of R and S

    $x\,(R \cup S)\,y = x\,R\,y \;\vee\; x\,S\,y$ $\vee \rightarrow$ OR

3) Difference of R and S

    $x\,(R - S)\,y = x\,R\,y \wedge x\,\cancel{S}\,y$

4) Complement of R

    $x\,(R')\,y = x\,\cancel{R}\,y$

Example 1

If A = {x, y, z}, B = { x, y, z}, C = {x , y} and D = {y, z}

R is the relation from A to B defined by R = {(x, X), (x, y), (y, z)} and S is a relation

from C to D defined by S = {(x, y), (y, z)}

Find R', R ∪ S, R ∩ S and R − S.

Solution :

The complement of R consists of all pairs of the Cartesian product

A x B that are not R. Thus

R' = {(x, Z, (y, X), (y, Y), (z, X), (z, Y), (z, Z)}

R $\cup$ S = {(x, X), (x, Y), (y, Z)}

R $\cap$ S = {x, Y), (y, Z)}

R – S = {(x, X)}

Example 2

If A = {2, 3, 5}, B = {6, 8, 10}, c = {2, 3} and D = {8, 10}. Suppose the

relation R from A to B is defined as

R = {(2, 6), (2, 8), (3, 10)} and the relation S from C to D is defined as

S = {(2, 8), (3, 10)}. Find R $\cup$ S, R $\cap$ S, R – S and R'.

Solution :

R $\cup$ S = {(2, 6), (2, 8), (3, 10)}

R $\cap$ S = {(2, 8), (3, 10)}

R – S = {(2, 6)}

R' = Set of all ordered pairs in A x B that are not in R

    = {(2, 10), (3, 6), (3, 8), (5, 6), (5, 8), (5, 10)}

2.4 TYPES OF RELATIONS

1) Identity relation (or) Diagonal relation in a set

The identity relation in a set A consists of all the ordered pairs (x, y) of A x A

for which x = y and it is denoted by I_A symbolically

I_A = {(x, y) : x $\in$ A, y $\in$ A, x = y}

Example

If A = {a, b, c, d} then identity relation in A is

I_A = {(a, a), (b, b), (c, c), (d, d)}

2) Universal Relation

A relation in a set A is said to be universal relation provided.

R = A x A

For Example

If A = {2, 3}, R = A x A

R = {(2, 2), (2, 3), (3, 2), (3,3)} is a universal relation.

3) Void Relation

A relation R in a set is said to be a void relation if R is a null set. (i.e) R = φ

For Example

If A = {2, 3, 5} and the relation R is defined as aRb, if and only if a divides b, then R = φ and hence A x A is a void relation

4. Inverse relation

Let R be any relation from a set A to a set B. The inverse relation denoted by R^{-1}, is a relation from B to A and is denoted by

R^{-1} = {(y, x) : x ∈ A, y ∈ B, (x, y) ∈ R}

In otherwords, the inverse relation is obtained by reversing each of the ordered pairs belong to R. Thus

$(x, y) \in R \Leftrightarrow (y, x) \in R^{-1}$ (or)

$x R y \Leftrightarrow y R^{-1} x$

Evidently, **the Range of R** is the **domain** of R^{-1} and vice versa. Then R and R^{-1} are both relations on A.

Example

Let A = {2, 4, 6}, B = {a, b} Then R = {(2, a), (2, b), (4, a)} is a relation from A to B. Find the inverse of the relation R.

R^{-1} = {(a, 2), (b, 2), (a, 4)}

= {(a, 2), (a, 4), (b, 2)}

Note

Dom (R) = Ran(R^{-1}) = {2, 4}

Ran (R) = Dom (R^{-1}) = {a, b}

$(R^{-1})^{-1}$ = R. If R is a relation on any set A, then R^{-1} is also the relation on A.

Properties of Relation and Types of Relation

(1) Reflexive relation [Each element is related to itself]

A relation R on a set A is reflexive if and only if each element in A is related to itself. i.e., aRa, for all a ∈ A. In other words for a ∈ A, (a, a) ∈ R.

A relation R on a set A is not reflexive if there is at least one element say b ∈ A such that b ∉ R.

Example

Let A = {1, 2, 3, 4} then the relation R = {(1,1), (2, 4), (3, 3), (4, 5), (4, 4)} on A is not reflexive because 2 ∈ A but (2, 2) ∉ R. **If A is reflexive each element of A is related to itself.**

R = {(1, 1), (2, 2), (3, 3), (4, 4)}

Here (2, 2) is not in R. So it is not reflexive.

Where as the another relation

$R_2 = \{(1, 1), (2, 2), (3, 3), (4, 4)\}$

is a reflexive relation on A

(2) Symmetric Relation

If any one element is related to any other element, then the 2nd element is related to the first.

A relation R on a set A is said to be symmetric, if whenever

a R b then b R a, if whenever (a, b) $\in$ R then (b, a) $\in$ R

The necessary and sufficient conditions for a relation R to be symmetric is

$R = R^{-1}$

Note :

A relation R on A is non-symmetric if there exist (a, b) $\in$ A such that (a, b) $\in$ R, but (b, a) $\notin$ R.

Example 1

A = {1, 2, 3} R = {1, 2} (2, 1), (3, 1), (1, 3)} it is **Symmetric**

Example 2

Let A = (1, 2, 3, 4) and

R = {(1, 3), (4, 2), (2, 4), (2, 3), (3, 1)}

The above relation is **not symmetric** because their exists elements 2, 3 belongs to A (i.e.) (2, 3) $\in$ A such that (2, 3) $\in$ R but (3, 2) $\notin$ R

Here (1, 3) $\in$ R $\Rightarrow$ (3, 1) $\in$ R, (4, 2) $\in$ R $\Rightarrow$ (2, 4) $\in$ R & (2, 3) $\in$ R $\Rightarrow$ (3, 2) $\notin$ R.

So the above relation is **not symmetric**.

However if R={(1,3),(4,2),(2,4),(3,1)} then it is a **symmetric** relation.

Also $R^{-1} = \{(3, 1), (2, 4), (4, 2), (1, 3)\}$

$R = R^{-1}$ when R is symmetric.

Similarly, $R = \{(1, 1), (2, 3), (3, 2)\}$ is a symmetric relation.

Anti Symmetric Relation

Let R be a relation on a set A. Then R is said to be anti-symmetric whenever (a, b) and (b, a) $\in$ R then a = b. If there exist (a, b) $\in$ A such that (a, b) $\in$ R and (b, a) $\in$ R but a $\neq$ b then R is not anti symmetric.

A relation R on a set A is anti-symmetric if $R \cap R^{-1} \subseteq I_A$

Where I_A denotes the identity relation on A.

Example 1

Let $A = \{1, 2, 3, 4\}$ and $R = \{(1, 1), (2, 3), (3, 2)\}$

Then $R^{-1} = \{(1, 1), (3, 2), (2, 3)\}$

and $R \cap R^{-1} = \{(1, 1), (2, 3), (3, 2)\}$

$R \cap R^{-1} \subseteq I_A$, where $I_A = \{(1, 1), (2, 2), (3, 3), (4, 4)\}$

Hence R is not anti-symmetric.

Example 2

Let $A = \{1, 2, 3\}$

$R_1 = \{(1, 1), (2, 1), (2, 2), (2, 3), (3, 2)\}$

Here $(2, 3) \in R_1$, $(3, 2) \in R_1$ but $2 \neq 3$.

$\therefore R_1$ is not anti-symmetric.

$R_2 = \{(1, 1)\}$

Here $(1, 1) \in R_2$, $(1, 1) \in R_2$ and $1 = 1$

R_2 is anti-symmetric.

Transitive Relation

If any one element is related to a second and that second element is related to a third, then the first is related to the third

A relation R on a set A is transitive if and only if for all a, b, c ∈ R, (a, b), (b, c) ∈ R then (a, c) ∈ R here a R b and b R c then a R c.

Example

A = (1, 2, 3}

R = {(1, 2), (2, 3), (1, 3)}

∴ it is transitive relation

Equivalence Relations

(1) (a, a) ∈ R for all a ∈ A [Reflexive]

(2) (a, b) ∈ R implies (b, a) ∈ R [Symmetric]

(3) (a, b) and (b, c) ∈ R implies (a, c) ∈ R [Transitive]

A relation R defined in a set A is said to be an equivalence relation if R is **symmetric, reflexive and transitive.**

Example

Let A = {1, 2, 3} and R is defined as R = {(1, 1), (2, 2), (3, 3), (1, 2), (2, 3)}

Then R is reflexive

Since (a, a) ∈ R for all a ∈ A. It is not symmetric since (1, 2) ∈ R but (2, 1)∉R. it is also not transitive since (1, 2)∈R and (2, 3)∈R but (1, 3)∉R.

Example

A = {1, 2, 3, 4} R = {(1, 1), (2, 2), (3, 3), (4, 4), (4, 1), (1, 4)}

It is reflexive, symmetric & transitive. So it is equivalence relation.

Partial Ordering Relations

A relation R on a set S is called a **partial ordering or partial order** if R is reflexive, antisymmetric and transitive. A set S together with a partial ordering R is called partially ordered set or poset.

Problems

1) A relation R called 'circular' if (a, b) ∈ R and (b, c) ∈ R ⇒ (c, a) ∈ R. Show that a relation is reflexive and circular, if and only if it is reflective, symmetric and transitive.

Solution

Let the relation R be reflexive and circular. Then we shall prove that R is reflexive, symmetric and transitive.

(a, b) ∈ R, (b, c) ∈ R ⇒ (c, a) ∈ R. since R is circular and (a, a) ∈ R since R is reflexive. We have

(c, a) ∈ R, (a, a) ∈ R ⇒ (a, c) ∈ R, since R is circular

This shows (a, c) ∈ R and (c, a) ∈ R. Hence R is Symmetric.

(a, b) ∈ R, (b, c) ∈ R ⇒ (c, a) ∈ R, since R is circular.

⇒ (a, c) ∈ R

Hence R is transitive. ∴ R is symmetric, transitive & reflexive so it s equivalence relation.

2.5 REPRESENTATION OF RELATIONS IN MATRIX FORM

Relation as a Directed Graph

Let R be a relation from a finite set A to itself. Draw a small circle for each element of A and label the circle with the corresponding element of A. These circles are called the **vertices** or **nodes (point or junction)**. Draw an arrow **(also called edge) (arcs or line or branch)** from vertex a_i to vertex b_j, if and only if $a_i \, R \, b_j$. This type of graph of relation R is called directed graph (or) diagram (digraph) of R diagraph G = (A, E)

Where

A→ It is made up of elements of A called vertices or nodes of A, Let A be a non-empty set A is called **vertex set.**

E → A subset E of A x A that contains the directed edges or arcs of G. E is called the **edge set**

Example

Let A = {1, 2, 3, 4} and

R = {(1,1), (1, 2), (2, 1), (2, 2), (2, 3), (2, 4), (3, 4), (4, 1), (4, 3)}

The diagraph of R is as shown

If a, b∈A and a, b∈E, there is an edge from a to b. Vertex a is called the **origin (or) source** edge with b, the **terminus (or) terminating vertex.** (a, a) is called a **loop** at a.

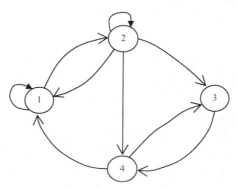

| In degree of vertex | : is the number of edges terminating at the vertex. |
| Out degree of vertex | : is the number of edges leaving the vertex. |

Example

Consider the above graph vertex 1 has indegree 3 and out degree 2. Similarly,

vertex 4 has indegree 2 and outdegree 2

Digraph of reflexive

(a, a) occur in the relation

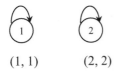

(1, 1)   (2, 2)

Digraph of symmetric

Here (b, a) is the relation whenever (a, b) is in the relation.

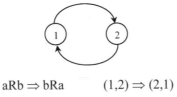

aRb ⇒ bRa   (1,2) ⇒ (2,1)

Digraph of transitive

a R b ⇒ b R c ⇒ a R c

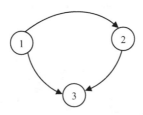

Relation as a Matrix

A relation R from a finite set A = {a_1, a_2, ..., a_m} to B = {b_1, b_2, ..., b_n}

containing m and n elements respectively. We define relation matrix.

M_R = [m_{ij}] of order m x n, for R whose elements are given by

$$m_{ij} = \begin{cases} 1 & \text{if } a_i \, R \, b_j \text{ or } (a_i, b_j) \in R \\ 0 & \text{otherwise (or) } (a_i, b_j) \notin R \end{cases}$$

The matrix M_R is also called the adjacency matrix (Boolean matrix (or) Relation Matrix).

Example

Let $A = \{a_1, a_2, a_3\}$, $B = \{b_1, b_2, b_3, b_4\}$

be two finite sets. Also, let the relation defined between them is

$R = \{(a_1, b_1), (a_1, b_4), (a_2, b_2), (a_2, b_3), (a_2, b_3), (a_3, b_1), (a_3, b_2)\}$

The matrix of the given relation is shown below :

Domain $= \{a_1, a_2, a_3\}$ Range $= \{b_1, b_2, b_3, b_4\}$

$$M_R = \begin{array}{c} \\ a_1 \\ a_2 \\ a_3 \end{array} \begin{array}{cccc} b_1 & b_2 & b_3 & b_4 \\ \left[\begin{array}{cccc} 1 & 0 & 0 & 1 \\ 0 & 1 & 1 & 0 \\ 1 & 1 & 0 & 0 \end{array}\right] \end{array} \longrightarrow \textbf{Range}$$

$\downarrow$ **Domain**

Example 2

Let $x = \{1, 2, 3, 4, 5\}$

$Y = \{1, 2, 3\}$, what is the graph of relation

$R = \{(x, y) : x \in X, y \in Y, x > y\}$, what is domain and range in this relation.

Solution

$R = \{(2, 1), (3, 1), (3, 2), (4, 3), (4, 2), (4, 1), (5, 3), (5, 2), (5, 1)\}$

Domain $= \{2, 3, 4, 5\}$

Range $= \{1, 2, 3\}$

$$\text{Matrix } M_R = \begin{array}{c} \\ 1 \\ 2 \\ 3 \\ 4 \\ 5 \end{array} \begin{array}{ccccc} 1 & 2 & 3 & 4 & 5 \\ \left(\begin{array}{ccccc} 0 & 0 & 0 & 0 & 0 \\ 1 & 0 & 0 & 0 & 0 \\ 1 & 1 & 0 & 0 & 0 \\ 1 & 1 & 1 & 0 & 0 \\ 1 & 1 & 1 & 0 & 0 \end{array} \right) \end{array}$$

It must be square matrix.

Diagraph

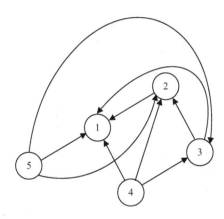

Matrix Representation of Relations

1. If R and S are relations on a set A represented by M_R and M_S respectively, then the matrix representing R∪S is the join of M_R and M_S obtained by putting 1 in the positions where either M_R or M_S has a 1 and denoted by $M_R \vee M_S$

(i.e.) $M_{R∪S} = M_R \vee M_S$ [∨ → Join operation]

Example

If R and S are relations on a set A represented by the matrices

$$M_R = \begin{bmatrix} 1 & 0 & 1 \\ 0 & 1 & 1 \\ 1 & 0 & 0 \end{bmatrix} \text{ and } M_S = \begin{bmatrix} 1 & 0 & 1 \\ 1 & 0 & 0 \\ 0 & 1 & 0 \end{bmatrix}$$

Respectively, then

$$M_{R \cup S} = M_R \vee M_S = \begin{bmatrix} 1 \vee 1 & 0 \vee 0 & 1 \vee 1 \\ 0 \vee 1 & 1 \vee 0 & 1 \vee 0 \\ 1 \vee 0 & 0 \vee 1 & 0 \vee 0 \end{bmatrix} = \begin{bmatrix} 1 & 0 & 1 \\ 1 & 1 & 1 \\ 1 & 1 & 0 \end{bmatrix}$$

Truth table for OR

P	Q	P∨Q
T	T	T
T	F	T
F	T	T
F	F	F

Note :

If either P or Q is True then True (value 1) else False (value 0).

2. The matrix representing R∩S is the meet of M_R and M_S obtained by putting 1 in the positions where both M_R and M_S have a_1 and denoted by $M_R \wedge M_S$.

3. [∧ is meet operation]

(ie) $M_{R \cap S} = M_R \wedge M_S$

The operations 'Join' and 'Meet' denoted by ∨ and ∧ respectively.

Example

Take the above example, $M_{R \cap S} = M_R \wedge M_S$

$$= \begin{bmatrix} 1 \wedge 1 & 0 \wedge 0 & 1 \wedge 1 \\ 0 \wedge 1 & 1 \wedge 0 & 1 \wedge 0 \\ 1 \wedge 0 & 0 \wedge 1 & 0 \wedge 0 \end{bmatrix} = \begin{bmatrix} 1 & 0 & 1 \\ 0 & 0 & 0 \\ 0 & 0 & 0 \end{bmatrix}$$

Truth Table for AND

P	Q	P∧Q
T	T	T
T	F	F
F	T	F
F	F	F

Note

If P and Q both are True then True (Value 1) else False (Value 0).

4. If R is a relation from a set A to a set B represented by M_R, then the matrix representing R^{-1} (the inverse of R) is M_R^T or M_R' the transpose of M_R.

Example

A = {2, 4, 6, 8} and B = {3, 5, 7} and if R is defined by

{(2, 3), (2, 5), (4, 5), (4, 7), (6, 3) (6, 7) (8, 7)}

Solution :

R is defined by {(2, 3), (2, 5), (4, 5), (4, 7), (6, 3) (6, 7) (8, 7)} then

$$M_R = \begin{array}{c} \\ 2 \\ 4 \\ 6 \\ 8 \end{array} \begin{array}{ccc} 3 & 5 & 7 \\ \left[\begin{array}{ccc} 1 & 1 & 0 \\ 0 & 1 & 1 \\ 1 & 0 & 1 \\ 0 & 0 & 1 \end{array}\right] \end{array}$$

Here   Domain = {2, 4, 6, 8} and Range = {3, 5, 7}

R^{-1} is denoted by {(3, 2), (5, 2), (5, 4), (7, 4), (3, 6), (7, 6), (7, 8)}

Domain   = {3, 5, 7},   Range   = {2, 4, 6, 8}

$$M_R^{-1} = \begin{array}{c} \\ 3 \\ 5 \\ 7 \end{array} \begin{array}{cccc} 2 & 4 & 6 & 8 \\ \left[\begin{array}{cccc} 1 & 0 & 1 & 0 \\ 1 & 1 & 0 & 0 \\ 0 & 1 & 1 & 1 \end{array}\right] \end{array} = M_R^T$$

5. If R is a relation from A to B and S is a relation from B to C, then the composition of relation R and S. R•S is represented by the Boolean products of matrices M_R and M_S denoted by $M_R•M_S$.

For addition we use + (or) ∨ operation, For multiplication we use • (or) ∧ operation.

Example

The matrix representing R•S

Where $M_R = \begin{bmatrix} 0 & 1 & 0 \\ 1 & 1 & 1 \\ 1 & 0 & 0 \end{bmatrix}$ and $M_S = \begin{bmatrix} 0 & 1 & 0 \\ 0 & 1 & 1 \\ 1 & 1 & 1 \end{bmatrix}$

Multiply the matrices

$M_{R•S} = M_R • M_S$

$$= \begin{bmatrix} 0+0+0 & 0+1+0 & 0+1+0 \\ 0+0+1 & 1+1+1 & 0+1+1 \\ 0+0+0 & 1+0+0 & 0+0+0 \end{bmatrix} = \begin{bmatrix} 0 & 1 & 1 \\ 1 & 1 & 1 \\ 0 & 1 & 0 \end{bmatrix}$$

Reflexive

6. Since the relation R on the set A = {a_1, a_2, ..., a_n} is reflexive if and only if (a_i,

a_i) $\in$ R for i = 1, 2, 3, ..., n, m_{ii} = 1 for i = 1, 2, 3, ..., n.

In otherwords, R is reflexive if all the elements in the principal diagonal of M_R

are equal to 1.

If all m_{ii} = 1 then relation is reflexive.

Thus $M_R = \begin{bmatrix} 1 & 0 & 1 \\ 0 & 1 & 0 \\ 0 & 0 & 1 \end{bmatrix}$ is the representation of reflexive relation R.

If all m_{ii} = 0, then the relation is irreflexive.

So $M_R = \begin{bmatrix} 0 & 0 & 1 \\ 0 & 0 & 0 \\ 1 & 1 & 0 \end{bmatrix}$

Hence reflexivity and irreflexivity depends only on diagonal.

7. Symmetric

One can relate symmetric property of a relation to properties of its matrix. If the representative matrix of a relation is symmetric with respect to the main diagonal.

(i.e.) $m_{ij} = m_{ji}$, for all values of i and j then the relation is **symmetric**.

A relation is antisymmetric if and only if $m_{ij} = 1$ $(i \neq j)$, then $m_{ij} = 0$. The following matrices illustrate the notation of symmetry and antisymmetry.

Symmetric   Antisymmetric

$$
\begin{matrix} a_{11} & a_{12} & a_{13} \\ a_{21} & a_{22} & a_{23} \\ a_{31} & a_{32} & a_{33} \end{matrix}
\quad
\begin{bmatrix} 1 & 0 & 1 \\ 0 & 1 & 0 \\ 1 & 0 & 0 \end{bmatrix}
\quad
\begin{bmatrix} 0 & 0 & 1 \\ 0 & 1 & 0 \\ 0 & 1 & 0 \end{bmatrix}
$$

8. Transitive

There is no simple way to test whether the relation R is a transitive by examining the matrix M_R. A relation R is transitive if and only if its matrix $M_R = [M_{ij}]$ has the property. If $M_{ij} = 1$ and $M_{jk} = 1$, then $M_{ik} = 1$. This statement simply means R is transitive if $M_R.M_R$ has 1 in position i, k. Thus the transitivity of R means that if $M_R^2 = M_R.M_R$ has a 1 in an any position then M_R must have a 1 in the same position. Thus, if $\mathbf{M_R^2 = M_R}$ the R is transitive.

Example

Let $A = \{1, 2, 3, 4\}$ and let R be a relation on A whose matrix is

$$
M_R \quad = \quad \begin{bmatrix} 1 & 1 & 1 & 1 \\ 0 & 0 & 0 & 0 \\ 1 & 1 & 1 & 1 \\ 0 & 1 & 0 & 0 \end{bmatrix}
$$

Show that R is transitive.

Solution

$$M_R^2 = M_R \bullet M_R$$

$$= \begin{bmatrix} 1 & 1 & 1 & 1 \\ 0 & 0 & 0 & 0 \\ 1 & 1 & 1 & 1 \\ 0 & 1 & 0 & 0 \end{bmatrix} \bullet \begin{bmatrix} 1 & 1 & 1 & 1 \\ 0 & 0 & 0 & 0 \\ 1 & 1 & 1 & 1 \\ 0 & 1 & 0 & 0 \end{bmatrix}$$

$$= \begin{bmatrix} 1 & 1 & 1 & 1 \\ 0 & 0 & 0 & 0 \\ 1 & 1 & 1 & 1 \\ 0 & 0 & 0 & 0 \end{bmatrix}$$

Here $M_R{}^2 \neq M_R$

$\therefore$ The relation is not transitive.

PROBLEMS IN REPRESENTATION OF RELATIONS

1. Describe the n arrow diagram of relation R from a finite set A to a finite set B.

   where the relation from

   $A = \{1, 2, 3, 4\}$ to set $B = \{x, y, z\}$

   defined by $R = \{(1, y), (1, z), (3, y), (4, x), (4, z)\}$

   Domain $= \{1, 3, 4\}$

   Range $= \{y, z, x\}$

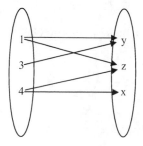

The above fig is called arrow diagram of R.

2. Let T be the relation from A = {1, 2, 3, 4, 5} to B = {red, white, blue, green}

   defined by T = {(1, red), (1, blue), (3, blue), (4, green)}

   a. Draw an arrow diagram of the relation T.

   b. Find the domain and range of T.

   c. Find the inverse T^{-1} and its arrow diagram

(a) Draw an arrow from x∈A and y∈B for each (x, y) ∈T.

   The arrow diagram is as follows

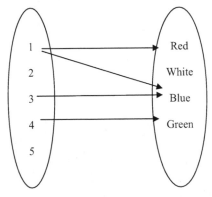

(b) The domain consists of the first elements of the ordered pairs of T and the range

   consists of the second elements.

   Hence dom (T) = {1, 3, 4} and range = {red, blue, green}.

c) Reverse the ordered pairs in T to obtain

   T^{-1} = {(red, 1), (blue, 1), (blue, 3), (green, 4)}

   Reverse the arrows in arrow diagram of T to obtain arrow diagram of T^{-1}.

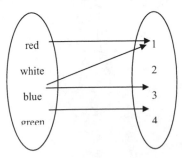

3) Find the relations determined by the following graphs

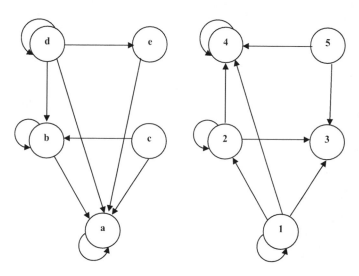

Solution

The relation shown in digraphs are

(i) R = {(a,a), (b,b), (d,d), (b,a), (d,a), (e,a), (c,a), (c,b) (d,b), (d,e)}

(ii) R = {(1,1), (2,2), (4,4), (1,2), (1,3), (1,4), (2,3), (2,4) (5,3), (5,4)}

4) Let R be a relation on the set A = {1, 2, 3, 4} defined by R = {(1,1), (1,2), (1,3),

(1,4), (2,2), (2,4), (3,3), (3,4), (4,4)}.

Construct the matrix and digraph of R.

Solution

Matrix of relation R

$$
\begin{array}{c} \\ 1 \\ 2 \\ 3 \\ 4 \end{array}
\begin{array}{cccc}
1 & 2 & 3 & 4 \\
\left[\begin{array}{cccc}
1 & 1 & 1 & 1 \\
0 & 1 & 0 & 1 \\
0 & 0 & 1 & 1 \\
0 & 0 & 0 & 1
\end{array}\right]
\end{array}
$$

Diagraph of relation R

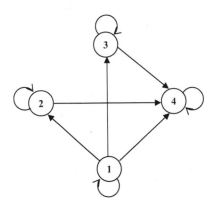

5) Let A = {a, b, c} be a non empty set, and R be the relation on A that has the matrix

$$M_R \quad = \quad \begin{bmatrix} 1 & 0 & 1 \\ 0 & 1 & 0 \\ 0 & 1 & 1 \end{bmatrix}$$

Construct the digraph of R, and list indegrees and outdegrees of all vertices.

Solution

$$\begin{array}{c} \\ \begin{array}{cc} & a \ \ b \ \ c \end{array} \\ \begin{array}{c} a \\ b \\ c \end{array} \begin{bmatrix} 1 & 0 & 1 \\ 0 & 1 & 0 \\ 0 & 1 & 1 \end{bmatrix} \end{array}$$

∴ Relation R = {(a,a), (a,c), (b,b), (c,b),(c,c)}

Digraph

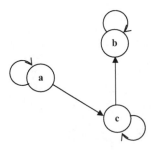

	a	b	c
Indegree	1	2	2
Outdegree	2	1	2

Cycle

A path that begins and ends at the same vertex is called a cycle.

Example

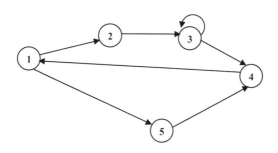

The sequence 1, 5, 4, 1 is the cycle of length 3.

The sequence 1, 2, 3, 4, 1 is the cycle of length 4.

2.6 COMPOSITION OF RELATIONS

If R is a relation from set A to set B and S is a relation from set B to set C. R is a subset of A x B and S is a subset of B x C, then the composition of R and S, denoted by R•S is defined by a(R•S)C, if some b∈B, we have a aRb and bRc.

R•S = {(a,c) : there exists some b∈B for which (a,b) ∈ R and (b,c) ∈ S}

NOTE

1. For the relation R•S, the domain is a subset of A and the range is the subset of C.

2. R•S is empty, if the intersection of the range of R and the domain of S is empty.

3. If R is a relation on a set A, then R•R, the composition of R with itself is always defined and sometimes denoted as R^2.

　　　　　　　　Pushpalatha Ramesh

Example

Let　R = {(1,1), (1,3), (3,2),(3,4),(4,2)}

and　S = {(2,1), (3,3), (3,4),(4,1)}

Composition of Relation

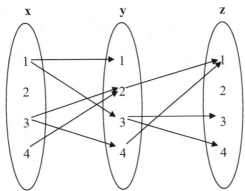

R•S　　　　　= Consider x and z then (1, 3), (1, 4), (3, 1), (4, 1)

x→y→z

Here any member (ordered pair) of R•S can be obtained only if the second element in the ordered pair of R agrees with the fist-element in the ordered pair of S.

Thus (1, 1) cannot combine with any member of S. (1, 3) in R can combine with (3, 3) and (3, 4) of S producing the members (1, 3) and (1, 4) respectively of R•S.

So　R•S　= {(1, 3), (1, 4), (3, 1), (4, 1)}

Similarly

S•R　　　　= {(2,1), (3,3), (3,4), (4,1)} {(1,1),(1,3),(3,2),(3,4),(4,2)}

S•R　　　　= {(2,3), (2,1), (3,2), (3,4),(4,1),(4,3)}

R•R　　　　= {(1,1), (1,3), (1,2), (1,4),(3,2)}

S•S　　　　= {(3,3), (3,4), (3,1)}

$(R \bullet S) \bullet R \quad = \{(1,2), (1,4), (3,1), (3,3),(4,1),(4,3)\}$

$R \bullet (S \bullet R) \quad = \{(1,2), (1,4), (3,1), (3,3),(4,1),(4,3)\}$

$R^3 = R \bullet R \bullet R = (R \bullet R) \bullet R \quad = R \bullet (R \bullet R)$

$\quad = \{(1,1), (1,3), (1,2), (1,4)\}$

Example 2

Let $A = \{1,2,3\}$, $B = \{a,b,c,d\}$, $C = \{x,y,z,w\}$ be three sets.

The relation R_1 from A to B and R_2 from B to C is defined as

$R_1 \quad = \{(1,a), (1,b), (3,c), (3,d)\}$

$R_2 \quad = \{(a,x), (b,x), (b,z), (d,w)\}$

Composition of Relations

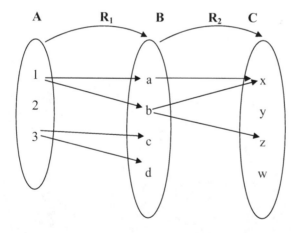

An arrow from 1 to a is followed by an arrow from a to x so $(1, x)$ is the first

element of $R_1 \bullet R_2$.

$R_1 \bullet R_2 \text{ (or) } R_1{}^\circ R_2 \quad = \quad \{(1, x), (1, z), (3, w)\}$

Power of R

(a) $R' = R$

(b) $R^{n+1} = R \bullet R^n$ for all +ve integers n.

Example

If $R = \{(1,2), (1,3), (2,4), (3,2)\}$ is a relation in a set $A = \{1,2,3,4\}$, Then

$$R^2 \quad = R \bullet R = \{(1,2),(1,3),(2,4),(3,2)\} \bullet \{(1,2),(1,3),(2,4),(3,2)\}$$

$$= \{(1,4),(1,2),(3,4)\}$$

$$R^3 \quad = R \bullet R^2$$

$$R^3 \quad = \{(1, 4)\} \text{ and for } n \geq 4, R^n = \phi$$

MATRIX REPRESENTATION OF COMPOSITION OF RELATIONS

Let $A = \{1, 2, 3\}$, $B = \{a, b, c, d\}$ and $C = \{x, y, z, w\}$ be three finite sets. The relation R_1 from A to B and the relation R_2 from B to C can be represented by the matrices $M_{R_1} = [M_{ij}]_{3 \times 4}$ and $M_{R_2} = [n_{ij}]_{4 \times 4}$ respectively. These matrices are defined as

$$M_{ij} \quad = \quad \begin{cases} 1 & \text{if } (i, j) \in R \\ 0 & \text{Otherwise} \end{cases}$$

$$M_{R_1} = \begin{array}{c} \\ 1 \\ 2 \\ 3 \end{array} \overset{\displaystyle a \;\; b \;\; c \;\; d}{\begin{bmatrix} 1 & 1 & 0 & 0 \\ 0 & 0 & 0 & 0 \\ 0 & 0 & 1 & 1 \end{bmatrix}}_{3 \times 4}$$

$$M_{R_2} = \begin{array}{c} \\ a \\ b \\ c \\ d \end{array} \overset{\displaystyle x \;\; y \;\; z \;\; w}{\begin{bmatrix} 1 & 0 & 0 & 0 \\ 1 & 0 & 1 & 0 \\ 0 & 0 & 0 & 0 \\ 0 & 0 & 0 & 1 \end{bmatrix}}_{4 \times 4}$$

Here M_{R_1} and M_{R_2} are given.

The composite relation $R_1 \bullet R_2$ from set A to C can also be obtained by multiplying two matrices M_{R_1} and M_{R_2} in the usual manner as shown below :

$$\begin{array}{c} \phantom{M_{R_1}} \\ M_{R_1} \bullet M_{R_2} \end{array} = \begin{array}{c} x \quad y \quad z \quad w \\ \begin{array}{c} 1 \\ 2 \\ 3 \end{array} \begin{bmatrix} 1 & 0 & 1 & 0 \\ 0 & 0 & 0 & 0 \\ 0 & 0 & 0 & 1 \end{bmatrix} \end{array}$$

The non-zero entries in matrix $M_{R_1} \bullet M_{R_2}$ indicate the relationships of particular elements in $R_1 \bullet R_2$

Standard Results

1. If R is a relation on A = $\{a_1, a_2, ..., a_n\}$ then $M_R^2 = M_R \bullet M_R$.

2. For n ≥ 2 and R a relation on a finite set, we have $M_R^n = M_R \bullet M_R ...... M_R$ (n factors).

Problems

Let R = {<1,2>, <3,4>,<2,2>} and S = {<4,2>, <2,5>, <3,1>, <1,3>} find R•S, S•R, R•(S•R), (R•S)•R, R•R, S•S and R•R•R.

Solution

R•S   = {<1,5>, <3,2>, <2,5>}

S•R   = {<4,2>, <3,2>, <1,4>}

Now R•S ≠ S•R

(R•S)•R   = {(3,2)}

R•(S•R)   = {<3,2>}   = (R•S)•R

R•R   = {<1,2>, <2,2>}

S•S   = {<4,5>, <3,3>, <1,1>}

R•R•R   = {<1,2>, <2,2>}

2) Let R and S be two relations on a set of +ve integers I. Find R•S, R•R, R•R•R and

R•S•R.

Where $R = \{<x, 2x> / x \in I\}$,

               $S = \{<x, 7x> / x \in I\}$

Solution

R•S $= \{(x, 14x> / x \in I\}$

S•R $= \{<x, 14x> / x \in I\}$

R•R $= \{<x, 4x> / x \in I\}$

R•R •R $= \{<x, 8x> / x \in I\}$

(R•S) •R $= \{x, 28x / x \in I\}$

3) If R and S be relations on a set A represented by the matrices.

$$M_R = \begin{bmatrix} 0 & 1 & 0 \\ 1 & 1 & 1 \\ 1 & 0 & 0 \end{bmatrix}$$

and $$M_S = \begin{bmatrix} 0 & 1 & 0 \\ 0 & 1 & 1 \\ 1 & 1 & 1 \end{bmatrix}$$

Find the matrices that represent

a) $R \cup S$ b) $R \cap S$ c) R•S   d) S•R   e) $R \oplus S$

a) $M_{R \cup S}$ $= M_R \vee M_S$

$$= \begin{bmatrix} 0 \vee 0 & 1 \vee 1 & 0 \vee 0 \\ 1 \vee 0 & 1 \vee 1 & 1 \vee 1 \\ 1 \vee 1 & 0 \vee 1 & 0 \vee 1 \end{bmatrix} = \begin{bmatrix} 0 & 1 & 0 \\ 0 & 1 & 1 \\ 1 & 1 & 1 \end{bmatrix}$$

Truth Table for OR

P	Q	PvQ
T	T	T
T	F	T
F	T	T
F	F	F

If either P or Q is true then true (value is 1) else false (value is 0).

b) $M_{R \cap S} = M_R \wedge M_S$

$$= \begin{bmatrix} 0 \wedge 0 & 1 \wedge 1 & 0 \wedge 0 \\ 1 \wedge 0 & 1 \wedge 1 & 1 \wedge 1 \\ 1 \wedge 1 & 0 \wedge 1 & 0 \wedge 1 \end{bmatrix} = \begin{bmatrix} 0 & 1 & 0 \\ 0 & 1 & 1 \\ 1 & 0 & 0 \end{bmatrix}$$

Truth Table for AND

P	Q	PvQ
T	T	T
T	F	F
F	T	F
F	F	F

If both P and Q are true then true (value is 1) else false (value is 0).

c) $M_{R \cdot S} = M_R \bullet M_S$ (Any one true then true)

$$= \begin{bmatrix} 0 \vee 0 \vee 0 & 0 \vee 1 \vee 0 & 0 \vee 1 \vee 0 \\ 0 \vee 0 \vee 1 & 1 \vee 1 \vee 1 & 0 \vee 1 \vee 1 \\ 0 \vee 0 \vee 0 & 1 \vee 0 \vee 0 & 0 \vee 0 \vee 0 \end{bmatrix} = \begin{bmatrix} 0 & 1 & 1 \\ 1 & 1 & 1 \\ 0 & 1 & 0 \end{bmatrix}$$

d) $M_{S \cdot R} = M_S \bullet M_R$

$$= \begin{bmatrix} 0 \vee 1 \vee 0 & 0 \vee 1 \vee 0 & 0 \vee 1 \vee 0 \\ 0 \vee 1 \vee 1 & 0 \vee 1 \vee 0 & 0 \vee 1 \vee 0 \\ 0 \vee 1 \vee 1 & 1 \vee 1 \vee 0 & 0 \vee 1 \vee 0 \end{bmatrix} = \begin{bmatrix} 1 & 1 & 1 \\ 1 & 1 & 1 \\ 1 & 1 & 1 \end{bmatrix}$$

e) $M_{R \oplus S} = M_{R \cup S} - M_{R \cap S}$

$$= \begin{bmatrix} 0 & 0 & 0 \\ 1 & 0 & 0 \\ 0 & 1 & 1 \end{bmatrix}$$

2.7 FUNCTIONS (OR) MAPPING (OR) TRANSFORMATIONS (OR)

CORRESPONDENCE

Definition : Functions

A function from a set A into a set B is a relation from A into B such that each element of A is related to exactly one element of the set B. The set A is called the **domain** of the function and the set B is called the **co-domain**. The phrase is related to exactly one element of the set B" means that if (a, b) $\in$ f and (a, c) $\in$ f then b = c. We write f : A→B. Further if a $\in$ A, the element in B which is assigned to 'a' is called the **image of a** and is denoted by f(a) which reads "f of a".

Example

Let f assign to each real number its square (i.e) for every real number x let f(x) $= x^2$. The domain and codomain of f are both real numbers. So we can write

$F : R^{\#} \to R^{\#}$

The image of -3 is 9 $\Rightarrow$ f(-3) $= (-3)^2 = 9$.

Define a function from a set A into a set B : Suppose that to each element of A there is assigned a unique element of B. The collection of such assignments is called a **function (or) mapping (or) transformations (or) correspondence.**

Definition

A relation f from a set X to another set y is called a function if for every $x \in X$ there is a unique $y \in Y$ such that $(x, y) \in f$.

In other words a function f from X to Y is an assignment of exactly one element of Y to every element of X.

If Y is the unique element of Y assigned by the function f to the element x of X, we write $f(x) = y$.

If f is a function from X to Y, we represent it as $f : X \to Y$ (or) $X \xrightarrow{f} Y$ then X is called domain of f denoted by D_f (its members are the 1st coordinates of the ordered pairs belongs to f) and set Y is called **codomain** of f.

If $(x, y) \in f$, it is to write $y = f(x)$ here y is called the image of x and x is called the **preimage (or) argument** of y.

Y is also called the **value of the function f at x.**

Range of Function

The set consisting of all the images of the elements of A under the function f is called the range of f. It is denoted by $f(A)$.

Thus range of $f = \{f(x) : \text{for all } x \in A\}$.

Note

a. The set A is the **domain** of f.

b. The set B is the **codomain** of f.

c. The set of all image values of f is called the image (or range) of f.

Example

(1) Let A = {1, 2, 3, 4, 5}, B = {0, 1, 2, 3, 5, 7, 9, 12, 13}, f is the function

   from A to B

f = {(1, 1), (2, 0), (3, 7), (4, 9), (5, 12)}.

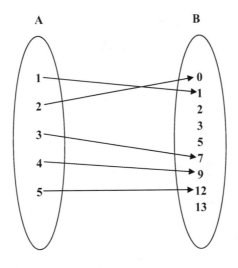

[**Note :** Each element of A has unique image in B and no element of A has two or

more images in B].

Here Domain	=	{1, 2, 3, 4, 5}
Codomain	=	{0, 1, 2, 3, 5, 7, 9, 12, 13}
Range of f (or) f(A)	=	{1, 0, 7, 9, 12}

Note :

   Some elements of B are not associated with any element of A.

(2) A = {1, 2, 3, 4, 5} B = {0, 1, 2, 3, 5, 7, 9, 12, 13} and f = {(1, 3), (2, 3), (3, 5),

(4, 9), (5, 9)} then f is a function from A to B.

Solution

Here each element of A has a unique image in B.

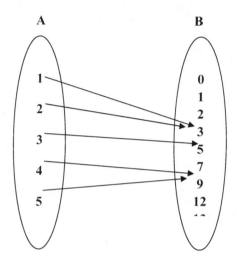

Domain	= {1, 2, 3, 4, 5}
Codomain	= {0, 1, 2, 3, 5, 7, 9, 12, 13}
Range of f (or) f(A)	= {3, 5, 9}

Note : Here the second component may repeat.

(3) Let A = {1, 2, 3, 4, 5}, B = {0, 1, 2, 3, 5, 7, 9, 12, 13} and f = {(1, 1),

(2, 13), (4, 7), (5, 12)}.

Here f is not a function because the element 3 of A has no image in B.

(4) The above A and B set and f = {(1, 1), (2, 3), (3, 5), (3, 7), (4, 9)} then f is

not a function because the different pairs (3, 5) and (3, 7) have same first

component.

(5) $f : A \to B$

$f(x) = x^2$

$x = 1,$ $f(1) = 1^2 = 1,$

$x = 2,$ $f(2) = 2^2 = 4,$

$x = 3,$ $f(3) = 3^2 = 9,$

$\therefore f = \{(1, 1), (2, 4), (3, 9)\}$

Domain $= \{1, 2, 3\}$

Range $= \{1, 4, 9\}$

Codomain $= \{1, 4, 9, 16\}$

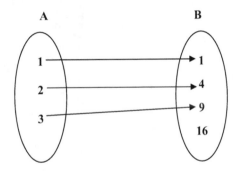

Image means it is the output of element A.

The image of 1 is 1.

The image of 2 is 4.

The image of 3 is 9.

(6) Let set $P = \{1, 2, 3\}, Q = \{2, 3, 4, 5\}$ function $f : P \to Q$ defined by $f(x) = x + 1.$

Solution

$x = 1, f(1) = 1 + 1 = 2$

$x = 2, f(1) = 2 + 1 = 3$

$x = 3, f(3) = 3 + 1 = 4$

$\therefore f = \{(1, 2), (2, 3), (3, 4)\}$

Domain $= \{1, 2, 3\}$

Range of function f(A) $= \{2, 3, 4\}$

Codomain $= \{2, 3, 4, 5\}$

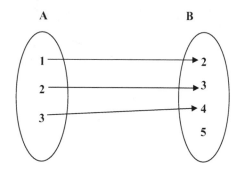

(7)   A = {-3, -1, 1, 3},   B = {0, 1, 2, 3, 4}

f : A→B is defined by $f(x)$ $= \dfrac{3-x}{2}$

Solution

From A = {-3, -1, 1, 3}

We know $f(x) = \dfrac{3-x}{2}$, substitute A values in the place of x, then we get,

$f(-3)$ $= \dfrac{3-(-3)}{2} = \dfrac{6}{2} = 3$

$f(-1)$ $= \dfrac{3-(-1)}{2} = \dfrac{4}{2} = 2$

$f(1)$ $= \dfrac{3-(1)}{2} = \dfrac{2}{2} = 1$

$f(3)$ $= \dfrac{3-3}{2} = \dfrac{0}{2} = 0$

f = {(-3, 3), (-1, 2), (1, 1), (3, 0)}

Domain (Set A)   = {-3, -1, 1, 3}

Codomain (Set B)   = {0, 1, 2, 3, 4}

Range of function f(A)   = {3, 2, 1, 0}

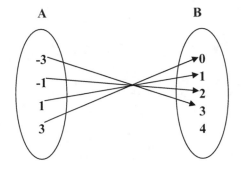

(8) Let I be the set of integers and A = {0, 1}. The relation between I and A defined as

f : I → A such that

$$f(x)=\begin{cases} 0 & \text{if } x \text{ is even} \\ 1 & \text{if } x \text{ is odd} \end{cases}$$

is a function because each set f(x) consists of a single element.

2.8 TYPES OF FUNCTIONS

The functions can be different types.

One-to-One Function (or) (injective) (or) injection

A function f : X→Y is called one-to-one (or) injective (or) injection, if distinct elements of X are mapped into distinct elements of Y. In otherwords, f is one-to-one if and only if $f(x_1) \neq f(x_2)$ whenever $x_1 \neq x_2$ (or) equivalently $f(x_1) = f(x_2)$ whenever $x_1 = x_2$.

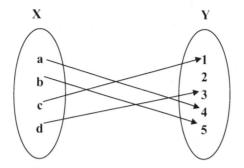

One-to-One (or) Injective

Example

Let $f : R^{\#} \to R^{\#}$ be defined by the formula $f(x) = x^2$ then $f(-2) = 4$, $f(2) = 4$ but

$2 \neq -2 \Rightarrow f$ is not injective.

Not Injective (Not One-to-One)

Example

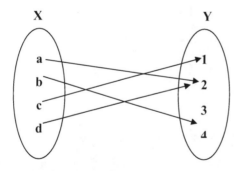

Since $f(a) = f(d) = 2$, but $a \neq d$.

Example 1

Let $A = \{1, 2, 3\}$, $B = \{a, b, c, d\}$ and let $f(1) = a$, $f(2) = b$, $f(3) = d$. Then f is

injective since the different elements 1, 2, 3 in A are assigned to the different elements

a, c, d respectively in B.

Example 2

If $f(x) = 3x - 1$ is one-to-one function because

$f(x_1) = f(x_2) \Rightarrow 3x_1 - 1 = 3x_2 - 1$

$\Rightarrow x_1 = x_2$

Many-One Function

A function f from A to B is said to be many-one if and only if two or more elements of A have same image in B.

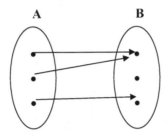

Many-One Function

Example

Let $f(x) = x^2$, x is any real number and $f : R \to R$, then f is many-one function.

For x = 1   then $f(1) = 1^2 = 1$ and

x = -1   then $f(-1) = (-1)^2 = 1$

So,   f = {(1, 1), (-1, 1)}

It shows two distinct number -1 and 1 are assigned to the same number 1 under f. Therefore f is many-one-function.

Into Function

A function f from A to B is called **Into** Function if any only if there exists at least one element in B which is not the image of any element in A (i.e) the range of f is a proper subset of co-domain of f.

Example

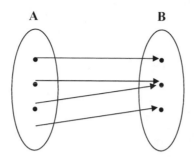

Onto Function (or) Surjective

A function f from A to B is **Onto (or) Surjective** if every element of B is the image of some element in A, that is B = range of f. It shows in figure

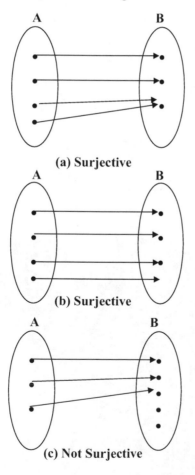

(a) Surjective

(b) Surjective

(c) Not Surjective

Note

To check whether

$Y = f(x)$ from a set A to set B is onto or not,

Write x in terms of y and see, if for every $Y \in B$, $x \in A$, if so it is onto otherwise it is into.

Bijective Function

A function f from A to B is said to be **Bijective or One-to-One Correspondence (or) Bijection**, if f is both **Injective and Surjective** (i.e) **One-to-One and Onto.**

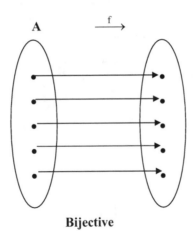

Bijective

Example

f be function from A to B

where

A   = {1, 2, 3, 4}

B   = {a, b, c, d}

f(1) = d,   f(2) = b,   f(3) = c,   f(4) = a.

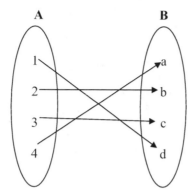

Then f is bijective function.

One-One-Onto (Bijective Function)

The above example, the function $f : A \rightarrow B$ is said to be **One-One Onto Function**, if to each element of A there corresponds one and only one elements of B and every element of B have one and only image in A. one-one and onto function are also called bijective.

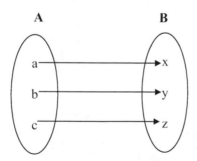

One-One Onto Function

One-One Into Function

The function $f : A \rightarrow B$ is said to be **One-One Into Function** if to each element of A there corresponds one element of B, but there are some element of B which do not correspond to any of the element of A as shown in fig.

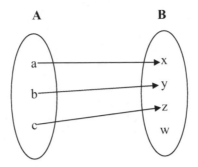

One-One Into Function

Many-One Into Function

The function f : A → B is said to be **Many-One Into Function**, if two or more elements of a set A corresponds to the same element of B and there are some elements in B which do not correspond to any of the elements of A as shown in fig.

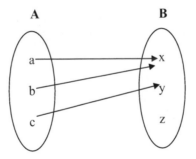

Many-One Into Function

Many-One Onto Function

The function f : A → B is said to be **Many-One Onto Function**, if each element in B is joined to atleast one element in A and two or more elements in A are joined to the same element in B as shown in fig.

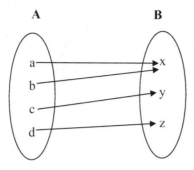

Example

Let A be the set of students siting on chairs in a classroom and let B be the set of chairs in the classroom. Let f be the correspondence which associates to each student the chair on which he sits.

Since every student has some chair to sit and no student can sit on two or more than two chairs, therefore for the function defined as f : A → B, the following cases may arise :

1. If every student get a separate chair and no chair is left vacant, then this is a case of a one-one-onto function.

2. If every student gets a separate chair and still some chairs are left vacant, it is a one-one into function.

3. If every student does not sit on a separate chair (i.e.) more than one student sit on a chair, no chair is left vacant, it is a many-one-onto function.

Equal Functions

Two functions f : A → B and g : A → B are said to be equal if and only if f(x) = g(x) for every x ∈ A and are written as f = g.

Constant Function

The function f : A → B is called a constant function, if some element y∈B is assigned to every element of A. (i.e.) f(x) = y for every x∈A. In otherwords, f : A → B is a constant function if the range of f consists of only one element.

Identity Function

Let A be any set, the function f : A → A defined by f(x) = x is said to be a identity function, if each element in A has a image itself. This is denoted by 'I_A'.

Difference between Function and Relation

Suppose A and B are two sets

Relation	Function
1. Every subset of A × B is a relation from A to B.	1. Let f be a function from A to B. Then by the definition of function, f is the subset of A × B in which each x ∈ A appears in one and only one ordered pair.
2. Every relation is not a function	2. Ever function is a relation
3. If R is a relation from A to B, the domain of R may be a subset of A.	3. If f is a function from A to B, then the domain of f is equal to A.
4. In a relation from A to B an element of A may be related to more than one element in B. Also there may be some elements in A which may not be related to any element in B.	4. But, in a function from A to B each element of A must be associated to one and only one element of B.

PRODUCT OR COMPOSITE OF FUNCTIONS

Definition

Let $f: A \rightarrow B$ and $g: B \rightarrow C$ be any 2 functions. Then the composition of f and g,

denoted by $g \circ f$, read as "g of f" results in a new function from A to C and is defined by

$(g \circ f)(x) = g(f(x))$ for all $x \in A$

$$g(f(x)) \quad = \quad h(x)$$

Figure illustrates the composition of the two functions f and g.

Example Problems

(1) Let $f : R \rightarrow R$ and $g : R \rightarrow R$ defined by $f(x) = 2x+1$, $g(x) = x^2 - 2$, find out $g \circ f$ and $f \circ g$.

Solution

$f \circ g(x) \qquad = f(g(x))$

$\qquad\qquad = f(x^2 - 2)$ [It is the form of f(x), here $x = x^2 - 2$. In the place of

$\qquad\qquad\qquad$ x, substitute $x^2 - 2$]

$\qquad\qquad = 2(x^2 - 2)$

$\qquad\qquad = 2x^2 - 4 + 1 = \qquad 2x^2 - 3$

$g \circ f(x) \qquad = g(f(x))$

$\qquad\qquad = g(2x + 1)$ [We know $g(x) = x^2 - 2$. So $g(2x+1) = (2x+1)^2 - 2$]

$\qquad\qquad = (2x + 1)^2 - 2 \qquad\qquad [(a+b)^2 = a^2 + 2ab + b^2]$

$\qquad\qquad = 4x^2 + 1 + 4x - 2 \quad = 4x^2 + 4x - 1$

(2) Let $f:R \rightarrow R$ and $g:R \rightarrow R$ defined by $f(x) = 4x-1$, $g(x) = \cos x$, find out $g \circ f$ and $f \circ g$.

Solution

$$
\begin{aligned}
g \circ f(x) \quad &= g(f(x)) \\
&= g(4x - 1) \qquad\qquad\qquad = \cos(4x - 1) \\[4pt]
f \circ g(x) \quad &= f(g(x)) \\
&= f(\cos x) \\
&= 4(\cos x) - 1 \qquad\qquad\qquad = 4\cos x - 1
\end{aligned}
$$

(3) Let $f : R \rightarrow R$ and $g : R \rightarrow R$ defined by $f(x) = 3x - 2$, $g(x) = 2x^2$, find $g \circ f$ and $f \circ g$.

Solution

$$
\begin{aligned}
g \circ f(x) \quad &= g(f(x)) \\
&= g(3x - 2) \\
&= 2(3x - 2)^2 \qquad\qquad [(a-b)^2 = a^2 - 2ab + b^2] \\
&= 2[(3x)^2 - 2 \times 3x \times 2 + (2)^2] \\
&= 2[9x^2 - 12x + 4] \\
&= 18x^2 - 24x + 8 \\[4pt]
f \circ g(x) \quad &= f(g(x)) \\
&= f(2x^2) \\
&= 3(2x^2) - 2 \\
&= 6x^2 - 2
\end{aligned}
$$

(4) Let A = {1, 2, 3}, B = {a, b} and C = {r, s} and f : A → B be defined by f(1) = a,

f(2) = a . f(3) = b and g : B → C be defined by g(a) = S, g(b) = r. Find g∘f.

Then   g∘f : A → C is defined by

$$g\circ f\,(1) \qquad = \qquad g(f(1)) \qquad = \qquad g(a) = S$$

$$g\circ f\,(2) \qquad = \qquad g(f(2)) \qquad = \qquad g(a) = S$$

$$g\circ f\,(3) \qquad = \qquad g(f(3)) \qquad = \qquad g(b) = r$$

(5) If f : R → R and g : R → R are defined by the formulas

$f(x) \quad = x + 2 \qquad$ for all x in R

$g(x) \quad = x^2 \qquad$ for all x in R

Find g∘f & f∘g

Then (g∘f) (x) $= g[f(x)] \qquad = g(x+2)$

$$= (x + 2)^2 \qquad = x^2 + 4x + 4$$

and   (f∘g) (x) $= f[g(x)] \qquad = f(x^2)$

$$= x^2 + 2$$

(6) Let A = {1, 2, 3} and f, g, h & s be functions from A to A given by

f   = {(1, 2), (2, 3), (3, 1)},   g   = {(1, 2), (2, 1), (3, 3)}

h   = {(1, 1), (2, 2), (3, 1)},   s   = {(1, 1), (2, 2), (3, 3)}

Find f∘g, g∘f, g∘s, s∘s, f∘s, f∘h∘g, s∘h∘g.

Solution

f(1) = 2	g(1) = 2	h(1) = 2	s(1) = 1
f(2) = 3	g(2) = 1	h(2) = 1	s(2) = 2
f(3) = 1	g(3) = 3	h(3) = 1	s(3) = 3

(1) f∘g(x)   =   f(g(x))

		f(g(1))		f(g(2))		f(g(3))
=		f(2)	=	f(1)	=	f(3)
=		3	=	2	=	1

    f∘g   =   {(1, 3), (2, 2), (3, 1)}

(2) g∘f(x)   =   g(f(x))

		g(f(1))		g(f(2))		g(f(3))
=		g(2)	=	g(3)	=	g(1)
=		1	=	3	=	2

    f∘g   =   {(1, 1), (2, 3), (3, 2)}

(3) g∘s(x)   =   g(s(x))

		g(s(1))		g(s(2))		g(s(3))
=		g(1)	=	g(2)	=	g(3)
=		2	=	1	=	3

    g∘s   =   {(1, 2), (2, 1), (3, 3)}

(4) s∘s(x)   =   s(s(x))

		s(s(1))		s(s(2))		s(s(3))
=		s(1)	=	s(2)	=	s(3)
=		1	=	2	=	3

    s∘s   =   {(1, 1), (2, 2), (3, 3)}

(5) f∘s(x)   =   f(s(x))

		f(s(1))		f(s(2))		f(s(3))
=		f(1)	=	f(2)	=	f(3)
=		2	=	3	=	1

    f∘s   =   {(1, 2), (2, 3), (3, 1)}

(6) $f \circ h \circ g$ $\qquad = \qquad f \circ (h \circ g)$

$\qquad h \circ g(x) \qquad = \qquad h \, [g(x)]$

$h(g(1))$		$h(g(2))$		$h(g(3))$
$= \quad h(2)$	$=$	$h(1)$	$=$	$h(3)$
$= \quad 2$	$=$	1	$=$	1

$\qquad h \circ g \qquad = \qquad \{(1, 2), (2, 1), (3, 1)\}$

$f \circ (h \circ g) \, (1) \qquad = \qquad f \, [h \circ g(1)] \qquad = \qquad f \, (2) = 3$

$f \circ (h \circ g) \, (2) \qquad = \qquad f \, [h \circ g(2)] \qquad = \qquad f \, (1) = 2$

$f \circ (h \circ g) \, (3) \qquad = \qquad f \, [h \circ g(3)] \qquad = \qquad f \, (1) = 2$

$\qquad \qquad f \circ h \circ g \qquad = \qquad \{(1, 3), (2, 2), (3, 2)\}$

Hence $s \circ h \circ g \qquad = \qquad \{(1, 2), (2, 1), (3, 1)\}$

(7) $\quad f(x) \quad = 5x + 2, \ g(x) = 2x - 3, \ h(x) = 3x + 1, \ $ Find $(f \circ g \circ h) \ \& \ (f \circ g) \circ h$

Solution

(i) $\quad f \circ (g \circ h)$

$(g \circ h) \qquad = \qquad g \, [h(x)]$

$\qquad \qquad = \qquad g(3x + 1)$

$\qquad \qquad = \qquad 2(3x + 1) - 3$

$\qquad \qquad = \qquad 6x + 2 - 3$

$\qquad \qquad = \qquad 6x - 1$

$f \circ (g \circ h) \qquad = \qquad f \circ [g \circ h(x)]$

$\qquad \qquad = \qquad f \, [6x - 1]$

$\qquad \qquad = \qquad 5(6x - 1) + 2$

$\qquad \qquad = \qquad 30x - 5 + 2$

$\qquad \qquad = \qquad 30x - 3$

$\therefore \ f \circ (g \circ h) \qquad = \qquad 30x - 3$

(ii)   (f∘g)∘h

(f∘g)	=	f[g(x)]
	=	f(2x - 3)
	=	5(2x - 3) + 2
	=	10x - 15 + 2
	=	10x - 13
(f∘g)∘h	=	(10x - 13)∘h
	=	3[10x − 13] + 1
	=	30x − 39 + 1
	=	30x − 38
∴ (f∘g)∘h	=	30x − 38

Inverse Function

(1) If $f : R \rightarrow R$ and $g : R \rightarrow R$ are defined as $f(x) = x^2 - 2$ and $g(x) = x + 4$. Find $g \circ f$ & $f \circ g$ and $f^{-1} \circ g^{-1}$.

Solution

g∘f	=	g[f(x)]		f∘g	=	f[g(x)]
	=	$g[x^2 - 2]$			=	f[x + 4]
	=	$x^2 - 2 + 4$			=	$(x + 4)^2 - 2$
	=	$x^2 + 2$			=	$x^2 + 16 + 8x - 2$
					=	$x^2 + 8x + 14$

$(g \circ f)^{-1}$	=	$f^{-1} \circ g^{-1}$

$f^{-1} \circ g^{-1}$	=	$(g \circ f)^{-1}$
	=	$(x^2 + 2)^{-1}$
∴ $(g \circ f)^{-1}$	=	$\dfrac{1}{x^2 + 2}$

(2) Let A = {1, 2, 3, 4} and B = {a, b, c, d} and let f = {(1, a), (2, a), (3, d), (4, c)}

show that f is a function but f^1 is not a function.

Solution

Here we have f(1) = a, f(2) = a, f(3) = d and f(4) = c.

Since each set f(n) is a single value, so f is a function.

Now f^1 = {(a, 1), (a, 2), (d, 3), (c, 4)} but f^1 is not a function.

Since $f^1(a)$ = {1, 2}   [So it is not a function].

(3) Show that the mapping f : R → R be defined by f(x) = ax + b where a, b, x ∈ R

a ≠ 0 is invertible defined its inverse.

Solution

For if x_1, x_2 ∈ R, then

$f(x_1) = f(x_2)$ $\Rightarrow ax_1 + b = ax_2 + b$

$\Rightarrow ax_1 = ax_2$

$\Rightarrow x_1 = x_2$

This proves f is one to one.

Again if y ∈ R

$y = f(x) \Rightarrow$ $y = ax + b$

$\therefore ax = y - b$

$\therefore x = \dfrac{y-b}{a}$

Thus for x ∈ R, so there exists $\left(\dfrac{y-b}{a}\right) \in R$, such that

$f\left(\dfrac{y-b}{a}\right)$ $=$ $a\left(\dfrac{(y-b)}{a}\right) + b$

$$= \quad y - b + b$$

$$= \quad y$$

Hence f is one-to-one and onto, therefore f^{-1} exists and it is defined by

$$f^{1}(y) \quad = \quad \frac{1}{a}(y-b)$$

(4) Find the formula for the inverse of $h(x) \quad = \quad \dfrac{2x-3}{5x-7}$

Set $y = h(x)$

Then interchange x and y as follows

$$y = \frac{2x-3}{5x-7} \text{ and then } x = \frac{2y-3}{5y-7}$$

Now solve for y in terms of x

$x[5y - 7]$	$=$	$2y - 3$
$5xy - 7x$	$=$	$2y - 3$
$5xy - 2y$	$=$	$7x - 3$
$(5x - 2)y$	$=$	$7x - 3$
$\therefore \quad y$	$=$	$\dfrac{7x-3}{5x-2}$

So $h^{-1}(x) \quad = \quad \dfrac{7x-3}{5x-2}$

2.9 PRINCIPLE OF MATHEMATICAL INDUCTION

The word induction means the method of inferring a general statement from the validity of particular cases.

Mathematical induction is a technique by which one can prove mathematical statements involving +ve integers.

A formal statement of principle of mathematical induction can be stated as follows.

Let S(n) be a statement that involves +ve integer n = 1, 2, 3....... Then S(n) is true for all +ve integer n provided that

(1) S(1) is true

(2) S(K+1) is true whenever S(K) is true so there are 3 steps to proof using the principle of mathematical induction

Step 1

Inductive Base

Verify that S(1) is true.

Step 2

Inductive Hypothesis

Assume that S(K) is true for an arbitrary value of K.

Step 3

Inductive step

Verify that S(K+1) is true on basis of the inductive hypothesis.

Example

(1) Prove that $1 + 2 + 3 + ... + n = \dfrac{n(n+1)}{2}$ by mathematical induction.

Proof :

Let S(n) be the given statement

(i.e) $1 + 2 + 3 + ... + n = \dfrac{n(n+1)}{2}$

(1) Inductive Base :

For n = 1, we have

L.H.S. n = 1

R.H.S.

$$S(1) = \frac{n(n+1)}{2} = \frac{1(1+1)}{2} = \frac{2}{2} = 1$$

L.H.S = RH.S

So S(1) is true. Hence S(n) is true for n = 1.

(2) Inductive Hypothesis :

Assume that

S(K) is true (i.e.) here n = K

$$1 + 2 + 3 + \dots + K = \frac{K(K+1)}{2}$$

(3) Inductive Step :

We wish to show the truth of S(K+1) (i.e.) here n = K+1

So

$$1 + 2 + 3 + \dots + K + K+1 \ = \frac{(K+1)[(K+1)+1]}{2}$$

$$= \frac{(K+1)(K+2)}{2}$$

$$= \frac{(K+1)(K+2)}{2} \text{ is true}$$

Now,

$$1 + 2 + 3 + \dots + K + K+1 \quad = (1 + 2 + 3 + \dots + K) + K+1$$

$$= \frac{K(K+1)}{2} + (K+1) \quad [S(K) \text{ being true}]$$

$$= \frac{K(K+1) + 2(K+1)}{2}$$

$$= \frac{K^2 + K + 2K + 2}{2} = \frac{K^2 + 3K + 2}{2}$$

$$= \frac{(K+1)(K+2)}{2}$$

$\therefore$ S(K+1) is true. Thus S(K) is true.

$\therefore$ By the principle of mathematical induction the theorem is true for all $n \in N$. In the above statement $K = n$, we can write $(n + 2)$ as $(n+1+1)$.

$$\therefore \frac{(n+1)(n+1+1)}{2} = \frac{n(n+1)}{2} \qquad \text{Where } (n+1) = n,$$

Hence proved.

(2) Prove by the principle of Mathematical Induction.

$$P(n) = 1 + 3 + 6 + \ldots \ldots \frac{n(n+1)}{2} = \frac{n(n+1)(n+2)}{6}$$

Solution

Let P(n) be the given statement

(1) Inductive Base

For $n = 1$, we have

R.H.S. $\qquad P(1) = \frac{1(1+1)(1+2)}{6} = \frac{2 \cdot 3}{6} = \frac{6}{6} = 1$

So P(1) is true.

L.H.S $\qquad \frac{n(n+1)}{2} = \frac{1(1+1)}{2} = \frac{2}{2} = 1$

L.H.S = R.H.S

Hence P(n) is true for n = 1.

(2) Inductive Hypothesis

Assuming that P(n) is true for n = K. Thus we get

$$P(K) = 1 + 3 + 6 + \ldots \frac{K(K+1)}{2} = \frac{K(K+1)(K+2)}{6}$$

(3) Inductive Step

We wish to show the truth of P(n) is true for n = K+1.

In L.H.S,

Adding (K+1) in the place of K $= \dfrac{(K+1)(K+1+1)}{2} = \dfrac{(K+1)(K+2)}{2}$

Then Adding the term $\dfrac{(K+1)(K+2)}{2}$ to both sides of P(K) we get

$$1 + 3 + 6 + \ldots \frac{K(K+1)}{2} + \frac{(K+1)(K+2)}{2} = \frac{K(K+1)(K+2)}{6} + \frac{(K+1)(K+2)}{2}$$

Consider the R.H.S. value, $\dfrac{K(K+1)(K+2)}{6} + \dfrac{3(K+1)(K+2)}{6}$

Here (K+1)(K+2) is common for both terms, take outside then we get

$$= \frac{(K+1)(K+2)(K+3)}{6}$$

This shows that P(n) is true for n = K, then it is also true for n = K+1.

Hence by mathematical induction it is true for every value of n.

$$= \frac{(K+1)(K+1+1)(K+1+2)}{6}$$

Replacing (K+1) by n.

$$= \frac{n(n+1)(n+2)}{6} = \text{R.H.S.}$$

Hence Proved.

(3) Prove $1^2 + 2^2 + ... + n^2 = \frac{n(n+1)(2n+1)}{6}$, for all $n \in N$.

Solution

Let P(n) denote the statement $1^2 + 2^2 + ... + n^2 = \frac{n(n+1)(2n+1)}{6}$

Step 1

Inductive Base : for n = 1

We have

L.H.S. P(1) = 1

R.H.S. of $P(1) = \frac{1(2)(3)}{6} = 1 = $ L.H.s. of P(1)

/ P(1) is true.

Step 2

Inductive Hypothesis :

Let P(K) for n = K

$$1^2 + 2^2 + ... + K^2 = \frac{K(K+1)(2K+1)}{6} \text{ be true.}$$

Step 3

Inductive Step

To prove P(K+1) put n = K+1

$$1^2 + 2^2 + ... + K^2 + (K+1)^2 = \frac{(K+1)(K+2)(2K+3)}{6} \text{ is true.}$$

Now

$$1^2 + 2^2 + ... + K^2 + (K+1)^2 = \frac{K(K+1)(2K+1)}{6} + (K+1)^2$$

(Since P(K) is true)

$$= \frac{K(K+1)(2K+1) + 6(K+1)^2}{6}$$

$$= (K+1)\left[\frac{K(2K+1) + 6(K+1)}{6}\right]$$

$$= \frac{(K+1)[2K^2 + K + 6K + 6]}{6}$$

$$= \frac{(K+1)[2K^2 + 7K + 6]}{6}$$

Since there is $2K^2$ so we can't factorize so split 7K

$$= \frac{(K+1)[2K^2 + 4K + 3K + 6]}{6}$$

$$= \frac{(K+1)[2K(K+2) + 3(K+2)]}{6}$$

Here (K+2) is common, take outside

$$\frac{(K+1)(K+2)(2K+3)}{6}$$

/ P(K+1) is true. Hence by principle of mathematical induction the statement is true

for all n ∈ N.

Put K+1 = n

$$= \frac{(K+1)(K+1+1)(2K+1+2)}{6} = \frac{(K+1)(K+1+1)(2(K+1)+1)}{6}$$

Put (K+1) = n

$$= \frac{n(n+1)\ 2(n)+1}{6} = \frac{n(n+1)(2n+1)}{6} = \text{R.H.S.}$$

Hence Proved.

(4) Prove that $1^3 + 2^3 + \ldots + n^3 = \left[\frac{n(n+1)}{2}\right]^2$

Solution

Let P(n) denote the statement

$$1^3 + 2^3 + \ldots + n^3 = \frac{n^2(n+1)^2}{4}$$

Step 1

Inductive base : for n =1

We have

L.H.S of $P(1) = 1^3 = 1$

R.H.S of $P(1) = \frac{1^2(1+1)^2}{4} = \frac{4}{4} = 1 = \text{L.H.S. of } P(1)$

/ P(1) is true.

Step 2

Inductive Hypothesis

Put n = K

Let $P(K) = 1^3 + 2^3 + \ldots + K^3 = \frac{K^2(K+1)^2}{4}$ be true

Step 3

Inductive Step :   To prove P(K+1)

Put n = K +1

Now

$$1^3 + 2^3 + ... + K^3 + (K+1)^3 = \frac{(K+1)^2(K+1+1)^2}{4} \quad \text{is true}$$

$$= \frac{(K+1)^2(K+2)^2}{4}$$

$$\therefore 1^3 + 2^3 + ... + K^3 + (K+1)^3$$

$$= \frac{K^2(K+1)^2}{4} + (K+1)^3 \quad [\therefore \text{P(K) is true}]$$

$$= \frac{K^2(K+1)^2 + 4(K+1)^3}{4}$$

$$= \frac{(K+1)^2 \left[K^2 + 4(K+1) \right]}{4}$$

$$= \frac{(K+1)^2(K^2 + 4K + 4)}{4}$$

$$= \frac{(K+1)^2(K+2)^2}{4}$$

$$\begin{array}{c} 4 \\ \diagup \diagdown \\ 2 \quad 2 \end{array}$$

$\therefore$ P(K+1) is true.

Thus P(K+1) is true if P(K) is true.

$\therefore$ By the principle of mathematical induction the statement is true for all $n \in$ N.

$$\frac{(K+1)^2(K+2)^2}{4} = \frac{(K+1)^2 + (K+1+1)^2}{4}$$

$$\text{Put } K + 1 = n \qquad = \frac{n^2(n+1)^2}{4} = \left[\frac{n(n+1)}{2} \right]^2$$

$\therefore 1^3 + 2^3 + ... + n^3 = \text{R.H.S}$

Hence it is proved.

(5) Let $P(n)$ is $8^n - 3^n$ is a multiple of 5 prove that $P(n)$ is a tautology over n.

Proof

$$P(n) = 8^n - 3^n$$

Step 1

For $n = 1$

$P(1) = 8^1 - 3^1 = 5$

$\therefore$ This is true for $n = 1$.

Step 2 :

$$P(n) = 8^n - 3^n$$

Assume that $P(n)$ is true.

Step 3 :

Prove that $P(n+1)$ is true.

$P(n+1)$ $\quad = 8^{n+1} - 3^{n+1}$ split $8^{n+1} = 8^n \cdot 8$

$\quad = 8^n \cdot 8 - 3^n \cdot 3$

$\quad = 8^n (5 + 3) - 3^n \cdot 3$

$\quad = 8^n \cdot 5 + 8^n \cdot 3 - 3^n \cdot 3$ $\qquad$ [Here 3 is common for 2nd & 3rd value]

$\quad = 8^n \cdot 5 + 3(8^n - 3^n)$

In step 2, we prove that $8^n - 3^n = $ true

$\quad = 8^n \cdot 5 + 3(T)$ $\qquad$ we know $P \cup T = P$ and $P \cap T = T$

$\quad = 8^n \cdot 5 + T$

$\quad = 8^n \cdot 5$

Which is also the multiples of 5 so it is proved.

(6) Let P(n) is $n^3 + 2n$ is a multiples of 3.

Prove that P(n) is a tautology over n.

Proof

Let $P(n) = n^3 + 2n$

Step 1

For n = 1

$P(1) = 1^3 + 2(1) = 1 + 2 + 3$

Step 2

Assume that P(n) is true and

$P(n) = n^3 + 2n$ so prove P(n+1) is true

Step 3

Let we prove that P(n+1) is true. $[(a+b)^3 = a^3 + b^3 + 3a^2b + 3ab^2]$

$P(n+1) \quad = (n+1)^3 + 2(n+1)$

$= n^3 + 1 + 3n^2.1 + 3n.1^2 + 2n + 2$

$= n^3 + 1 + 3n^2 + 3n + 2n + 2$

$= n^3 + 3n^2 + 2n + 3n + 3$

$= n^3 + 2n + 3n^2 + 3n + 3$

$= T + 3(n^2 + n + 1)$

$= 3(n^2 + n + 1) \qquad\qquad [n^3 + 2n = true = T]$

The result is multiples of 3

$\therefore$ Hence Proved

(7) Prove that $\dfrac{1}{1\cdot 2}+\dfrac{1}{2\cdot 3}+......+\dfrac{1}{n(n+1)}=\dfrac{n}{n+1}$

Proof

Let $\dfrac{1}{1\cdot 2}+\dfrac{1}{2\cdot 3}+......+\dfrac{1}{n(n+1)}=\dfrac{n}{n+1}$

Step 1

For $n=1$

$$\frac{1}{n(n+1)}=\frac{1}{1(2)}=\frac{1}{2}$$

Step 2

Let us assume $P(n)$ is true and we will prove for $P(n+1)$

Adding $\dfrac{1}{(n+1)(n+2)}$ on both sides we get

$$\frac{1}{1\cdot 2}+\frac{1}{2\cdot 3}+......+\frac{1}{n(n+1)}+\frac{1}{(n+1)(n+2)}$$

$$=\frac{n}{(n+1)}+\frac{1}{(n+1)(n+2)}$$

$$=\frac{n(n+2)+1}{(n+1)(n+2)}=\frac{n^2+2n+1}{(n+1)(n+2)}$$

$$=\frac{(n+1)^2}{(n+1)(n+2)}=\frac{n+1}{n+2}$$

$$=\frac{n+1}{n+1+1}$$

Replace n+1 by n

$$=\frac{n}{n+1}$$

$\therefore \dfrac{1}{1\cdot 2}+\dfrac{1}{2\cdot 3}+......+\dfrac{1}{n(n+1)}=\dfrac{n}{(n+1)}$

Hence proved.

CHAPTER – III

3. BOOLEAN ALGEBRA

Boolean Algebra is an algebra of logic. George Boole (1815-1864) who invented a symbolic way of manipulating logic symbols which became known as Boolean Algebra.

3.1 DEFINITION

Let B be a set on which are defined two binary operations + and * and a unary operation denoted as' ; let 0 and 1 denote two distinct elements of B. Then <B, +, *, ', 0, 1> is called Boolean algebra.

Axioms of Boolean Algebra

If a, b, c ∈ B then

(1) Commutative Laws

(a) $a + b = b + a$

(b) $a \cdot b = b \cdot a$

The operations + and * are called sum and product. Instead of * we use •. a' is the complement of a.

(2) Distributive Law

(a) $a + (b.c) = (a + b).(a+c)$

(b) $a \cdot (b+c) = (a \cdot b) + (a \cdot c)$

(3) Identity Laws

(a) $a + 0 = a$ (b) $a \cdot 1 = a$

(4) Complement Laws

(a) $a + a' = 1$ (b) $a \cdot a' = 0$

Basic Theorems

Let a, b, c, $\in$ B, then

(1) Idempotent Laws

(a) $a + a = a$ (b) $a \cdot a = a$

(2) Boundedness Laws (or) Null Laws

(a) $a + 1 = 1$ (b) $a \cdot 0 = 0$

(3) Absorption Laws

(a) $a + (a \cdot b) = a$

(b) $a \cdot (a + b) = a$

(4) Associative Laws

(a) $(a + b) + c = a + (b + c)$

(b) $(a \cdot b) \cdot c = a \cdot (b \cdot c)$

(5) Uniqueness of Complement

$a + x = 1$ and $a \cdot x = 0$ then $x = a'$

(6) Involution Law $(a')' = a$

(7) (a) $0' = 1$ (b) $1' = 0$

(8) De-Morgan's Law

De-Morgan's theorem can be stated as

(a) The complement of the sum is the product of the complements.

$(a+b)' = a' \cdot b'$ ------------ (1)

(b) The complement of the product is the sum of the complements.

$$(a . b)' = a' + b' \qquad\qquad \text{------------ (2)}$$

Theorem 1

Prove $a + a = a$

Proof

$a = a + 0$	by Identity law
$= a + aa'$	using Complement law
$= (a+a) (a+a')$	using Distributive law
$= (a+a) . 1$	using Complement law
$= a + a$	using Identity law

Hence proved

Theorem 2

Prove $a . a = a$

Proof

$a . a = a . a + 0$	by Identity law
$= a.a + a.a'$	using Complement law
$= a . (a+a')$	using Distributive law
$= a . 1 = a$	using Complement and Identity law

Hence proved

Theorem 3

Prove $a + 1 = 1$

Proof

$a + 1 = a + a + a'$ by Complement law

$\quad = (a + a) + a'$ using Associative law

$\quad = a + a'$ using Idempotent law

$\quad = 1$ using Complement law

Hence proved

Theorem 4

Prove $a + (a.b) = a$

Proof

$a + (a.b) = a \cdot 1 + a \cdot b$ by Identity law

$\quad = a(1+b)$ using Distributive law

$\quad = a \cdot 1$ using Boundedness law

$\quad = a$ using Identity law

Hence proved

3.2 KARNAUGH MAP

- Boolean function can be implemented by many methods but there are complexities.

- The map method provides a simple straight forward procedure for minimizing Boolean functions.

- This method may be regarded either as a pictorial form of truth table or as an extension of the Venn diagram.

- The map method first proposed by Veitch & simply modified by Karnaugh is also known as "Veitch Diagram" or "Karnaugh Map".

- The map is a diagram made up of squares each square represents one minterm.

- Any Boolean function can be expressed as a sum of minterms.

Two-Variable Map

x \ y	0	1
0	m_0	m_1
1	m_2	m_3

Example

(i)

x \ y	0	1
0		
1		1

Here, 0 $\rightarrow$ x' or $\bar{x}$ in row

0    $\rightarrow$ y' or $\bar{y}$ in column

1    $\rightarrow$ x in row

1    $\rightarrow$ y in column

F = x y

(ii) Simplify the Boolean function

F = x'y + xy' + xy

x \ y	0	1
0		1
1	1	1

F = x + y

Three-Variable Map

x \ y	00	01	11	10
0	m_0	m_1	m_3	m_2
1	m_4	m_5	m_7	m_6

Example

(i) Simplify the Boolean function

$F = x'yz + x'yz' + xy'z' + xy'z$

x \ y	00	01	11	10
0			1	1
1	1	1		

Note

$$00 \to \bar{x}\,\bar{y}, \quad 01 \to \bar{x}\,y, \quad 11 \to x\,y, \quad 10 \to x\,\bar{y}$$

Ans : $F = x'y + xy'$

(ii) Simplify the Boolean function

$F = A'C + A'B + AB'C + BC$

x \ y	00	01	11	10
0		1	1	1
1		1	1	

Ans : $F = C + A'B$

(iii) Simplify the Boolean function

$F = x'yz + xy'z' + xyz + xyz'$

x \ y	00	01	11	10
0			1	
1	1		1	1

Ans : $F = yz + xz'$

Four-Variable Map

wx \ yz	00	01	11	10
00	m_0	m_1	m_3	m_2
01	m_4	m_5	m_7	m_6
11	m_{12}	m_{13}	m_{15}	m_{14}
10	m_8	m_9	m_{11}	m_{10}

Example

(i) $F(w, x, y, z)$ = $\Sigma(0, 1, 2, 4, 5, 6, 8, 9, 12, 13, 14)$

wx \ yz	00	01	11	10
00	1	1		1
11	1	1		1
11	1	1		1
10	1	1		

Ans : $F = y' + w'z' + xz'$

(ii) Simplify the Boolean function $F = A'B'C' + B'CD' + A'BCD' + AB'C'$

yz wx	00	01	11	10
00	1	1		1
01				1
11				
10	1	1		1

Ans : $F = B'C' + B'D' + A'CD'$

5 Variable Map

CDE AB	000	001	011	010	110	111	101	100
00	0	1	3	2	6	7	5	4
01	8	9	11	10	14	15	13	12
11	24	25	27	26	30	31	29	28
10	16	17	19	18	22	23	21	20

3.3 SUM OF PRODUCT

(i) $f(a, b, c, d) = \sum(1,3,5,7,9,11,13,15)$

CD \ AB	0 0 $\overline{A}\,\overline{B}$	0 1 $\overline{A}B$	1 1 AB	1 0 $A\overline{B}$
00 $\overline{C}\,\overline{D}$	0	1 1	1 3	2
01 $\overline{C}D$	4	1 5	1 7	6
11 CD	12	1 13	1 15	14
10 $C\overline{D}$	8	1 9	1 11	10

(Write the common factors)

$$= B\overline{C} + BC = B\left[\overline{C} + C\right] \qquad = B \qquad\qquad \left[\because \overline{C} + C = 1\right]$$

(ii) $f(a, b, c, d) = \sum(0,5,7,8,12,14)$

CD \ AB	0 0 $\overline{A}\,\overline{B}$	0 1 $\overline{A}B$	1 1 AB	1 0 $A\overline{B}$
00 $\overline{C}\,\overline{D}$	1 0	1	3	2
01 $\overline{C}D$	4	1 5	1 7	6
11 CD	1 12	13	15	1 14
10 $C\overline{D}$	1 8	9	11	10

Note

$$\overline{C}\,\overline{D}\,\overline{A}\,\overline{B} = 0 \rightarrow 0000,\ 5 \rightarrow 0101,\ 7 \rightarrow 0111,\ 8 \rightarrow 1000 \text{ and so on.}$$
$$\text{(Write the common factors)}$$

$$= \overline{A}\,\overline{B}\,\overline{D} + B\overline{C}D + \overline{B}CD$$

3.4 PRODUCT OF SUM

$f(a, b, c, d) = \sum(0,2,4,6,8,10,12,14)$

CD \ AB	0 0 $\overline{A}\,\overline{B}$	0 1 $\overline{A}\,B$	1 1 $A\,B$	1 0 $A\,\overline{B}$
00 $\overline{C}\,\overline{D}$	0 0	1	3	0 2
01 $\overline{C}\,D$	0 4	5	7	0 6
11 $C\,D$	0 12	13	15	0 14
10 $C\,\overline{D}$	0 8	9	11	0 10

$$\Rightarrow \left(\overline{A} + \overline{B}\right).\left(A + \overline{B}\right)$$

According to De-Morgan's Law

Complement the above result

$$\Rightarrow \overline{\left(\overline{A} + \overline{B}\right)}.\overline{\left(A + \overline{B}\right)}$$

$$\Rightarrow (A + B).(\overline{A} + B)$$

CHAPTER - IV

4. MATHEMATICAL LOGIC

Logic is the discipline that deals with the methods of reasoning.

4.1 INTRODUCTION

PROPOSITIONS

- A declarative sentence (or) assertion which is true or false but not both is called a propositions (or) statement.

- Sentences which are exclamatory, interrogative (or) imperative in nature are not propositions.

- Lower case letters such as p, q, r are used to denote propositions.

Example 1

1) New Delhi is the capital city of India

2) $2 + 2 = 3$ 1) & 2) are propositions

Example 2

1) How beautiful is Rose ?

2) What time is it ?

3) Take a cup of Coffee these are not propositions as they are not declarative in nature.

If a proposition is true denoted by T or 1. If a preposition is false denoted by F or 0.

Proposition which donot contain any of the logical operators or connectives are called atomic (primary (or) primitive) propositions.

Many mathematical statements which can be constructed by combining one or more atomic statements using connectives are called molecular (or) compound proposition (or) composite.

TYPES OF PROPOSITIONS

Definition I :

A proposition consisting of just one subject and one predicate is called a **Simple Proposition.**

Example

1. Ram is Blind

2. Line L and L' are parallel

3. The flower is not red

Definition II :

A proposition consisting of two or more simple proposition in the form of single sentence is called **compound proposition.**

Example

1. Some men are stupid and pigs can fly

2. Quadrilateral ABCD is a square and each side of this quadrilateral is 4 cm long.

4.2 CONNECTIVES

The word and phrases (or symbols) used to form compound propositions are called connectives. There are five basic connectives called Negation, Conjunction, Disjunction, Implication (or) Conditional and Equivalence (or) Biconditional. So, to combine simple propositions to form compound propositions by using logical connectives such as

Symbol	Connective Word	Name
¬, ~, '	Not	Negation
∧	And	Conjunction
∨	Or	Disjunction
⇒	If …… then	Implication (or) Conditional
⇔	If and only if	Equivalence (or) Biconditional
~(∧) ↑	Nand	
~(∨) ↓	Nor	

BASIC LOGICAL OPERATIONS

Definition : Connectives

For the systematic usage of certain keywords 'and', 'or', 'not', 'if ….. then', 'if and only if', which are called sentential connectives.

Definition 1 : Conjunction

The process of joining two statements or propositions p and q using connective "and" produces a new statement denoted by p∧q. The statement p∧q is called the conjunction of statements p and q.

Note : p∧q = T, True value, when both p and q are true. Otherwise F-value.

Example

p   : Today is Sunday

q   : Government offices are working.

Then conjunction of p & q is

⇒ p∧q : Today is Sunday and government offices are working.

Truth Table for p∧q

P	q	p∧q
T	T	T
T	F	F
F	T	F
F	F	F

AND Gate Symbol

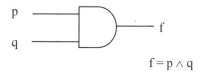

$$f = p \wedge q$$

Meaning p • q

Note

Truth table is a table that displays the relationships between the truth values of sub propositions and that of compound and proposition constructed from them.

Definition 2 : Disjunction

Here the connective has 2 different meaning.

i) Inclusive Disjunction (OR)

The process of joining the two statements (or) propositions p and q by the connective "OR" produces a new statement denoted by 'p∨q' which is read as "p OR q".

Truth Table for p∨q

P	Q	p∨q
T	T	T
T	F	T
F	T	T
F	F	F

OR Gate Symbol

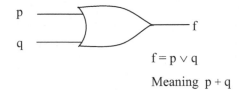

$$f = p \vee q$$

Meaning p + q

Note :

The statement p∨q has the truth value F only when both P and Q have the truth value F. Otherwise it is True T (Any one true it is true)

Example 1

p   : 21 is divisible by 3

q   : 21 is divisible by 7

p∨q   : 21 is divisible by 3 OR 21 is divisible by 7

Example 2

For disjunction

p   : I shall buy a TV set

q   : I shall buy a car

then p∨q   : I shall buy a TV set OR I shall buy a car

(ii) Exclusive Disjunction (XOR) Symbol is   ∨

The process of joining the two statements p and q by "XOR" produces a new statement denoted by p⊕q, which is read as "p XOR q"

Truth Table for XOR

p	q	(p∨q) or (p⊕q)
T	T	F
T	F	T
F	T	T
F	F	F

XOR Gate Symbol

$$f = p \oplus q$$

$$\text{Meaning} = p'q + pq'$$

Definition 3 : Negation (Unary Operation)

If p denotes a statement or proposition then the negation of ¬p is written as ¬p and read as 'not p' ¬p is also denoted as p', $\bar{p}$ and ~p. if p is true then ¬p is false and p is false then ¬p is true.

Example 1 :

p   : London is a city.

¬p   : London is not a city.

Example 2 :

p   : The door is locked.

¬p   : The door is not locked

Truth Table for ¬p

p	¬p
T	F
F	T

¬p → The Negation of p

Example Problems

(1) Construct a Truth Table for p∨¬q

Solution :

p	q	¬q	p∨¬q
T	T	F	T
T	F	T	T
F	T	F	F
T	T	F	T

(2) Construct a Truth Table for p∧⅂p

Solution

p	⅂p	p∧⅂p
T	F	F
F	T	F

(3) Draw a truth table of (pvq) ∨ ⅂p

Solution

p	⅂p	pvq	⅂p	(pvq) ∨ ⅂p
T	T	T	F	T
T	F	T	F	T
F	T	T	T	T
F	F	F	T	T

(4) Draw a truth table of ⅂(⅂pv⅂q)

Solution

p	q	⅂p	⅂q	⅂pv⅂q	⅂(⅂pv⅂q)
T	T	F	F	F	T
T	F	F	T	T	F
F	T	T	F	T	F
F	F	T	T	T	F

(5) What is the truth table of pv(q∧r) if the truth table value of p and q are True and that of r is false.

Solution

p	q	r	q∧r	pv(q∧r)
T	T	F	F	T

(6) Construct a Truth table for the formula   (⅂pvq)∧(⅂qvp)

Solution

P	q	⅂p	(⅂pvq)	⅂q	(⅂qvp)	(⅂pvq) ∧ (⅂qvp)
T	T	F	T	F	T	T
T	F	F	F	T	T	F
F	T	T	T	F	F	F
F	F	T	T	T	T	T

(7) Construct a Truth table for the formula, $(p \wedge q) \vee (\neg p \wedge q) \vee (p \wedge \neg q) \vee (\neg p \wedge \neg q)$

Solution :

$(p \wedge q) \vee (\neg p \wedge q) \vee (p \wedge \neg q) \vee (\neg p \wedge \neg q)$ ----- (1)

$(p \wedge q) \vee (\neg p \wedge q)$ ----- (2)

$(p \wedge \neg q) \vee (\neg p \wedge \neg q)$ ----- (3)

p	q	p∧q	¬p	¬p∧q	¬q	p∧¬q	¬p∧¬q	(2)	(3)	(1)
T	T	T	F	F	F	F	F	T	F	T
T	F	F	F	F	T	T	F	F	T	T
F	T	F	T	T	F	F	F	T	F	T
F	F	F	T	F	T	F	T	F	T	T

4.3 DERIVED CONNECTIVES

NAND CONNECTIVES

NAND

It is the negation after Anding of two statements of for example if p and q are two statements then Nanding of p and q denoted by p↑q is a false statement when both p and q are true, otherwise true.

Truth table for p↑q

P	q	p∧q	p↑q (or) ~(p∧q)
T	T	T	F
T	F	F	T
F	T	F	T
F	F	F	T

NAND Gate Symbol

$f = (pq)'$

NOR (or) Joint Denial

It is the negation after ORing of two statements. For example if p and q are two statements then NORing of p and q denoted by p↓q is a true statement when both p and q are false, otherwise false.

Truth table for p↓q

P	q	p∨q	~ (p∨q) or (p↓q)
T	T	T	F
F	T	T	F
T	F	T	F
F	F	F	T

NOR GATE SYMBOL

$$f = (p + q)'$$

XOR (Exclusive Disjunction) Symbol is   ∨

The process of joining the two statements p and q by "XOR" produces a new statement denoted by p⊕q, which is read as "p XOR q".

If p and q are two statements then XORing of p and q denoted by p⊕q is a true statement when either p or q is true but not both and vice versa.

Truth Table for XOR

p	q	(p∨q) or (p⊕q)
T	T	F
T	F	T
F	T	T
F	F	F

XOR Gate Symbol

$$f = p \oplus q$$

$$\text{Meaning} = p'q + pq'$$

XNOR (Exclusive NOR)

Definition

The process of joining the two statements p and q by "XNOR" produces a new statement denoted by $(p \oplus q)'$, which is read as "p XNOR q".

If p and q are two statements then XNORing of p and q denoted by $(p \oplus q)'$ is a false statement when either p or q is true but not both and vice versa.

Truth Table for XNOR

P	q	~(p⊕q) or (p⊕q)'
T	T	T
T	F	F
F	T	F
F	F	T

XNOR (Exclusive NOR) Gate Symbol

$$f \quad = (p \oplus q)'$$

$$= pq + p'q'$$

DUALITY LAW

Two statements A and B duals of each other of either one can be obtained from the other by replacing $\wedge$ by $\vee$ and $\vee$ by $\wedge$. The connecting $\vee$ and $\wedge$ are called duals of each other.

Example

i) $(p \vee q) \wedge r = (p \wedge q) \vee r$;

ii) $(p \wedge q) \vee t \rightarrow (p \vee q) \wedge t$

NEGATION OF COMPOUND STATEMENTS

When a compound statement is regreted, the logical connective changes from **OR to AND** and from **AND to OR**.

For example

$\sim(p \vee q) \qquad = \sim p \wedge \sim q$

$\sim(p \wedge q) \qquad = \sim p \vee \sim q$

The following relations are based on above laws

(a) $\sim(p \wedge \sim q) = \sim p \vee \sim(\sim q) \qquad = \sim p \vee q$

(b) $\sim(\sim p \wedge q) = \sim(\sim p) \vee \sim q \qquad = p \vee \sim q$

(c) $\sim(\sim p \vee \sim q) = \sim(\sim p) \wedge \sim(\sim q) \qquad = p \wedge q$

4.4 TRUTH TABLES FOR CONNECTIVES

EXAMPLE PROBLEMS FOR BASIC LOGICAL OPERATION

a) With the help of truth table prove that

$\sim p \vee \sim q = \sim (p \wedge q)$

Solution   **Truth Table**

p (1)	q (2)	$\sim$p (3)	$\sim$q (4)	$\sim$p$\vee\sim$q (5)	p$\wedge$q (6)	$\sim$(p$\wedge$q) (7)
T	T	F	F	F	T	F
T	F	F	T	T	F	T
F	T	T	F	T	F	T
F	F	T	T	T	F	T

Note : The decimal number 3 has equivalent binary value is 11. Here 1 for T(True) an 0 for F(False).

Example

$0 = 00 = FF$

$1 = 01 = FT$

$2 = 10 = TF$

$3 = 11 = TT$

Since values in the column (5) and (7) are identical therefore

$\sim p \vee \sim q = \sim (p \wedge q)$

b) With the help of truth table prove that, $\sim (p \vee q) = \sim p \wedge \sim q$

Solution   **Truth Table**

p 1	q 2	p$\vee$q 3	$\sim$(p$\vee$q) 4	$\sim$p 5	$\sim$q 6	$\sim$p$\wedge\sim$q 7
T	T	T	F	F	F	F
T	F	T	F	F	T	F
F	T	T	F	T	F	F
F	F	F	T	T	T	T

Since values in columns (4) and (7) are identical, therefore $\sim (p \vee q) = \sim p \wedge \sim q$.

(c) With the help of truth table prove that, $p \lor q = \sim(\sim p \land \sim q)$

Solution   **Truth Table**

p 1	q 2	p∨q 3	~p 4	~q 5	~p∧~q 6	~(~p∧~q) 7
T	T	T	F	F	F	T
T	F	T	F	T	F	T
F	T	T	T	F	F	T
F	F	F	T	T	T	F

Since values in columns (3) and (7) are identical, therefore $p \lor q = \sim(\sim p \land \sim q)$.

(d) With the help of truth table prove that, $p \lor \sim q = (p \lor q) \land \sim(p \land q)$

Solution   **Truth Table**

p 1	q 2	p∨~q 3	p∨q 4	p∧q 5	~(p∨q) 6	(p∨q) ∧ ~(p∧q) 7
T	T	T	T	T	F	F
T	F	T	T	F	T	T
F	T	F	T	F	T	T
F	F	T	F	F	T	F

Since values in columns (3) and (7) are identical, therefore $p \lor \sim q = (p \lor q) \land \sim(p \land q)$

(e) With the help of truth table prove that, $\sim(p \land q) = \sim p \lor \sim q$

Solution   **Truth Table**

p 1	q 2	p∧q 3	~(p∧q) 4	~p 5	~q 6	~p∨~q 7
T	T	T	F	F	F	F
T	F	F	T	F	T	T
F	T	F	T	T	F	T
F	F	F	T	T	T	T

Since values in columns (4) and (7) are identical, therefore $\sim(p \land q) = \sim p \lor \sim q$.

Example problems for Derived connectives (NAND, NOR, XOR)

a) Make truth tables for $(p \downarrow q) \wedge (p \downarrow r)$

Solution   **Truth Table**

Here p, q and r are given, so we have 7 combinations from decimal numbers 0 to 7.

p	q	r	p↓q	p↓r	(p↓q) ∧ (p↓r)
T	T	T	F	F	F
T	T	F	F	F	F
T	F	T	F	F	F
T	F	F	F	F	F
F	T	T	F	F	F
F	T	F	F	T	F
F	F	T	T	F	F
F	F	F	T	T	T

Here $p \downarrow q \rightarrow \sim (p \vee r)$

$p \downarrow r = \sim (p \vee r)$

The decimal number 7 has equivalent binary value 111, so we put TTT.

Here 1 for T (True) and 0 for F (False)

Example

					Note :	
0	=	000	=	FFF		
1	=	001	=	FFT		
2	=	010	=	FTF		
3	=	011	=	FTT	p∧q	→ If both True then True else False
4	=	100	=	TFF	p∨q	→ If any one true then True else False
5	=	101	=	TFT		
6	=	110	=	TTF		
7	=	111	=	TTT		

(b) Make the Truth Table for p↑q↑r

Solution   **Truth Table**

p	q	r	p∧q	~(p∧r) = p↑q	p↑q↑r = ~[(~(p∧q))∧r]
T	T	T	T	F	T
T	T	F	T	F	T
T	F	T	F	T	F
T	F	F	F	T	T
F	T	T	F	T	F
F	T	F	F	T	T
F	F	T	F	T	F
F	F	F	F	T	T

(3) Make the truth table for p⊕q⊕r

Solution   **Truth Table**

p	q	r	p⊕q	p⊕q⊕r
T	T	T	F	T
T	T	F	F	F
T	F	T	T	F
T	F	F	T	T
F	T	T	T	F
F	T	F	T	T
F	F	T	F	T
F	F	F	F	F

Note : In XOR if both same then False else True.

(4) If p and q are two statements then show that the statement $(p\uparrow q)\oplus(p\uparrow q)$ is

equivalent to $(p\lor q)\land(p\downarrow q)$

Solution

The equivalence of two compound statement is shown in the truth table.

Truth Table for Equivalence

p	Q	p↑q	(p↑q)⊕(p↑q)	p∨q	p↓q	(p∨q)∧(p↓q)
1	2	3	4	5	6	7
T	T	F	F	T	F	F
T	F	T	F	T	F	F
F	T	T	F	T	F	F
F	F	T	F	F	T	F

Note :

XOR   : If both same then False else True.

p∨q   : If any one True then True else False.

p∧q   : If both True then True else False.

Since values in Columns (4) and (7) are same, therefore two statements are

equivalent.

(5) If p and q are two statements, then show that $p\oplus q$ is equivalent to $(p\land\sim q)\lor(\sim p\land q)$.

Solution

Truth Table for Equivalence

p	q	p⊕q	~p	~q	p∧~q	~p∧q	(p∧~q)∨(~p∧q)
1	2	3	4	5	6	7	8
T	T	F	F	F	F	F	F
T	F	T	F	T	T	F	T
F	T	T	T	F	F	T	T
F	F	F	T	T	F	F	F

Note : $p \oplus q \rightarrow$ XOR if both same then false else true.

Since values in column (3) and (8) are same, therefore two compound statements are equivalent.

(6) If p and q are two statements, then show that the statement $(p \oplus q) \vee (p \downarrow q)$ is equivalent to $p \uparrow q$.

Solution

The equivalence of two compound statements is shown in the truth table.

Truth Table for Equivalence

p 1	q 2	p⊕q 3	p↓q = ~(p∨q) 4	(p⊕q)∨(p↓q) 5	(p↑q) = ~(p∧q) 6
T	T	F	F	F	F
T	F	T	F	T	T
F	T	T	F	T	T
F	F	F	T	T	T

Since values in column (5) and (6) are same, therefore two compound statements are equivalent.

(7) Using the below statements

R   : Mark is Rich

H   : Mark is Happy

Write the following statement in symbolic form.

(i) Mark is Poor but Happy

Solution   **Note :**

⌐R ∧ H   but, both → and

(ii) Mark is Rich (or) Unhappy

Solution

R ∨ ⌐H

(iii) Mark is neither rich nor happy

Solution

⌐R ∧ ⌐H

(iv) Mark is Poor (or) he is both Rich and Unhappy

Solution

⌐R ∨ (R ∧ ⌐H)

(8) Given the truth values of p & q as T and those of r & s as F. Find the truth values of the following.

(i) p ∨ (q∧r)

p	q	r	q∧r	p∨(q∧r)
T	T	F	F	T

(ii) (p∧(q∧r)) ∨ 7((p∨q) ∧ (r∨s))   ----   (1)

p	q	r	s	q∧r	p∧ (q∧r)	p∨q	r∨s	(p∨q)∧ (r∨s)	7[(p∨q)∧ (r∨s)]	(1)
T	T	F	F	F	F	T	F	F	T	T

LOGICAL EQUIVALENCE

Two statements are said to be logical equivalent (or equal) if they have same identical truth values we will denote logical equivalence by the symbol "=".

Example

~(p∧q) and ~p∨~q.

Their truth tables are

(1)

p	q	p∧q	~p(p∧q)
T	T	T	F
T	F	F	T
F	T	F	T
F	F	F	T

(2)

p	q	~p	~q	~p∧~q
T	T	F	F	F
T	F	F	T	T
F	T	T	F	T
F	F	T	T	T

Hence ~(p∧q) = ~p∨~q

4.5 CONDITIONAL STATEMENT (OR) CONDITIONAL PROPOSITION

DEFINITION

If p and q are two statements then the statement p→q which is read as if "P then Q" is called a conditional statement.

In this conditional statement p is called the **hypothesis (or) antecedent (or) premise.** The statement q is called the **conclusion (or) consequent.**

"If ..... then",It is a conditional connective

Here p is condition and q is executable statement. "If p and then q", here the computer executes q and on the condition that P is true. Otherwise the computer goes to next instruction in the program sequence.

Example

"If p then q else r", q is executed when p is true and r is executed when p is false.

The connective if ..... then is denoted by $\rightarrow$ (or) $\Rightarrow$ and can be read as follows:

(i) p implies q

(ii) p is sufficient for q

(iii) p only if q

(iv) q is necessary for p

(v) q is consequence of p

Truth table for p $\rightarrow$ q

p	q	p→q
T	T	T
T	F	F
F	T	T
F	F	T

Note : The statement p→q is false if p is true and q is false and otherwise all other options are true.

Example Problems

(1) Draw the truth table for $(p \rightarrow q) \wedge (q \rightarrow p)$

Solution

p	q	p→q	q→p	$(p \rightarrow q) \wedge (q \rightarrow p)$
T	T	T	T	T
T	F	F	T	F
F	T	T	F	F
F	F	T	F	T

(2) Draw the truth table for $(q \wedge (p \rightarrow q)) \rightarrow p$

Solution

p	q	p→q	q ∧ (p→q)	q∧(p→q)→p
T	T	T	T	T
T	F	F	F	T
F	T	T	T	F
F	F	T	F	T

4.6 BI-CONDITIONAL STATEMENT

DEFINITION

If p and q are any two statements $p \rightleftarrows q$ which is read as "p if and only if q" is called bi-conditional statement (or) bi-conditional propositions.

Note : Which is true when p and q have the same truth values and is false otherwise.

↔ (or) $\rightleftarrows$ symbol is used for bi-conditional statement.

Truth Table for $p \rightleftarrows q$

p	q	p⇄q
T	T	T
T	F	F
F	T	F
F	F	T

Example for Bi-conditional Statements

(i) A candidate passes the examination with first class if and only if he get at least 60% marks in aggregate.

(ii) 7 > 5 if and only if 7- 5 is positive.

EXAMPLE PROBLEMS

(1) Show that the truth values for $\lnot(p \land q) \rightleftarrows (\lnot p \lor \lnot q)$ are independent of their components.

Solution

$$\lnot(p \land q) \rightleftarrows (\lnot p \lor \lnot q) \quad \text{----- (1)}$$

p	q	$\lnot$p	$\lnot$q	(p$\land$q)	$\lnot$(p$\land$q)	$\lnot$p$\lor\lnot$q	(1)
T	T	F	F	T	F	F	T
T	F	F	T	F	T	T	T
F	T	T	F	F	T	T	T
F	F	T	T	F	T	T	T

From the last column truth values are independent of their components.

(2) Draw a truth table for $(p \land (p \to q)) \to q$ and show that are independent of their components.

Solution

p	q	p$\to$q	p$\land$(p$\to$q)	(p$\land$(p$\to$q))$\to$q
T	T	T	T	T
T	F	F	F	T
F	T	T	F	T
F	F	T	F	T

From the last column truth values are independent of their components.

(3) Show that the truth values for $(p{\to}q)\rightleftarrows(\neg p{\vee}q)$ are independent of their components.

Solution

$(p{\to}q)\rightleftarrows(\neg p{\vee}q)$ ----- (1)

p	q	p→q	¬p	¬p∨q	(p→q)⇄¬p∨q (1)
T	T	T	F	T	T
T	F	F	F	F	T
F	T	T	T	T	T
F	F	T	T	T	T

From last column truth values are independent of their components.

(4) Show that the truth values of $((p{\to}q){\wedge}(q{\to}r))\to(p{\to}r)$

Solution

$((p{\to}q){\wedge}(q{\to}r))\to(p{\to}r)$ ------ (1)

p	q	r	p→q	q→r	(p→q)∧(q→r)	p→r	(1)
T	T	T	T	T	T	T	T
T	T	F	T	F	F	F	T
T	F	T	F	T	F	T	T
T	F	F	F	T	F	F	T
F	T	T	T	T	T	T	T
F	T	F	T	F	F	T	T
F	F	T	T	T	T	T	T
F	F	F	T	T	T	T	T

From the last column truth values are independent of their components.

(5) Show that the truth values of $(p \rightleftarrows q) \rightleftarrows ((p \wedge q) \vee (\neg p \wedge \neg q))$ are independent of their

components.

Solution

$$(p \rightleftarrows q) \rightleftarrows ((p \wedge q) \vee (\neg p \wedge \neg q)) \quad \text{------- (1)}$$

p	q	p⇄q	¬p	¬q	(p∧q)	¬p∧¬q	(p∧q)∨(¬p∧¬q)	(1)
T	T	T	F	F	T	F	T	T
T	F	F	F	T	F	F	F	T
F	T	F	T	F	F	F	F	T
F	F	T	T	T	F	T	T	T

From the last column truth values are independent of their components.

(6) Draw truth table for $(q \wedge (p \rightarrow q)) \rightarrow p$.

Solution

$$(q \wedge (p \rightarrow q)) \rightarrow p \quad \text{------ (1)}$$

p	q	p→q	q∧(p→q)	(1)
T	T	T	T	T
T	F	F	F	T
F	T	T	T	F
F	F	T	F	T

(7) Given the truth values of p and q as T and those of r and s as F. Find the truth

values of the following.

(a) $(\neg(p \wedge q) \vee \neg r) \vee ((q \rightleftarrows \neg p) \rightarrow (r \vee \neg s))$

Solution

$$(\neg(p \wedge q) \vee \neg r) \quad \text{------ (1)}$$

Truth Table for Equation (1)

p	Q	r	s	$\neg$r	$\neg$s	$\neg$p	$\neg$q	p$\wedge$q	$\neg$(p$\wedge$q)	($\neg$ (p$\wedge$q)$\vee$ $\neg$r) (1)
T	T	F	F	T	T	F	F	T	F	T

$$(1) \vee ((q\rightleftarrows \neg p) \rightarrow (r\vee \neg s)) \ \text{------} \ (2)$$

Truth Table for Equation (2)

q$\rightleftarrows$$\neg$p	r$\vee$$\neg$s	((q$\rightleftarrows$$\neg$p)$\rightarrow$(r$\vee$$\neg$s))	Required Result (2)
F	T	T	T

(b) (p$\rightleftarrows$r)$\wedge$($\neg$q$\rightarrow$s)

Solution

$$(p\rightleftarrows r)\wedge(\neg q\rightarrow s) \ \text{-------} \ (1)$$

p $\rightleftarrows$ r	$\neg$q$\rightarrow$s	(1)
F	T	F

(c) (p$\vee$(q$\rightarrow$(r$\wedge$$\neg$p))) $\rightleftarrows$ (q$\vee$$\neg$s)

Solution

(r$\wedge$$\neg$p)	(q$\rightarrow$(r$\wedge$$\neg$p))	P$\vee$(q$\rightarrow$(r$\wedge$$\neg$p))	(q$\vee$$\neg$s)	(p$\vee$(q$\rightarrow$(r$\wedge$$\neg$p))) $\rightleftarrows$ (q$\vee$$\neg$s)
F	F	T	T	T

4.7 ORDER OF PRECEDENCE FOR LOGICAL CONNECTIVES

We will generally use parentheses to specify the order in which logical operators

in a compound proposition are to be applied.

Example

(p∨q)∧(⌐r) is the conjunction of p∨q and ⌐r. To avoid the use of an excessive number of parentheses we adopt an order of precedence for the logical operators given as follows.

(i) The negation operator has precedence over all other logical operators. Thus ⌐p∧q means (⌐p)∧q, ⌐(p∧q).

(ii) The conjunction operator (∧) has precedence over the disjunction operator (∨) thus p∧q∨r means (p∧q)∨r but not p∧(q∨r).

(iii) The conditional and biconditional operators →, ⇄ have lower precedence than other operators. Among them → has precedence over ⇄.

Definition

Well Formed Formula

A statement formula is an expression which is a string consisting of variables, parentheses and connective symbols.

A well formed formula can be generated by the following rules.

1. A statement variable standing alone is a well formed formula.

2. If A is a well formed formula then ⌐A is a well formed formula.

3. If A & B are well formed formulas then (A∧B), (A∨B), (A→B) and (A⇄B) are well formed formulas.

4. A string of symbols containing the statement variables, connectives & parenthesis is a well formed formula, if and only if it can be obtained by applying the values of rules (1), (2) & (3) finitely many times.

Example

(i)   ((p→q) → (∧q)) is not a Well Formed Formula as ∧q is not a formula.

(ii) (p→q → is not a Well Formed Formula. Because) parentheses is missing. But

      (p→q) is a Well Formed Formula.

(iii) ⌐(P→q) → is a Well Formed Formula.

(iv) ((p→q)→(r∧q) is a Well Formed Formula.

(v)   (p∧q) → q) is not a Well Formed Formula because the parentheses in the

      beginning is missing.

CONDITION PROPOSITION

Example Problems

Prove that $p \Rightarrow q = \sim p \vee q$.

p	q	p⇒q	~p	~p∨q
T	T	T	F	T
T	F	F	F	F
F	T	T	T	T
F	F	T	T	T

$\therefore p \Rightarrow q = \sim p \vee q$

4.8 CONVERSE, INVERSE AND CONTRAPOSITIVE PROPOSITIONS

Definition

If $p \Rightarrow q$ is the direct proposition, then

(a) $q \Rightarrow p$ is called its **converse**

(b) The proposition $\sim p \Rightarrow \sim q$ is called its **inverse** and

(C) The proposition $\sim q \Rightarrow \sim p$ is called its **Contrapositive**.

We have

p	q	p $\Rightarrow$ q	~p	~q	~q $\Rightarrow$ ~p
T	T	T	F	F	T
T	F	F	F	T	F
F	T	T	T	F	T
F	F	T	T	T	T

$\therefore$ p$\Rightarrow$q = ~q $\Rightarrow$ ~p

(i.e) Direct statement = contrapositive

Again we have

Prove q$\Rightarrow$p = ~p$\Rightarrow$~q

Converse = Inverse

p	q	q $\Rightarrow$ p	~p	~q	~p $\Rightarrow$ ~q
T	T	T	F	F	T
T	F	T	F	T	T
F	T	F	T	F	F
F	F	T	T	T	T

$\therefore$ q $\Rightarrow$ p = ~p $\Rightarrow$ ~q

(i.e) Converse = Inverse

4.9 TAUTOLOGIES AND CONTRADICTIONS

Definition : Tautology

A compound proposition that is always true for all possible truth values of its variables or in other words contain only T in the last column of its truth table is called a tautology.

Definition : Contradiction (or) Fallacy

A compound proposition that is always false for all possible values of its variables (or) in other words contain only F in the last column of its truth table is called a contradiction.

Definition : Contingency

Propositions that is neither a tautology nor a contradiction is called contingency.

A compound proposition $p = p(p_1, p_2, p_3, \ldots, p_n)$ where $p_1, p_2, p_3, \ldots, p_n$ are variables (elemental propositions) is called a tautology. If it is true for every truth assignment for $p_1, p_2, p_3, \ldots, p_n$ suppose p is called a contradiction (or) fallacy, if it is false for every truth assignment for $p_1, p_2, p_3, \ldots, p_n$ for example, $p \lor \neg p$ is a tautology, whereas $p \land \neg p$ is a contradiction shown in table.

p	¬p	p∨¬p	P∧¬p
T	F	T	F
F	T	T	F

Tautology   Contradiction

Note

(1) The negation of tautology is a contradiction and the negation of a contradiction is a tautology

(2) If $P(p_1, p_2, p_3, \ldots, p_n)$ is a tautology then $P(q_1, q_2, q_3, \ldots, q_n)$ is also a tautology, where $q_1, q_2, q_3, \ldots, q_n$ are any set of propositions. This is known as the **Principle of Substitution**.

(3) If a proposition is neither a tautology nor a contradiction, it is called a contingency.

Example Problems

(1) From the formulas given below select those which are well formed according to definition and indicate which ones are tautologies (or) contradictions.

(a) $(p \rightarrow (p \lor q))$

(b) $((p \rightarrow (\neg p)) \rightarrow \neg p)$

(c) $((\neg q \wedge p) \wedge q)$

(d) $((p \rightarrow (q \rightarrow r)) \rightarrow ((p \rightarrow q) \rightarrow (p \rightarrow r)))$

(e) $((\neg p \rightarrow q) \rightarrow (q \rightarrow p)))$

(f) $((p \wedge q) \rightleftarrows p)$

Solution

(a)

p	q	p∨q	p→(p∨q)
T	T	T	T
T	F	T	T
F	T	T	T
F	F	F	T

All true in last column.

∴ Formula is a Tautology & Well Formed Formula.

(b)

p	¬p	(p→(¬p))	(p→(¬p)→ ¬p
T	F	F	T
F	T	T	T

All true in last column.

∴ Formula is a Tautology & Well Formed Formula.

(c)

p	q	¬q	¬q∧p	(¬q∧p)∧q
T	T	F	F	F
T	F	T	T	F
F	T	F	F	F
F	F	T	F	F

All false in last column.

∴ Formula is a Contradiction & Well Formed Formula.

(d) $((p\rightarrow(q\rightarrow r)) \rightarrow ((p\rightarrow q) \rightarrow (p\rightarrow r)))$

Solution

$((p\rightarrow(q\rightarrow r)) \rightarrow ((p\rightarrow q) \rightarrow (p\rightarrow r)))$ -------- (1)

p	q	r	q→r	p→((q→r))	p→q	p→r	((p→q)→(p→r)	(1)
T	T	T	T	T	T	T	T	T
T	T	F	F	F	T	F	F	T
T	F	T	T	T	F	T	T	T
T	F	F	T	T	F	F	T	T
F	T	T	T	T	T	T	T	T
F	T	F	F	T	T	T	T	T
F	F	T	T	T	T	T	T	T
F	F	F	T	T	T	T	T	T

All true in last column.

∴ Formula is a Tautology & Well Formed Formula.

(e) $((\neg p\rightarrow q) \rightarrow (q \rightarrow p)))$ is not a Well Formed Formula because of extra one closing parentheses.

(f) $((p\wedge q) \rightleftarrows p)$

p	q	p∧q	(p∧q) ⇄ p
T	T	T	T
T	F	F	F
F	T	F	T
F	F	F	T

∴ Formula is not a Tautology.

The (f) problem is an example for **contingency**. Neither Tautology nor contradiction.

Exercise Problems

1. Establish $\sim(p \wedge q) \rightleftarrows (\sim p \vee \sim q)$ as tautology.

   Ans : Tautology

2. $(P \wedge Q) \Rightarrow (P \vee Q)$ is a tautology.

   But $(P \vee Q) \Rightarrow (P \wedge Q)$ is not

   Ans : Not Tautology.

3. $P \vee \sim(P \wedge Q)$ show that it is a tautology

   Ans : Tautology

4. Show that $(P \wedge Q) \wedge \sim(P \vee Q)$ is a fallacy (or) contradiction

   Ans : Contradiction

(1) Write the following statement in symbolic form

If either Ramu takes calculus or Gopu takes sociology, then Karthi will take English.

Solution

Let   P : Ramu takes Calculus

         Q : Gopu takes Sociology

         R : Karthi will take English

Required Formula

$(P \vee Q) \rightarrow R$

Note :   "if then" $\rightarrow$ Conditional Connective.

                "if and only if" $\rightarrow$ Bi-Conditional Connective.

4.10 EQUIVALENCE OF FORMULAE

ALGEBRA OF PREPOSITIONS

Laws of Algebra of Propositions

S.No	Name of the Law	Primal Form	Dual Form
1.	Idempotent Law	(a) p∨p ≡ p	(b) p∧p ≡ p
2.	Identity Law	(a) p∨F ≡ p	p∧T ≡ p
3.	Dominant Law	p∨T ≡ T	p∧F ≡ F
4.	Complement Law	p∨⌐p ≡ T	p∧⌐p ≡ F
5.	Commutative Law	P∨q ≡ q∨p	p∧q ≡ q∧p
6.	Associative Law	(p∨q)∨r ≡ p∨(q∨r)	(p∧q)∧r ≡ p∧(q∧r) p∧(q∧r) ≡ (p∧q)∨(p∧r)
7.	Distributive Law	p∨(q∧r) ≡ (p∨q)∧(p∨r)	p∧(q∨r) ≡ (p∧q)∨(p∧r)
8.	Absorption Law	p∨(p∧q) ≡ p	p∧(p∨q) ≡ p
9.	Demorgan's Law	⌐(p∨q) ≡ ⌐p∧⌐q	⌐(p∧q) ≡ ⌐p∨⌐q
10.	Operations with F and T	F∨p = p	T∧p = p
11.	Operations with F and T	~F = T	~T = F
12.	Double Negation (or) Double Complementation	(1) ~(~p) = p (2) p∨⌐p = T (3) p∧⌐p = F (4) p∨T = T, p∧T = p (5) p∨F = p, p∧F = F	
13.	Contra Positive	(1) p⇒q ≡ ⌐q ⇒ ⌐p (2) p⇒q ≡ (⌐p∨q)	

Note :   ⌐p, p′, ~p

(⌐, ′, ~) All symbols denote negation of p.

EQUIVALENCES INVOLVING CONDITIONS

1. $p \rightarrow q$ $\qquad \equiv \neg p \vee q$

2. $p \rightarrow q$ $\qquad \equiv \neg q \rightarrow \neg p$

3. $p \vee q$ $\qquad \equiv \neg p \rightarrow \neg q$

4. $p \wedge q$ $\qquad \equiv \neg(p \rightarrow \neg q)$

5. $\neg(p \rightarrow q)$ $\qquad \equiv p \wedge \neg q$

6. $(p \rightarrow q) \wedge (p \rightarrow r)$ $\qquad \equiv p \rightarrow (q \wedge r)$

7. $(p \rightarrow r) \wedge (q \rightarrow r)$ $\qquad \equiv (p \vee q) \rightarrow r$

8. $(p \rightarrow r) \vee (q \rightarrow r)$ $\qquad \equiv (p \vee q) \rightarrow r$

9. $(p \rightarrow r) \vee (q \rightarrow r)$ $\qquad \equiv (p \wedge q) \rightarrow r$

EQUIVALENCES INVOLVING BI-CONDITIONS

1. $p \leftrightarrow q$ $\qquad \equiv (p \rightarrow q) \wedge (q \rightarrow p)$

2. $p \leftrightarrow q$ $\qquad \equiv \neg p \rightarrow \neg q$

3. $p \leftrightarrow q$ $\qquad \equiv (p \wedge q) \vee (\neg p \wedge \neg q)$

4. $\neg(p \leftrightarrow q)$ $\qquad \equiv (p \leftrightarrow \neg q)$

Example Problems

1) Prove $(p \to q) \Leftrightarrow (\neg p \vee q)$

Solution   **Note :**

       $(p \to q)$ ------- (1) $\Leftrightarrow$ read as equivalent to

       $(\neg p \vee q)$ ------- (2)

p	q	(1) $p \to q$	$\neg p$	(2) $\neg p \vee q$
T	T	T	F	T
T	F	F	T	F
F	T	T	F	T
F	F	T	F	T

From (1) & (2)

$\therefore (p \to q) \Leftrightarrow \neg p \vee q$

(2) Show that $p \to (q \to r) \Leftrightarrow p \to (\neg q \vee r) \Leftrightarrow (p \wedge q) \to r$

Proof

We know the following formulas

$p \to q \Leftrightarrow \neg p \vee q$ ------- (1)

$(p \vee q) \vee r = p \vee (q \vee r)$ ------- (2) Associative Law

$\neg(p \wedge q) = \neg p \vee \neg q$ -------- (3) Demorgan's Law

From formula 1 we get

$q \to r \Leftrightarrow \neg q \vee r$

Consider LHS of the given problem is $p \to (q \to r)$ is replaced by

$\Leftrightarrow p \to (\neg q \vee r)$. Again apply the same formula then we get

$\Leftrightarrow \neg p \vee (\neg q \vee r)$

$\Leftrightarrow (\neg p \vee \neg q) \vee r$ (by Associative Law)

$\Leftrightarrow \daleth(p \wedge q) \vee r$ (by Demargon's Law)

The above result is in the form of formula 1

$p \rightarrow q \Leftrightarrow \daleth p \vee q$

Therefore we replace

    $\daleth(p \wedge q) \vee r$ as $(p \wedge q) \rightarrow r$

(3) Show that $\{p \wedge (\daleth p \vee q)\} \vee \{q \wedge \daleth(p \wedge q)\} = q$

Proof

LHS

    $= \{p \wedge (\daleth p \vee q\} \vee \{q \wedge \daleth(p \wedge q)\}$

    $= \{(p \wedge \daleth p) \vee (p \wedge q)\} \vee \{q \wedge (\daleth p \vee \daleth q)\}$

    $= F \vee (p \wedge q) \vee (q \wedge \daleth p) \vee (q \wedge \daleth q)$

    $= F \vee (p \wedge q) \vee (q \wedge \daleth p) \vee F$

    $= p \wedge q \vee q \wedge \daleth p$

    $= q \wedge (p \vee \daleth p)$

    $= q \wedge T = q = R.H.S$

(4) Show that $\{p \wedge \daleth q\} \wedge \{\sim p \vee \sim q)\} \vee q = T$

Proof

    LHS

    $= \{(p \vee \sim q) \wedge \sim p \vee \sim q)\} \vee q$

    $= \{(p \vee \sim q) \wedge \sim p \vee (p \vee \sim q) \wedge \sim q\} \vee q$

    $= \{(p \wedge \sim p) \vee (\sim q \wedge \sim p) \vee (p \vee \sim q) \vee (\sim q \wedge \sim q)\} \vee q$

    $= \{F \vee (\sim q \wedge \sim p) \vee (p \wedge \sim q) \vee \sim q\} \vee q$

$= (\sim q \wedge \sim p) \vee (p \wedge \sim q) \vee \sim q \vee q$

$= (\sim q \wedge \sim p) \vee (p \wedge \sim q) \vee T$

$= T$

Hence $\{(p \vee \sim q) \wedge \sim p \vee \sim q\} \vee q$ is a tautology.

(5) Prove the following equivalences without using truth table

$p \rightarrow (q \rightarrow r) \Leftrightarrow (p \wedge q) \rightarrow r$

Proof

LHS

$\Leftrightarrow p \rightarrow (q \rightarrow r)$ we know $p \rightarrow q \Leftrightarrow \daleth p \vee q$

$\Leftrightarrow p \rightarrow (\daleth q \vee r)$

$\Leftrightarrow \daleth p \vee (\daleth q \vee r)$

$\Leftrightarrow (\daleth p \vee \daleth q) \vee r)$

$\Leftrightarrow \daleth (p \wedge q) \vee r$

By demargen's law

$\Leftrightarrow (p \wedge q) \rightarrow r$

$= RHS$

LHS $=$ RHS

Hence Proved.

(6) Prove the following equivalences without using truth table

(1) $p \rightarrow (q \rightarrow r) \Leftrightarrow (p \wedge q) \rightarrow r$

Proof

$\Leftrightarrow p \rightarrow (q \rightarrow r)$ $[p \rightarrow q \Leftrightarrow \daleth p \vee q]$

$\Leftrightarrow p \rightarrow (\daleth q \vee r)$ $[\therefore p \rightarrow q \Leftrightarrow \daleth p \vee q]$

$\Leftrightarrow \neg p \vee (\neg q \vee r)$

$\Leftrightarrow (\neg p \vee \neg q) \vee r \qquad [\therefore$ Associative Law$]$

$\Leftrightarrow \neg (p \wedge q) \vee r$ [By Demargan's law]

$\Leftrightarrow (p \wedge q) \rightarrow r \ [p \rightarrow q \Leftrightarrow \neg p \vee q]$

= RHS

Hence Proved.

4.11 TAUTOLOGICAL IMPLICATIONS

Definition

A statement A is said to Tautologically imply a statement B if and only if $A \rightarrow B$ is a "**Tautology**".

A compound proposition $A(P_1, P_2, ..., P_n)$. If B is true whenever A is true or equivalently if and only if $A \rightarrow B$ is a tautology. This is denoted by $A \Rightarrow B$, need as "A implies B".

Note :

$\Rightarrow$ is not a connective and $A \Rightarrow B$ is not a proposition.

Example Problems

(1) Show that the following implications

(a) $(p \wedge q) \rightarrow (p \rightarrow q)$

(b) $(p \rightarrow (q \rightarrow p))$

(c) $q \Rightarrow (q \rightarrow p)$

(d) $(p \rightarrow (q \rightarrow r)) \rightarrow (p \rightarrow q) \rightarrow (p \rightarrow r)$

Proof

(a) $(p \wedge q) \to (p \to q)$

> $p \to q$ if p is true and q is false then false else true

p	q	p∧q	p→q	(p∧q)→(p→q)
T	T	T	T	T
T	F	F	F	T
F	T	F	T	T
F	F	F	T	T

All true values in the last column

> $\therefore (p \wedge q) \Rightarrow p \to q$ is a Tautology.

(b) $(p \to (q \to p))$

Solution

p	q	Q→p	p→(q→p)
T	T	T	T
T	F	T	T
F	T	F	T
F	F	T	T

All true values in the last column

$\therefore p \Rightarrow (q \to p)$ is a Tautology

(c) $q \Rightarrow (q \to p)$

Solution

p	q	q→p	q→(q→p)
T	T	T	T
T	F	T	T
F	T	F	F
F	F	T	T

There are not all true values in the last column.

$\therefore$ It is not a Tautology.

(d) $(p\rightarrow(q\rightarrow r)) \rightarrow (p\rightarrow q) \rightarrow (p\rightarrow r)$

p	q	r	q→r	p→ (q→r)	p→q	p→r	(p→q)→ (p→r)	(p→(q→r))→ (p→q)→(p→r)
T	T	T	T	T	T	T	T	T
T	T	F	F	F	T	F	F	T
T	F	T	T	T	F	T	T	T
T	F	F	T	T	F	F	T	T
F	T	T	T	T	T	T	T	T
F	T	F	F	T	T	T	T	T
F	F	T	T	T	T	T	T	T
F	F	F	T	T	T	T	T	T

All true values in the last column

∴ $(p\rightarrow(q\rightarrow r)) \Rightarrow (p\rightarrow q)\rightarrow(p\rightarrow r)$ is a Tautology.

(2) Show the following equivalences

(a) $p\rightarrow(q\rightarrow p) \Leftrightarrow \neg p\rightarrow(p\rightarrow q)$

(b) $p\rightarrow(q\vee r) \Leftrightarrow (p\rightarrow q)\vee(p\rightarrow r)$

(c) $(p\rightarrow q)\wedge(r\rightarrow q)\Leftrightarrow(p\vee r)\rightarrow q$

(d) $\neg (p\rightleftarrows q) \Leftrightarrow (p\vee q)\wedge(p\wedge q)$

(a) $p\rightarrow(q\rightarrow p) \Leftrightarrow \neg p\rightarrow(p\rightarrow q)$

Proof

$p\rightarrow(q\rightarrow p) \Leftrightarrow \neg p\rightarrow(p\rightarrow q)$ -------- (1)

p	q	(q→p)	p→(q→p)	7p	p→q	7p→(p→q)	(1)
T	T	T	T	F	T	T	T
T	F	T	T	F	F	T	T
F	T	F	T	T	T	T	T
F	F	T	T	T	T	T	T

All true values in last column, ∴ $p\rightarrow(q\rightarrow p)\Leftrightarrow\neg p\rightarrow(p\rightarrow q)$ is a Tautology.

(b) $p \to (q \lor r) \Leftrightarrow (p \to q) \lor (p \to r)$

Proof

$$p \to (q \lor r) \Leftrightarrow (p \to q) \lor (p \to r) \text{ ------ (1)}$$

p	q	r	q∨r	p→(q∨r)	p→q	p→r	(p→q)∨(p→r)	(1)
T	T	T	T	T	T	T	T	T
T	T	F	T	T	T	F	T	T
T	F	T	T	T	F	T	T	T
T	F	F	F	F	F	F	F	T
F	T	T	T	T	T	T	T	T
F	T	F	T	T	T	T	T	T
F	F	T	T	T	T	T	T	T
F	F	F	F	T	T	T	T	T

All true values in last column, $\therefore$ $p \to (q \lor r) \Leftrightarrow (p \to q) \lor (p \to r)$ is a tautology.

Exercise Problems

(a) $(p \to q) \land (r \to q) \Leftrightarrow (p \lor r) \to q$ [Ans : Last column is T, so it is a tautology]

(b) $\daleth(p \rightleftarrows q) \Leftrightarrow (p \lor q) \land (p \land q)$ [Ans : Last column is true so it is a tautology]

Some important implications which can be proved by the truth tables are given in table.

Implications

1. $p \land q \Rightarrow p$ ⎫   Conjunctions

2. $p \land q \Rightarrow q$ ⎭   Simplifications

3. $p \Rightarrow p \lor q$ Disjunctive - Addition

4. $\daleth p \Rightarrow p \to q$

5. $q \Rightarrow p \to q$

6. $\daleth(p \to q) \Rightarrow p$

7. $\daleth(p \to q) \Rightarrow \daleth q$

8. $p \wedge (p \rightarrow q) \Rightarrow q$

9. $\neg q \wedge (p \rightarrow q) \Rightarrow \neg p$

10. $\neg p \wedge (p \vee q) \Rightarrow q$

11. $(p \rightarrow q) \wedge (q \rightarrow r) \Rightarrow p \rightarrow r$

12. $(p \vee q) \wedge (p \rightarrow r) \wedge (q \rightarrow r) \Rightarrow r$

Example Problems

(1) Show that following implications with out constructing the truth table

(a) $(p \rightarrow q) \Rightarrow p \rightarrow (p \wedge q)$

(b) $(p \rightarrow q) \rightarrow q \Rightarrow (p \vee q)$

(c) $((p \vee \neg p) \rightarrow q) \rightarrow ((p \vee \neg p) \rightarrow r) \Rightarrow (q \rightarrow r)$

(d) $(q \rightarrow (p \wedge \neg p)) \rightarrow (r \rightarrow (p \wedge \neg p)) \Rightarrow (r \rightarrow q)$

a) Solution

Consider

$(p \rightarrow q) \Rightarrow p \rightarrow (p \wedge q)$ [by formula, $p \rightarrow q = \neg (p \vee q)$]

$\Leftrightarrow (\neg p \vee q) \Rightarrow \neg p \vee (p \wedge q)$

$\Leftrightarrow (\neg p \vee q) \Rightarrow ((\neg p \vee p) \wedge (\neg p \vee q))$

$\Leftrightarrow (\neg p \vee q) \Rightarrow (T \wedge (\neg p \vee q))$ $[\because p \vee \neg p = T]$

$\Leftrightarrow (\neg p \vee q) \Rightarrow (\neg p \vee q)$ $[\because T \wedge p = p]$

The above statement is in the form $p \rightarrow q$ $[\because p \rightarrow q = \neg (p \vee q)]$

$\Leftrightarrow \neg (\neg p \vee q) \vee (\neg p \vee q)$

$\Leftrightarrow T$ [since $\neg p \vee p = T$]

Hence Proved.

(b) $(p \to q) \to q \Rightarrow p \lor q$

Solution

Consider

$(p \to q) \to q \Rightarrow (p \lor q)$

$\Rightarrow \neg(p \to q) \lor q \Rightarrow (p \lor q)$

$\Rightarrow \neg(\neg p \lor q) \lor q \Rightarrow (p \lor q)$ [By formula, $p \Rightarrow q = \neg p \lor q$]

$\Rightarrow (p \lor q) \lor q \to (p \lor q)$ $[p = \neg(\neg p)]$

$\Rightarrow p \lor (q \lor q) \to (p \lor q)$ [According to Associative Law, $p \lor (q \lor r) = (p \lor q) \lor r$]

$\Rightarrow p \lor q \to p \lor q$ [According to Idempotent Law, $p \lor p = p$]

$\Rightarrow \neg(p \lor q) \lor (p \lor q)$ $[p \to q = \neg p \lor q]$

$\Rightarrow T$ $[\therefore \neg p \lor p = T]$

Hence Proved.

(2) Show that p is equivalent to the following formulas

(1) $\neg \neg P$

Solution

p	$\neg p$	$\neg \neg p$
T	F	T
F	T	F

$\therefore$ p is equation to $\neg \neg P$.

(2) $p \Rightarrow p \land p$

Solution

p	p	p∧p
T	T	T
F	F	F

$\therefore p \Rightarrow p \land p$

(3) $p \Rightarrow p \vee p$

Solution

p	p	p∨p
T	T	T
F	F	F

∴ $p \Rightarrow p \vee p$

(4) Show that $\daleth(p \wedge q) \Rightarrow \daleth p \vee \daleth q$

Proof

p	q	p∧q	⏋(p∧q)	⏋p	⏋q	⏋p∨⏋q
T	T	T	F	F	F	F
T	F	F	T	F	T	T
F	T	F	T	T	F	T
F	F	F	T	T	T	T

From 4th and 7th column $\daleth(p \wedge q) \Rightarrow \daleth p \vee \daleth q$

Exercise Problems

(1) Show that

    (a) $p \Rightarrow (p \wedge q) \vee (p \wedge \daleth q)$

    (b) $p \Rightarrow (p \vee q) \wedge (p \vee \daleth q)$

    (c) $p \Rightarrow p \wedge (p \vee q)$

(2) Show that following equivalences

    (a) $\daleth(p \vee q) \Rightarrow \daleth p \vee \daleth q$

    (b) $\daleth(p \rightarrow q) \Rightarrow p \wedge \daleth q$

    (c) $\daleth(p \rightleftarrows q) \Rightarrow (p \wedge \daleth q) \vee (\daleth p \wedge q)$

4.12 NORMAL FORMS

Definition 1 : Satisfiable

If A has the truth table T for atleast one combination of truth values assigned to P_1, P_2, ..., P_n, then A is said to be **Satisfiable**.

Definition 2 : Decision Problem

The problem of determining in a finite number of steps, whether a given statement formula is a Tautology (or) a Contradiction (or) atleast satisfiable is known as a **Decision Problem**.

Definition : Disjunctive Normal Form

1. We use the word "**Product**" in the place of "**Conjunction**" and "**Sum**" in the place of "**Disjunction**".

2. A product of the variables and their negations in a formula is called an "**Elementary Product**".

   Example

   $p, \neg p \wedge q, \neg q \wedge p \wedge \neg p, p \wedge \neg p$ and $q \wedge \neg p$.   [Note : $\wedge \rightarrow$ Product]

3. A sum of the variables and their negations is called an "**Elementary Sum**".

   Example for Elementary sum of two variables

   $p, \neg p \vee q, \neg q \vee p \vee \neg p, p \vee \neg p$ and $q \vee \neg p$ [Note : $\vee \rightarrow$ Sum]

A formula which is equivalent to a given formula and which consists of a sum of elementary products is called a "Disjunctive Normal Form" of the given formula.

Example

Obtain disjunctive normal forms of

$p \wedge (p \rightarrow q)$ $\Rightarrow p(\neg p \vee q)$

$\Leftrightarrow (p \wedge \neg p) \vee (p \wedge q)$ [By Distributive Law$\rightarrow p \wedge (q \vee r) = (p \wedge q) \vee (p \wedge q)$]

Hence the result.

Conjunctive Normal Forms

Definition :

A formula which is equivalent to a given formula and which consists of a product of elementary sum is called a "Conjunctive Normal Form" of the given formula.

Example

Obtain a conjunctive normal form of the formula given $p \wedge (p \rightarrow q)$

Solution

$p \wedge (p \rightarrow q) \Leftrightarrow p \wedge (\neg p \vee q)$

Hence the result.

4.13 PRINCIPAL DISJUNCTIVE NORMAL FORM (P D N F)

(SUM OF THE PRODUCTS CANONICAL FORM)

Truth Table

P	Q	Minterm
T	T	$P \wedge Q$
T	F	$P \wedge \neg Q$
F	T	$\neg P \wedge Q$
F	F	$\neg P \wedge \neg Q$

Definition

For a given formula an Equivalent Formula

    Consisting of disjunction of "Minterms" only is known as its **Principal Disjunctive Normal Form (or) Sum of Products Canonical.**

Example

(Min terms) (or) Boolean conjunctions $p \wedge q$, $p \wedge \neg q$, $\neg p \wedge q$ and $\neg p \wedge \neg q$.

Steps for PDNF

1. Only consider the truth values (T) in the truth table for the required column.

2. Write the corresponding Minterm values for that required column.

3. Connect those Minterm values by $\vee$ symbol.

Example Problems

(1) The truth table for $p \rightarrow q$, $p \vee q$ and $\neg(p \wedge q)$ are given below, obtain the Principal Disjunctive Normal Forms of those formulas.

p	q	p∧q	p→q	p∨q	¬(p∧q)	Minterm
T	T	T	T	T	F	P∧Q
T	F	F	F	T	T	P∧7Q
F	T	F	T	T	T	7P∧Q
F	F	F	T	F	T	7P∧7Q

Solution

(1) $p \rightarrow q$

Consider Truth values T in the column $p \rightarrow q$ and then write the corresponding Minterm values, which are connected by $\vee$ symbol.

$\Rightarrow (p \wedge q) \vee (\neg p \wedge q) \vee (\neg p \wedge \neg q)$

(2) $p \lor q$

Consider Truth values T in the column $p \lor q$ and then write the corresponding Minterm

values, which are connected by $\lor$ symbol.

$\Rightarrow (p \land q) \lor (p \land \neg q) \lor (\neg p \land q)$

(3) $\neg(p \land q)$

Consider Truth values T in the column $\neg(p \land q)$ and then write the corresponding

Minterm values, which are connected by $\lor$ symbol.

$\Rightarrow (p \land \neg q) \lor (\neg p \land q) \lor (\neg p \land \neg q)$

(2) Obtain the Principal Disjunctive Normal Form [P D N F] for $\neg p \lor q$

Solution

Construct the truth table for $\neg p \lor q$

p	q	Minterm	$\neg p$	$\neg p \lor q$
T	T	$p \land q$	F	T
T	F	$p \land \neg q$	F	F
F	T	$\neg p \land q$	T	T
F	F	$\neg p \land \neg q$	T	T

The Principal Disjunctive Normal Form of $\neg p \lor q$ is

(Consider Truth values T in the column $\neg p \lor q$ and then write the corresponding

Minterm values, which are connected by $\lor$ symbol).

$(p \land q) \lor (\neg p \land q) \lor (\neg p \land \neg q)$

(3) Obtain the Principal Disjunctive Normal Form [P D N F] for $(p \wedge q) \vee (\neg p \wedge r) \vee (q \wedge r)$.

Solution

Construct the truth table for $(p \wedge q) \vee (\neg p \wedge r) \vee (q \wedge r)$

p	q	r	Minterm	p∧q	¬p∧r	q∧r	(p∧q)∨(¬p∧q)∨(q∧r)
T	T	T	p∧q∧r	T	F	T	T
T	T	F	p∧q∧¬r	T	F	F	T
T	F	T	p∧¬q∧r	F	F	F	F
T	F	F	p∧¬q∧¬r	F	F	F	F
F	T	T	¬p∧q∧r	F	T	T	T
F	T	F	¬p∧q∧¬r	F	F	F	F
F	F	T	¬p∧¬q∧r	F	T	F	T
F	F	F	¬p∧¬q∧¬r	F	F	F	F

The Principal Disjunctive Normal Form of $(p \wedge q) \vee (\neg p \wedge r) \vee (q \wedge r)$ is,

(Consider Truth values T in the column $(p \wedge q) \vee (\neg p \wedge r) \vee (q \wedge r)$ and then write the corresponding Minterm values, which are connected by $\vee$ symbol).

$(p \wedge q \wedge r) \vee (p \wedge q \wedge \neg r) \vee (\neg p \wedge q \wedge r) \vee (\neg p \wedge \neg q \wedge r)$

(4) By not using truth table directly, find Principal Disjunctive Normal Form for

(1) $p \wedge (p \to q)$

$\Leftrightarrow p \wedge (\neg p \vee q)$ [By formula, $p \to q \Rightarrow \neg p \vee q$]

$\Leftrightarrow (p \wedge \neg p) \vee (p \vee q)$

Which is the required Principal Disjunctive Normal Form (P D N F).

(2) $\neg p \vee q$

$\Leftrightarrow (\neg p \wedge (q \vee \neg q)) \vee (q \wedge (p \vee \neg p))$ $[\because (q \wedge \neg q) \Rightarrow T \ \& \ (p \wedge \neg p) \Rightarrow T]$

$\Leftrightarrow (\neg p \wedge q) \vee (\neg p \wedge \neg q) \vee ((q \wedge p) \vee (q \wedge \neg p))$ [By Distribution Laws]

$\Leftrightarrow (\neg p \wedge q) \vee (\neg p \wedge \neg q) \vee (q \wedge p)$

Which is the required Principal Disjunctive Normal Form (P D N F).

(3) $\lnot(p \land q) \Leftrightarrow \lnot(p \land q) \land T$

$\Leftrightarrow (\lnot p \lor \lnot q) \land T$

$\Leftrightarrow (\lnot p \land T) \lor (\lnot q \land T)$

$\Leftrightarrow (\lnot p \land (q \lor \lnot q)) \lor (\lnot q \land (p \lor \lnot p))$

$\Leftrightarrow (\lnot p \land q) \lor (\lnot p \land \lnot q) \lor (\lnot q \land p) \lor (\lnot q \land \lnot p)$

$\Leftrightarrow (\lnot p \land q) \lor (\lnot p \land \lnot q) \lor (\lnot q \land p)$

Which is the required Principal Disjunctive Normal Form (P D N F).

(4) $p \rightarrow q \Rightarrow (\lnot p \lor q)$

$\Leftrightarrow (\lnot p \lor q) \land T$ (Since $() \land T \Rightarrow ()$)

$\Leftrightarrow (7p \land T) \lor (q \land T)$ (By Associative Law)

$\Leftrightarrow \lnot p \land (q \lor \lnot q) \lor (q \land (p \lor \lnot p))$

$\Leftrightarrow (\lnot p \land q) \lor (\lnot p \land \lnot q) \lor (q \land p) \lor (q \land \lnot p)$

$\Leftrightarrow (p \land q) \lor (\lnot p \land \lnot q) \lor (\lnot p \lor q)$

Which is the required Principal Disjunctive Normal Form (P D N F).

4.14 PRINCIPAL CONJUNCTIVE NORMAL FORM (P C N F)

(PRODUCTS OF SUMS CANONICAL FORM)

Truth Table

p	q	Maxterm
t	t	$p \lor q$
t	f	$p \lor \lnot q$
f	t	$\lnot p \lor q$
f	f	$\lnot p \lor \lnot q$

Definition of PCNF

For a given formula, an equivalent formula consisting of conjunctions of Maxterms only is known as its **Principal Conjunctive Normal Form (Or) Product Of Sums Canonical Form.**

Example

Maxterms   p∨q, p∨⌐q, ⌐p∨⌐q

Steps for PCNF

1. Only consider the false values (F) in the truth table for the required column.

2. Write the corresponding Maxterm values for that required column.

3. Connect those Maxterm values by ∧ symbol.

Example Problems

(1) Obtain Principal Conjunctive Normal Form for p∧(⌐p∨q)

Solution

Construct Truth table for p∧(⌐p∨q)

p	q	Maxterm	⌐p	⌐p∨q	p∧(⌐p∨q)
T	T	p∨q	F	T	T
T	F	p∨⌐q	F	F	F
F	T	⌐p∨q	T	T	F
F	F	⌐p∨⌐q	T	T	F

(Consider False values (F) in the column p∧(⌐p∨q) and then write the corresponding Maxterm values, which are connected by ∧ symbol).

A ⇒ (p∨⌐q)∧(⌐p∨q) ∧ (⌐p∨⌐q)

∴ The required Principal Conjunctive Normal Form is −A [negation of A]

-A $\Rightarrow \daleth((p\vee\daleth q)\wedge(\daleth p\vee q)\wedge(\daleth p\vee\daleth q))$

$\Leftrightarrow (\daleth p\vee q)\wedge(p\vee\daleth q)\wedge(p\vee q)$

(2) Obtain Principal Conjunctive Normal Form (PCNF) for $\daleth(p\vee q)$

Solution

Construct Truth table for $\daleth(p\vee q)$

p	q	**Maxterm**	p∨q	$\daleth$(p∨q)
T	T	p∨q	T	F
T	F	p∨$\daleth$q	T	F
F	T	$\daleth$p∨q	T	F
F	F	$\daleth$p∨$\daleth$q	F	T

(Consider False values (F) in the column $\daleth(p\vee q)$ and then write the corresponding

Maxterm values, which are connected by $\wedge$ symbol).

$A \Rightarrow (p\vee q)\wedge(p\vee\daleth q)\wedge(\daleth p\vee q)$

∴ The required Principal Conjunctive Normal Form is –A (negation of A)

$\Rightarrow \daleth[(p\vee q)\wedge(p\vee\daleth q)\wedge(7p\vee q)]$

$\Rightarrow (\daleth p\vee\daleth q)\wedge(\daleth p\vee q)\wedge(p\vee\daleth q)]$

(3) Obtain Principal Conjunctive Normal Form (P C N F) for $q\wedge(p\vee\daleth q)$

Solution

Construct Truth table for $q\wedge(p\vee\daleth q)$

p	q	**Maxterm**	$\daleth$q	p∨$\daleth$q	q∧(p∨$\daleth$q)
T	T	p∨q	F	T	T
T	F	p∨$\daleth$q	T	T	F
F	T	$\daleth$p∨q	F	F	F
F	F	$\daleth$p∨$\daleth$q	T	T	F

(Consider False values (F) in the column q∧(p∨⅂q) and then write the corresponding Maxterm values, which are connected by ∧ symbol).

$$A \Rightarrow (p\vee \urcorner q)\wedge(\urcorner p\vee q)\wedge(\urcorner p\vee \urcorner q)$$

∴ The required Principal Conjunctive Normal Form is –A [negation of A]

$$\Rightarrow \urcorner [(p\vee \urcorner q)\wedge(\urcorner p\vee q)\wedge(\urcorner p\vee \urcorner q)]$$

$$\Rightarrow (\urcorner p\vee q)\wedge(p\vee \urcorner q)\wedge(p\vee q)$$

(4) By not using truth table directly, find Principal Conjunctive Normal Form P C N F for

(a) ⅂(p∨q)

Solution

$$\urcorner(p\vee q) \Rightarrow \urcorner p \wedge \urcorner q$$

$$\Leftrightarrow (\urcorner p\vee F)\wedge(\urcorner q\vee F) \qquad [\text{By formula } () \vee F = ()]$$

$$\Leftrightarrow \urcorner p\vee(q\wedge \urcorner q)\wedge(\urcorner q\vee(p\wedge \urcorner p)) \qquad [\text{By formula } p \wedge \urcorner p = F]$$

$$\Leftrightarrow (\urcorner p\vee q)\wedge(\urcorner p\vee \urcorner q)\wedge(\urcorner q\vee p)\wedge(\urcorner q\vee \urcorner p)$$

$$\Leftrightarrow (\urcorner p\vee q)\wedge(\urcorner p\vee \urcorner q)\wedge(\urcorner q\vee p)$$

Which is a required Principal Conjunctive Normal Form (P C N F).

(b) ⅂(p→q)

Solution

$$\Rightarrow \urcorner(\urcorner p\vee q) \qquad [\text{By formula } p\to q \Rightarrow \urcorner p\vee q]$$

$$\Leftrightarrow (p\to\wedge \urcorner q)$$

$$\Leftrightarrow (p\vee F)\wedge(\urcorner q\vee F)$$

$$\Leftrightarrow p\vee(q\wedge \urcorner q)\wedge(\urcorner q\vee(p\wedge \urcorner p))$$

$\Leftrightarrow (p \lor q) \land (p \lor \daleth q) \land (\daleth q \lor p) \land (\daleth q \land \daleth p)$

$\Leftrightarrow (p \lor q) \land (p \lor \daleth q) \land (\daleth q \lor \daleth p)$

Which is a required Principal Conjunctive Normal Form.

Example Problems

(1) Obtain Principal Disjunctive Normal Form (P D N F) & Principal Conjunctive Normal Form (P C N F) for $(q \rightarrow p) \land (\daleth p \land q)$.

$\Leftrightarrow (\daleth q \lor p) \land (\daleth p \land q)$ [By formula $q \rightarrow p \Rightarrow \daleth q \lor p$]

$\Leftrightarrow (\daleth q \lor p) \land (\daleth p \lor (\daleth q \land q) \land q \lor (\daleth p \land p))$

$\Leftrightarrow (\daleth q \lor p) \land (\daleth p \lor \daleth q) \land (\daleth p \lor q) \land (q \lor \daleth p) \land (q \lor p)$

$\Leftrightarrow (\daleth q \lor p) \land (q \lor p) \land (q \lor \daleth p) \land (\daleth p \lor \daleth q)$

Which is a required P C N F. Here all terms are available in P C N F so we cannot able to find P D N F.

(2) Obtain Principal Disjunctive Normal Form (P D N F) & Principal Conjunctive Normal Form (P C N F) for $A \Leftrightarrow (p \land q) \lor (\daleth p \land q \land r)$.

Solution

p	q	r	$\daleth p$	$\daleth p \land q$	$\daleth p \land q \land r$	$p \land q$	$(p \land q) \lor (\daleth p \land q \land r)$	Minterm	Maxterm
T	T	T	F	F	F	T	T	$p \land q \land r$	
T	T	F	F	F	F	T	T	$p \land q \land \daleth r$	
T	F	T	F	F	F	F	F		$p \lor \daleth q \lor r$
T	F	F	F	F	F	F	F		$p \lor \daleth q \lor \daleth r$
F	T	T	T	T	T	F	T	$\daleth p \land q \land r$	
F	T	F	T	T	F	F	F		$\daleth p \lor q \lor \daleth r$
F	F	T	T	F	F	F	F		$\daleth p \lor \daleth q \lor r$
F	F	F	T	F	F	F	F		$\daleth p \lor \daleth q \lor \daleth r$

PDNF

(Consider Truth values (T) in the column $(p \wedge q) \vee (\neg p \wedge q \wedge r)$ and then write the corresponding Minterm values, which are connected by $\vee$ symbol).

The Principal Disjunctive Normal Form is $(p \wedge q \wedge r) \vee (p \wedge q \wedge \neg r) \vee (\neg p \wedge q \wedge r)$

PCNF

(Consider False values (F) in the column $(p \wedge q) \vee (\neg p \wedge q \wedge r)$ and then write the corresponding Maxterm values, which are connected by $\wedge$ symbol).

The Principal Conjunctive Normal Form is

Consider the false values and corresponding Maxterms values

$A \Rightarrow (p \vee \neg q \vee r) \wedge (p \vee \neg q \vee \neg r) \wedge (\neg p \vee q \vee \neg r) \wedge (\neg p \vee \neg q \vee r) \wedge (\neg p \vee \neg q \vee \neg r)$

$A \Rightarrow \neg A \Rightarrow \neg(A)$ we get

$\Rightarrow (\neg p \vee q \vee \neg r) \wedge (\neg p \vee q \vee r) \wedge (p \vee \neg q \vee r) \wedge (p \vee q \vee \neg r) \wedge (p \vee q \vee r)$.

4.15 INDIRECT METHOD OF PROOF

Proofs that are not direct are called **Indirect**.

The two main types of indirect proof both use the negation of the conclusion.

(1) First type of proof is

Contra Positive Proof

(2) Second type of indirect proof is known as proof by contradiction (or) reduction absurdum proof.

The indirect method is based on the equivalence $(P_1 \wedge P_2 \wedge \ldots \ldots \wedge P_n) \Rightarrow q$,

$\Leftrightarrow (P_1 \wedge P_2 \wedge \ldots \ldots \wedge P_n) \Rightarrow (\sim q)$,

Example

Let the following statements be true.

- If I am lazy, then I do not study.

- I study or I enjoy myself

- I do not enjoy myself

Show that the statement 'I am not lazy' is a true statement.

Solution

Let p, q, r represent the statements.

p   : I am lazy

q   : I study

r   : I enjoy myself

Consider premises that the statements

$p \Rightarrow \sim q$ (If I am lazy I do not study)

$q \vee r$ (I study or I enjoy myself)

and $\sim r$ (I do not enjoy myself)

are true. Then we shall prove that the statement $p \sim P$ (I am not lazy) is true. Assuming that P is true, since P is true and $p \Rightarrow \sim q$, then $\sim q$ is true.

$\therefore$ q is false. Also r is false.

But either q or r is true. This is not possible. This contradiction implies that the assumption that p is true is false and $\sim p$ is true.

RULES OF INFERENCE

Rule P

A premise can be introduced at any point of derivation.

Rule T

We may introduce a formula S in a derivation if S is tautologically implied by any one or more of the preceding formulae in the derivation.

We use the following table of implications and Equivalences.

Implications

I_1 $P \wedge Q$ $\Rightarrow P$ ⎫

I_2 $P \wedge Q$ $\Rightarrow Q$ ⎬ Conjuctiv4e (Simplification)

I_3 P $\Rightarrow P \vee Q$ ⎫

I_4 Q $\Rightarrow P \vee Q$ ⎬ Disjunctive (Addition)

I_5 $7P$ $\Rightarrow P \rightarrow Q$

I_6 Q $\Rightarrow P \rightarrow Q$

I_7 $7(P \rightarrow Q)$ $\Rightarrow P$

I_8 $7(P \rightarrow Q)$ $\Rightarrow 7Q$

I_9 P, Q $\Rightarrow P \wedge Q$

I_{10} $7P, P \vee Q$ $\Rightarrow Q$ (disjunctive syllogism)

I_{11} $P, P \rightarrow Q$ $\Rightarrow Q$ (modus ponens)

I_{12} $7Q, P \rightarrow Q$ $\Rightarrow 7P$ (modus tollens)

I_{13} $P \rightarrow Q, Q \rightarrow R \Rightarrow P \rightarrow R$ (hypothetical syllogism)

I_{14} $P \vee Q, P \rightarrow Q, Q \rightarrow R \Rightarrow R$ (dilemma)

I_{15} $P \rightarrow R, Q \rightarrow R \Rightarrow (P \lor Q) \rightarrow R$

$(P \leftrightarrow Q) \Leftrightarrow ((P \rightarrow Q) \land (Q \rightarrow P)) \Leftrightarrow ((P \land Q) \lor (7P \land 7Q))$

Biconditional Equivalences

E_1	$77P$	$\Leftrightarrow$	P	(Double Negation)
E_2	$P \land Q$	$\Leftrightarrow$	$Q \land P$	
E_3	$P \lor Q$	$\Leftrightarrow$	$Q \lor P$	(Commutative Laws)
E_4	$(P \land Q) \land R$	$\Leftrightarrow$	$P \land (Q \land R)$	
E_5	$(P \lor Q) \lor R$	$\Leftrightarrow$	$P \lor (Q \lor R)$	(Associative Laws)
E_6	$P \land (Q \lor R)$	$\Leftrightarrow$	$(P \land Q) \lor (P \land R)$	
E_7	$P \lor (Q \land R)$	$\Leftrightarrow$	$(P \lor Q) \land (P \lor R)$	(Distributive Laws)
E_8	$7(P \land Q)$	$\Leftrightarrow$	$7P \lor 7Q$	
E_9	$7(P \lor Q)$	$\Leftrightarrow$	$7P \land 7Q$	DCM Organ's Law
E_{10}	$P \lor P$	$\Leftrightarrow$	P	
E_{11}	$P \land P$	$\Leftrightarrow$	P	
E_{12}	$R \lor (P \land 7P)$	$\Leftrightarrow$	R	
E_{13}	$R \land (P \lor 7P)$	$\Leftrightarrow$	R	
E_{14}	$R \lor (P \lor 7P)$	$\Leftrightarrow$	T	
E_{15}	$R \land (P \land 7P)$	$\Leftrightarrow$	F	
E_{16}	$P \rightarrow Q$	$\Leftrightarrow$	$7P \lor Q$	
E_{17}	$7(P \rightarrow Q)$	$\Leftrightarrow$	$P \land 7Q$	
E_{18}	$P \rightarrow Q$	$\Leftrightarrow$	$7Q \rightarrow 7P$	
E_{19}	$P \rightarrow (Q \rightarrow R)$	$\Leftrightarrow$	$(P \land Q) \rightarrow R$	

E_{20} $7(P \rightleftarrows Q)$ $\Leftrightarrow$ $\rightleftarrows 7Q$

E_{21} $(P \rightleftarrows Q)$ $\Leftrightarrow$ $(P \rightarrow Q) \wedge (Q \rightarrow P)$

E_{22} $(P \rightleftarrows Q)$ $\Leftrightarrow$ $(P \wedge Q) \vee (7P \wedge 7Q)$

The technique of indirect method of proof runs as follows

1. Introduce the negation of the desired conclusion as a new premise.

2. From the new premise, together with the given premises, derive a contradiction

3. Assert the desired conclusion as a logical inference from the premises.

The following example illustrates this method.

Example Problem 1

Using indirect method of proof, derive P→7S from P→QvR, Q→7P, S→7R, P

Solution

The desired result is P→7S, its negation is P∧S.

(P∧S↔7(7P∨7S) ↔ 7(P→7S)) is a tautology. This follows from the law of

negation for implication. Here P∧S as an additional premise.

[1]	(1)	P→QvR	Premise [Rule P]
[2]	(2)	P	Premise [Rule P]
[1, 2]	(3)	QvR	T, (1), (2), modus ponens
[4]	(4)	S→7R	P
[5]	(5)	P∧S	P (new premise)
[5]	(6)	S	T, (5) and simplification
[4, 5]	(7)	7R	T, (4), (6) modus ponens
[1, 2, 4, 5]	(8)	Q	T, (3), (7), I_{10}
[9]	[9]	Q→7P	P
[1, 2, 4, 5, 9]	(10)	7P	T, (8) (9) modus ponens
[1, 2, 4, 5, 9]	(11)	P∧7P	T, (2), (10) contradiction

Thus additional premise P∧S and the given premises together lead to a contradiction.

So 7(P∧S) is derivable from P→Q∨R, Q→7P, S→7R, P.

Problem 2) Prove by indirect method that

(7Q), P → Q, P∨T ⇒ T   [q, p & t are small letters]

Solution

The desired result is t,. Include its negation 7t as a new premise.

[1]	(1)	P∨t	P (Premise)
[2]	(2)	7t	P (additional Premise)
[1, 2]	(3)	p	T, (1), (2), I_{10} disjunctive syllogism
[4]	(4)	P→Q	P (Premise)
[1, 2, 4]	(5)	Q	T, (3) (4) modus I_{11} ponens
[6]	(6)	7Q	P (Premise)
[1,2, 4, 6]	(7)	Q∧7R	T, (5), (6) contradiction

Here q is true 7q is false.

Both present so contradiction.

Thus the new premise, together with the given premise, leads to a contradiction. (7q), p → q, p∨t ⇒ t

Problem 3) Using indirect proof, show that p→q, q→r, 7(p∧r), p∨r ⇒ r.

Solution

The desired result is r. Include 7r as a new premise.

[1]	(1)	Q→R	P
[2]	(2)	7R	P (Additional Premise)
[1, 2]	(3)	7Q	T, (1), (2), I_{12} modus tollens

[4]	(4)	P→Q	P
[1, 2, 4]	(5)	7P	T, (3) (4) I_{12} (modus tollens)
[6]	(6)	P∨R	P
[1,2, 4, 6]	(7)	R	T, (5), (6) I_{10} (disjunction syllogism)
[1,2, 4, 6, 2]	(8)	R∧7R	T, (2), (7) contradiction

Thus we get a contradiction

Therefore we get p→q, q→r, p∨r→r.

We note that the other premise 7(p∧r) will not yield a contradiction with r.

4) a→b, 7(b∨c) ⇒ 7a

The indirect proof of this theorem is

[1]	(1)	a	Negation of the conclusion
[2]	(2)	a→b	Premise
[1, 2]	(3)	b	(1), (2), modus ponens (I_{11})
[3]	(4)	b∨c	(3) disjunctive addition I_3
[5]	(5)	7(b∨c)	Premise
[3, 5]	(6)	(b∨c) ∧ 7(b∨c)	T, (5), (6) contradiction

4.16 PREDICATE CALCULUS (OR) PREDICATE LOGIC

Predicate :

Consider the statement "x is greater than 10", it has two parts first part, the variable x, is the **"Subject"** of the statement. The second part "is greater than 10" which is called the **"Predicate"**.

We can denote the above statement by the notation P(x).

When P → denotes the predicate "is greater than 10"

x → is a variable (subject)

so P(x) is called the propositional function at x.

Suppose value has been assigned to the variable x, the statement P(x) becomes a proposition and has the truth value True (or) False. Consider the example,

P(15) {=15 > 10} and P(5) {=5>10} are T and F respectively.

The logic based on the analysis of predicates in any statement is called predicate logic or predicate calculus.

Note :

Any statement of the type "P is Q" where Q is the predicate and P is the subject can be denoted by Q(P).

Example 1

Let R denote the predicate "is red" and let P denote the subject "This Painting". Then the statement is "This Painting is Red" = R(P).

Example 2

Connectives can also be used in predicates.

Example

"John is a bachelor and this painting is red" can be qritten as

B(j) ∧ R(P)

Here this painting (sub) denoted by P is red (predicated) denoted by R.

Here B is Bachelor (Pre)

J → John (Sub)

Example 3

Consider the statement

(a) Jack is taller than Jill

Here   Predicate $\rightarrow$ "is taller than" $\rightarrow$ G

Subject $\rightarrow$ Jack, Jill

So we write the statement is $G(J_1, J_2)$

Here we consider two types of statement functions.

1) A simple statement function of one variable is defined to be an expression consisting of a predicate symbol and an individual variable.

We call $H(x)$ as a function

Ex 1   is the example for this

Ex 2   X is taller than Y [Mr.Miller is taller than Mr.fox $G(m, f)$]

Is denoted by $G(x, y)$

It is called a function of two variables.

2) Compound Statement

With the help of two simple statements we can form a compound statement.

Example

$M(x)$: X is a man

$H(Y)$: Y is a mortal

Then $M(x) \wedge H(y)$: x is a man and y is a mortal

QUANTIFIERS

Certain statements involve words that indicate quantity such as "all", some none (or) one. They answer the questions how many? such words indicate quantity. They are called quantifiers.

Let us consider the statement

1) For all x if x is a man then x is a mortal.

2) For every x if x is an apple then x is red.

3) For all x if x is an integer, then x is either +ve or negative.

We symbolize "for all x" by the symbol "($\forall$x)".

Example

All roses are red, this can be understood as for every x. If x is a rose then x is red.

If we denote R(x) : x is rose and P(x) : x is red, then we can write above statement

as

(x) (R(x) $\rightarrow$ P(x)) Here (x) is called universal quantifier.

The above statement is also written as ($\forall$x) (R(x) $\rightarrow$ P(x)).

The symbols (x) (or) ($\forall$x) are called "universal quantifiers".

We use universal quantifiers for those statement of form

"All P are Q"

Universal Quantifiers

For all x, for every x

For each x, every thing x is such that, each thing x is such that

Example

(ii) Consider the statements

Some men are tall

The quantifier "some" is existential quantifier. Denote it by the symbol ($\exists$x),

which is a reversed E followed by the variable symbol x.

Existential Quantifier

For some x, there is atleast one) There exists x such that

1) There is atleast one X such that x is green can be denoted by

$(\exists x)\,(G(x))$

2) Some thing is not green → There is atleast one X such that x is not green can be

denoted by $(\exists x)\,(7G(x))$

1) Everything is green $(\forall x)\,(G(x))$

2) Nothing is green $(\forall x)\,(7G(x))$

Problems

1) Write each of following in symbolic form (Assume that the universe consists of

literally every thing)

a) All men are giants

b) No men are giants

c) Some men are giants

d) Some men are not giants

Solution

We assume that the universe consists of objects some of which are not men.

Let   M(x) :   X is a man and

      G(x) :   X is a giant

Statement (a) means

For all x, if x is a man, then x is a giant, so (a) is

$(\forall x)\,[M(x) \rightarrow G(x)]$

Statement (b) means

For all x, if x is a man, then x is not a giant and it is represented by

$(\forall x) [M(x) \rightarrow 7G(x)]$

Statement (c) means

"there is an x, such that x is a man and x is a giant". It is written as

$(\exists x) [M(x) \wedge G(x)]$

Statement (d) means

"there is an x, such that x is a man and x is not a giant

So it is

$(\exists x) [M(x) \wedge 7G(x)]$

2) Write the following sentences in the closed form. (Assume that the universe consists of literally every thing).

a) Some people who trust others are rewarded.

b) If any one is good then John is good.

c) He is ambitions or no one is ambitions

d) Some one is teasing

e) It is not true that all roads lead to Rome.

Solution

Let $P(x)$: x is person

$T(x)$: x trusts others

$R(x)$: x is rewarded

$G(x)$: x is good

$A(x)$: x is ambitions

$Q(x)$: x is teasing

S(x)   : x is road

L(x)   : x lead to Rome

Then

a) Some people who trust others are rewarded can be rephrased as "There is one x such that x is a person, x trusts others and X is rewarded".

Symbolic Form

$(\exists x)\ [P(x) \wedge T(x) \wedge R(x)]$

b) "If any one is good then John is good can be worded as

"If there is one x such that x is a person and x is good, then John is good".

Symbolic Form

$(\exists x)\ [P(x) \wedge G(x)] \quad \rightarrow \quad G(John)$

c) "He" represents a particular person.

Let that person be y. So the statement is

"y is ambitious or for all x, if x is a person then x is not ambitious".

So

$A[y] \vee (\forall x)\ [P(x) \rightarrow 7A(x)]$

d) "Some one is teasing can be written as

There is one x such that x is a person and x is teasing and it is

$(\exists x)\ [P(x) \wedge Q(x)]$

e) The statement e can be written as

$7(\forall x)\ [S(x) \rightarrow L(x)]$

(or) $(\exists x)\ [S(x) \wedge 7L(x)]$

4.17 BOUND AND FREE VARIABLES

Definition

In any formula the part containing (x) P(x) (or) (∃x) P(x) such a part is called

the x bound part of the formula. Any variable appearing in an x bound part of the

formula is called bound variable. Otherwise it is called free. Any formula immediately

following (x) or (∀x) or (∃x) is called the scope f the quantifier.

Example

(x) P(x) ∧ Q(x)

In this all x in P(x) is bound whereas the x in Q(x) is free. The scope (x) is P(x).

Problems

Indicate free and bound variables. Also indicate the scope of the quantifier in

a) (x) [P(x) ∧ R(x)] → (x) P(x) ∧ q(x)

Ans

All occurrences of x is P(x) ∧ R(x) is bound occurrence. The occurrences of x

in P(x) is bound the occurrence of x and Q(x) is tree. The scope of (x) → for L.H.S. is

P(x) ∧ R(x).

and scope of (x) → for RH.S is P(x)

2) (∀x) P(x, y) [Scope of ∀(x) = P(x, y)]

Both occurrences of x are bound occurrences while the occurrence of y is free.

(∃x) P(x) ∧ Q(x) [P(x) is the scope of ∃x]

3) The first two occurrences of x are bound, while the third occurrence of x is free.

4.18 INFERENCE THEORY FOR PREDICATE CALCULUS

1) Universal Specification

   $(x) A(x) \Rightarrow A(y)$

2) Universal Generalisation

   $A(y) \Rightarrow (x) A(x)$

3) Existential Specification

   $(\exists x) A(x) \Rightarrow A(y)$

4) Existential Generalisation

   $A(y) \Rightarrow (\exists x)A(x)$

5) $7(x) A(x) \quad = \quad (\exists x) 7A(x)$

6) $7(\exists x) A(x) \quad = \quad (x) 7A(x)$

Problems

Show that $(\exists x)$ follows logically from the premises.

$(x) (H(x) \to M(x))$ and $(\exists x) H(x)$

Ans

1. $(\exists x) H(x)$	Rule P
2. $H(y)$	Existential Specification
3. $(x) (H(x) \to M(x))$	P
4. $H(y) \to M(y)$	Universal Generalization
5. $M(y)$	Rule (Modus Ponens)
6. $(\exists x) M(x)$	Existential Generalisation

2) Prove that $(\exists x)\, P(x) \wedge Q(x) \Rightarrow (\exists x)\, P(x) \wedge (\exists x)\, Q(x)$

Ans

    1. $(\exists x)\, P(x) \wedge Q(x)$ Rule P

    2. $P(y) \wedge Q(x)$ Existential Specification

    3. $P(y)$ Rule T (I_1 Conjunctive Simplification)

    4. $Q(y)$ Rule T (I_2 Conjunctive Simplification)

    5. $(\exists x)\, P(x)$ Existential Generalization

    6. $(\exists x)\, Q(x)$ Existential Generalization

    7. $(\exists x)\, P(x) \wedge (\exists x)\, Q(x)$ Rule T

CHAPTER – V

5. GRAPH THEORY

5.1 GRAPHS

A graph G consists of a set of objects $V = \{v_1, v_2, \ldots\ldots, v_n\}$ called **Vertices** (also called **Points** or **Nodes**) and other set $E = \{e_1, e_2, \ldots.., e_n\}$ whose elements are called **Edges** also called **Lines** or **Arcs**.

The set V(G) is called the vertex set of G.

The set E(G) is called the edge set of G. The graph G with vertices V and Edges E is written as $G = (V, E)$.

Example

Let $V = \{1, 2, 3, 4\}$ and $E = \{\{1, 2\}, \{1, 3\}, \{3, 2\}, \{4, 4\}\}$

Then G(V, E) is a graph.

Let $V = \{1, 2, 3, 4\}$ and $B = \{\{1, 5\}, \{2, 3\}\}$

Then G(V, E) is not a graph, as 5 is not in V.

Adjacent Nodes

Any pair of nodes that is connected by an edge in a graph is called **Adjacent Nodes**.

Isolated Node

In a graph a node that is not adjacent to another node is called an **Isolated Node**. A graph which contains only isolated node is called a **Null Graph** (i.e.) set of edges in a null graph is empty.

Finite & Infinite Graph

A graph G(V, E) is said to be **Finite**, it has a finite number of vertices and finite number of edges. Otherwise it is **Infinite Graph**.

If G is finite, V(G) denotes the number of vertices in G and is called the **Order** of G.

If G is finite E(G) denotes the number of edges in G is called the size of G.

Incident

The edge e that joints the nodes u and v is said to be incident on each of its end points u and v.

Undirected Graph : An Undirected Graph G consists of set V of vertices and a set E of edges such that each edge $e \in E$ is associated with an unordered pair of vertices.

Undirected Graph

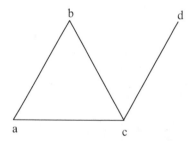

If each edge of the graph G has no direction then the graph is called undirected graph.

5.2 DIRECTED GRAPH (OR) DIGRAPH

G consists of a set V of vertices and a set E of edges such that $e \in E$ is associated with an ordered pair of vertices. In other words if each edge of the graph G has a direction then the graph is called **Directed Graph**.

Suppose

e = (u, v) is a directed edge in a digraph, then

i.   u is called the **Initial Vertex** of e and v is the **Terminal Vertex** of e.

ii. e is said to be incident from u, and to be incident to v.

iii. u is adjacent to v, and v is adjacent from u.

Directed Graph

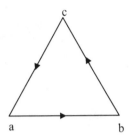

5.3 TYPES OF GRAPHS

1. **Null Graph :** A graph which contains only isolated node is called a **Null Graph** (i.e.) the set of edges in a null graph is empty. Null graph is denoted on n vertices by N_n.

   Example

   N_4 is shown in Fig.

   Null Graph

   Each vertex of a null graph is isolated.

2. **Complete Graph :** A simple graph G with n vertices is said to be a **Complete Graph** if the degree of every vertex is n-1.

   A simple graph G is said to be complete if every vertex in G is connected with every other vertex.

Example

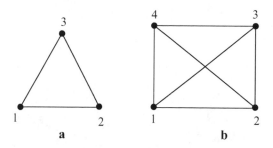

In Fig.a, Vertex 1 is connected to vertex 2 and 3, vertex 2 is connected to 3 and 1, vertex 3 is connected to 2 and 1.

In fig b. vertex 1 is connected to vertices 2 & 3

vertex 2 is connected to vertices 3, 1 & 4

vertex 3 is connected to vertices 2, 4 & 3

vertex 4 is connected to vertices 3, 1 & 2

So it is complete graph.

3. Regular Graph : A graph in which all vertices are of equal degree is called **Regular Graph**, if the degree of each vertex is r, then the graph is called a regular graph of degree r.

[A graph in which every vertex has the **Same Degree** is called a **Regular Graph**]

4. Degree of a Vertex

The number of edges incident on a vertex v_i is called the degree of a vertex.

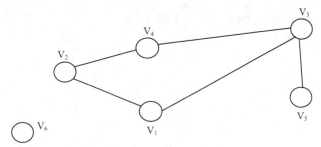

Degree of vertex $V_2 = 2$

Degree of vertex $V_6 = 0$

Example

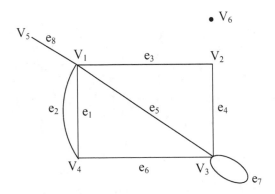

$d(V_i)$ said to be the degree of the vertex V_i of graph G. If $d(V_i)$ is number of edges incident at the vertex V_i edge e_7 is called **Self Loop**. Self loop counted twice.

$d(V_1) = 5, \ d(V_2) = 2, \ d(V_3) = 5, \ d(V_4) = 3, d(V_5) = 1, \ d(V_6) = 0$

5. Isolated Vertex

A vertex having no incident edge is called an **Isolated Vertex**. In otherwords, isolated vertices are those with zero degree.

6. Pendant or End Vertex

A vertex of degree one, is called **Pendant Vertex** or an **End Vertex**.

A vertex with **Zero Indegree** is called a **Source**.

A vertex with **Zero Outdegree** is called a **Sink**.

7. Cycles

The cycle C_n, $n \geq 3$ consists of n vertices $V_1, V_2, ..., V_n$ and edges $\{V_1, V_2\}$, $\{V_2, V_3\}, ..., \{V_{n-1}, V_n\}$ and $\{V_n, V_1\}$.

The cycles C_3, C_4, C_5 and C_6 are shown in fig.

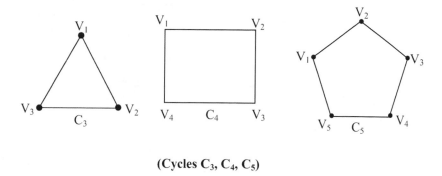

(Cycles C_3, C_4, C_5)

8. Wheels

The wheel W_n is obtained when an additional vertex to the cycle C_n, for $n \geq 3$ and connect this new vertex to each of n vertices in C_n, by new edges.

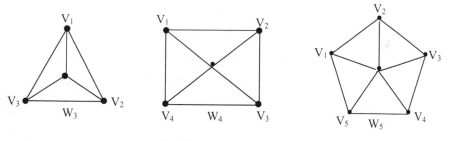

The Wheels W_3, W_4 & W_5

9. Subgraph

A graph H is said to be a subgraph of G if all the vertices and all the edges of H are in G.

1. Every graph is its own subgraph.

2. A single vertex in a graph G is a subgraph of G.

3. A single edge in G, together with its end vertices, is also a sub graph of G.

4. A subgraph of a subgraph G is a subgraph of G.

Example

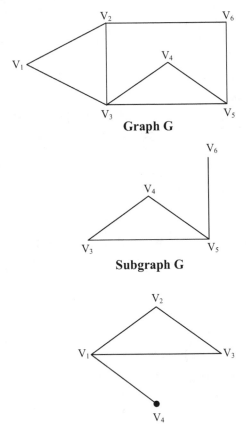

Graph G

Subgraph G

Not a Subgraph of G

Isomorphism

Two graphs G and G′ are said to be Isomorphic if there is a one-one correspondence between their vertices and between their edges. Such that the incidence relationship is preserved if G and G′ are isomorphic then G and G′ have.

1. The same number of vertices.

2. The same number of edges.

3. An equal number of vertices with d given degree.

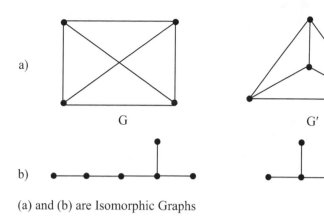

a)

G   G'

b)

(a) and (b) are Isomorphic Graphs

(c) Non-Isomorphic

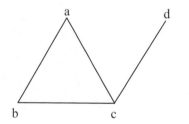   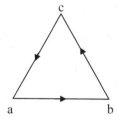

Simple Graph

A graph which has neither loops nor multiple edges (i.e.) where each edge connects two distinct vertices and no two edges connect the same pair of vertices is called a **Simple Graph**. Here multiple edge means parallel edges, Pair of nodes joined by more than one edge are called **Multiple Edges**.

Example

Un Directed Simple Graph   **Directed Simple Graph**

Multipgraph

Any graph which contains some multiple edges is called a **Multigraph**.

Note

In a multigraph, no loops are allowed.

A) Undirected Multigraph

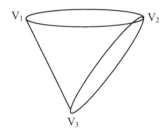

b) Directed Multigraph

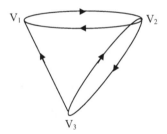

Pseudograph

A graph in which loops and multiple edges are allowed is called a **Pseudograph**.

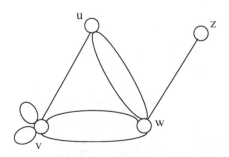

Undirected Pseudograph

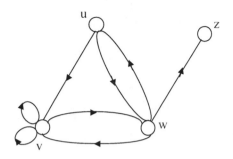

Directed Pseudograph

Walks, Paths and Circuits

A finite alternating sequence of vertices and edges of a graph G beginning and ending with vertices, such that each edge is incident with vertices preceding and following it is called a **Walk** of the graph G walk is also called **Edge Train** or **Chain**.

Note

No edge appears more than once in a walk but a vertex may appear more than once.

Vertices with which a walk begins or ends are called its **Terminal Vertices**.

If a walk begins and ends with the same vertex then it is called a **Closed Walk**. Otherwise the walk is called **Open**.

If no vertex appears more than once in an open walk than it is called a **Path**.

The number of edges in a path is called the **Length of the Path**.

Circuit

It is defined as a closed walk in which no vertex appears more than once [except the initial and final vertex i.e. **Terminal Vertices**]

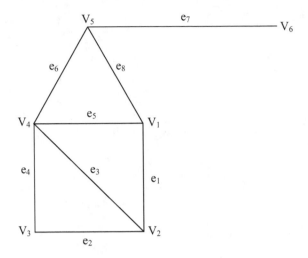

Here

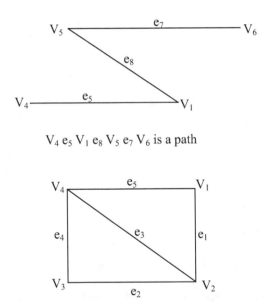

V_4 e_5 V_1 e_8 V_5 e_7 V_6 is a path

V_4 e_5 V_1 e_1 V_2 e_3 V_4 e_4 V_3 is an Open Walk but not a path because here vertex v_4 appears more than once (no vertex appears more than once an **Open Walk** (i.e.) **Path**).

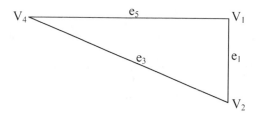

$V_2 \, e_3 \, V_4 \, e_5 \, V_1 \, e_1 \, V_2$ is a circuit or **Closed Walk.**

Connected Graph

A graph G is said to be connected if there is **atleast one path between every pair of vertices in G.** otherwise G is said to be **disconnected.**

Here disconnected graph consists of two or more **connected subgraphs.** Connected subgraph of a graph G is called a **component of the graph G.**

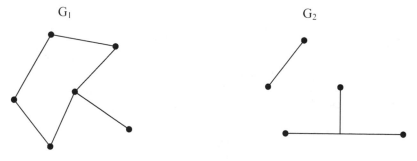

Connected Graph G1   **Disconnected Graph. It has two components**

Euler Graphs

If some closed walk in a graph G contains all the edges of G then the walk is called an **Euler Line** and the graph is called an **Euler Graph.**

[A path of a graph G is said to be **Eulerian** if it contains **all the edges of the graph.** If the path becomes a **circuit** then it is called **Eulerian circuit.** An Eulerian graph if it has Eulerian path].

Hamiltonian Graph and Circuits

A Hamiltonian circuit in a connected graph G is defined as a **closed walk** that traverses every vertex of G **exactly once except starting vertex**. A graph having **Hamiltonian Circuit** is called **Hamiltonian Graph**.

Example

Let G be a graph shown in fig. verify G has an Eulerian circuit.

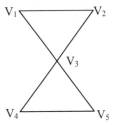

Solution

G is connected and all the vertices are having even degree

$$\deg (V_1) = \deg (V_2) = \deg (V_3) = \deg (V_4) = \deg (V_5) = 2$$

The G has a Eulerian circuit.

$$V_1 - V_3 - V_5 - V_4 - V_3 - V_2 - V_1$$

It is Eulerian circuit.

Hamiltonian

(Visit every vertex exactly once except starting vertex)

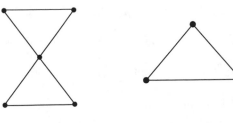

Non-Hamiltonian   **Hamiltonian**

5.4 DEFINITIONS OF PATHS, REACHABILITY AND CONNECTEDNESS

Any sequence of edges of a digraph such that the **Terminal Vertex (or) Node** of any edge in the sequence is the **Initial Node** of the edge, if any, appearing next in the sequence defines a **path of the graph**.

$$V_1 \rightarrow V_2 \rightarrow V_3 \rightarrow V_4$$

Length of the Path

The number of edges appearing in the sequence of a path is called **the length of the path**.

Simple Path

A **Simple Path** is a path in a digraph in which the edges are all distinct.

Elementary Path

An **Elementary Path** is a path in which all the nodes through which it travels are distinct.

Cycle

A path originates and ends in the same node is called a **Cycle (or) Circuit**.

Simple Cycle

Simple Cycle is a cycle if its path is simple.

Elementary Cycle

Elementary Cycle is a cycle if its path is elementary (but the initial node is the only node which appears twice).

Acyclic

Any simple digraph which does not have any cycle is called **Acyclic**.

Example 1

Determine the paths in the graph given below

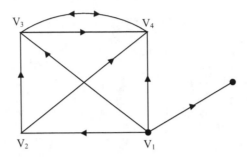

Solution

P_1 : V_1V_4

P_2 : $V_1V_2V_3V_4$

P_3 : $V_1V_2V_4V_3V_4$

P_4 : $V_1V_2V_3V_4V_3V_4$

Path	Type	Length
V_1V_4	Elementary	1
$V_1V_2V_3V_4$	Elementary	3
$V_1V_2V_4V_3V_4$	Simple	4
$V_1V_2V_3V_4V_3V_4$	Neither Simple Nor Elementary	5

Example 2

Find some simple and elementary cycles in the graph given below

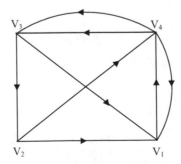

Solution

C_1 : $V_1V_4V_3V_2V_1$

C_4 : $V_1V_4V_3V_4V_1$

Cycle	Type
C_1	Elementary
C_2	Simple

Reachable

A node V of a simple digraph is said to be reachable (accessible) from u if there is a path from u to v.

Example 1

Determine the reachability and accessibility of each vertex from every other vertex for the following graph G.

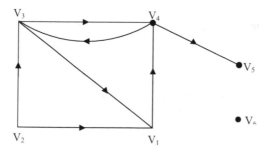

Solution

Reachability of V_j from V_i						
V_i / V_j	V_1	V_2	V_3	V_4	V_5	V_6
V_1	Yes	No	Yes	Yes	Yes	No
V_2	Yes	Yes	Yes	Yes	Yes	No
V_3	Yes	No	Yes	Yes	Yes	No
V_4	Yes	No	Yes	Yes	Yes	No
V_5	No	No	No	No	Yes	No
V_6	No	No	No	No	No	Yes

Consider the vertex V_1 in row, compared with all column vertices.

V_1 to V_1, so V_1 is Possible, put yes in the table

V_1 to V_4 to V_3, so V_3 is Possible, put yes in the table

V_1 to V_4 so V_4 is Possible, put yes in the table

V_1 to V_4 to V_5 so V_5 is Possible, put yes in the table

5.5 MATRIX REPRESENTATION OF GRAPHS

Adjacency Matrix

$$a_{ij} \quad = \quad \begin{cases} 1 & \text{if there is an edge between } i^{th} \text{ and } j^{th} \text{ vertices} \\ 0 & \text{if there is no edge between them} \end{cases}$$

Example 1

Find the Adjacency matrix of the given graph.

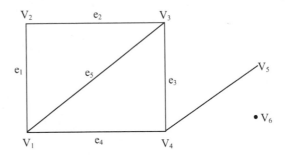

$$A = \begin{array}{c} \\ V_1 \\ V_2 \\ V_3 \\ V_4 \\ V_5 \\ V_6 \end{array} \begin{array}{c} V_1\ V_2\ V_3\ V_4\ V_5\ V_6 \\ \begin{bmatrix} 0 & 1 & 1 & 1 & 0 & 0 \\ 1 & 0 & 1 & 0 & 0 & 0 \\ 1 & 1 & 0 & 1 & 0 & 0 \\ 1 & 0 & 1 & 0 & 1 & 0 \\ 0 & 0 & 0 & 1 & 0 & 0 \\ 0 & 0 & 0 & 0 & 0 & 0 \end{bmatrix} \end{array}$$ where A is adjacency matrix of the given graph.

Example 2

Find $Y = A + A^2 + A^3 + A^4$ where A is adjacency matrix of the following graph

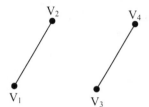

Solution

$$A = \begin{array}{c} \\ V_1 \\ V_2 \\ V_3 \\ V_4 \end{array} \begin{array}{cccc} V_1 & V_2 & V_3 & V_4 \\ \begin{bmatrix} 0 & 1 & 0 & 0 \\ 1 & 0 & 0 & 0 \\ 0 & 0 & 0 & 1 \\ 0 & 0 & 1 & 0 \end{bmatrix} \end{array}$$

$$A^2 = A \cdot A = \begin{bmatrix} 1 & 0 & 0 & 0 \\ 0 & 1 & 0 & 0 \\ 0 & 0 & 1 & 0 \\ 0 & 0 & 0 & 1 \end{bmatrix}$$

$$A^3 = \begin{bmatrix} 0 & 1 & 0 & 0 \\ 1 & 0 & 0 & 0 \\ 0 & 0 & 0 & 1 \\ 0 & 0 & 1 & 0 \end{bmatrix}$$

$$A^4 = \begin{bmatrix} 1 & 0 & 0 & 0 \\ 0 & 1 & 0 & 0 \\ 0 & 0 & 1 & 0 \\ 0 & 0 & 0 & 1 \end{bmatrix}$$

$$Y = A + A^2 + A^3 + A^4$$

$$= \begin{bmatrix} 2 & 2 & 0 & 0 \\ 2 & 2 & 0 & 0 \\ 0 & 0 & 2 & 2 \\ 0 & 0 & 2 & 2 \end{bmatrix}$$

Example 3

The given graph is undirected graph.

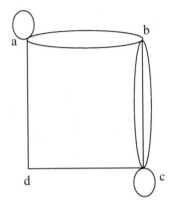

$$
\text{Then} \quad
\begin{array}{c}
 \\
a \\
b \\
c \\
d
\end{array}
\begin{array}{cccc}
a & b & c & d \\
\begin{pmatrix}
1 & 2 & 0 & 1 \\
2 & 0 & 3 & 0 \\
1 & 3 & 1 & 1 \\
1 & 0 & 1 & 0
\end{pmatrix}
\end{array}
$$

The given graph is directed graph

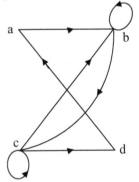

$$
\text{Then} \quad
\begin{array}{c}
 \\
a \\
b \\
c \\
d
\end{array}
\begin{array}{cccc}
a & b & c & d \\
\begin{pmatrix}
0 & 1 & 0 & 0 \\
0 & 1 & 1 & 0 \\
0 & 1 & 1 & 1 \\
1 & 0 & 0 & 0
\end{pmatrix}
\end{array}
$$

Incidence Matrix

$$b_{ij} = \begin{cases} 1 & \text{if the } j^{th} \text{ edge is incident on } i^{th} \text{ vertex} \\ 0 & \text{Otherwise} \end{cases}$$

Example 1

Construct the incidence matrix B for the following graph G and give your observations regarding the entries of B.

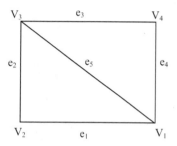

Solution

$$\begin{array}{c|ccccc} & e_1 & e_2 & e_3 & e_4 & e_5 \\ \hline V_1 & 1 & 0 & 0 & 1 & 1 \\ V_2 & 1 & 1 & 0 & 0 & 0 \\ V_3 & 0 & 1 & 1 & 0 & 1 \\ V_4 & 0 & 0 & 1 & 1 & 0 \end{array} = B$$

Note : Edges incident on particular vertex.

Example

Example 2

For the diagraph given below write down the Incidence matrix A and Adjacency matrix X

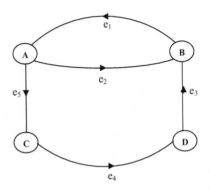

Solution

$$
\begin{array}{c}
\quad\quad A\ B\ C\ D \\
X = \begin{array}{c} A \\ B \\ C \\ D \end{array}
\left[\begin{array}{cccc}
0 & 1 & 1 & 0 \\
1 & 0 & 0 & 0 \\
0 & 0 & 0 & 1 \\
0 & 1 & 0 & 0
\end{array} \right]
\end{array}
$$

Note

There is an edge between i^{th} and j^{th} vertices $= 1$

There is no edge between i^{th} and j^{th} vertices $= 0$

Incidence Matrix

$$
\begin{array}{c}
\quad\quad e_1\ \ e_2\ \ e_3\ \ e_4\ \ e_5 \\
A = \begin{array}{c} A \\ B \\ C \\ D \end{array}
\left[\begin{array}{ccccc}
-1 & 1 & 0 & 0 & 1 \\
1 & -1 & -1 & 0 & 0 \\
0 & 0 & 0 & 1 & -1 \\
0 & 0 & 1 & -1 & 0
\end{array} \right]
\end{array}
$$

Note

For Incidence matrix,

Out degree edge $= 1$

In degree edge $= -1$

Path Matrix or Reachability

Let G = G (V, E) be a directed graph.

$$P_{ij} = \begin{cases} 1 & \text{if there is a path from } V_i \text{ to } V_j \\ 0 & \text{Otherwise} \end{cases}$$

Example 1

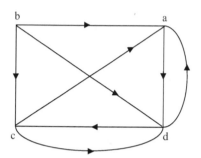

Solution

$$P = \begin{matrix} & \begin{matrix} a & b & c & d \end{matrix} \\ \begin{matrix} a \\ b \\ c \\ d \end{matrix} & \begin{pmatrix} 1 & 0 & 1 & 1 \\ 1 & 0 & 1 & 1 \\ 1 & 0 & 1 & 1 \\ 1 & 0 & 1 & 1 \end{pmatrix} \end{matrix}$$

a → d → c → a is example for path.

5.6 SHORTEST PATH IN A WEIGHTED GRAPH ALGORITHM

Dijkstra's Shortest Path Algorithm

Dijkstra's Algorithm seems to be the most efficient one among several algorithms proposed for the shortest path between a specified vertex pair.

Let the problem be to find the shortest path from vertex 'a' to vertex 'b' in a connected weighted graph.

Let w(i, j) > 0 denote the weight of the edge (i, j) of the graph and let the label of any vertex x ∈ G be denoted by L(x).

(1) Initialisation Set L(a) = 0. For all vertices x ≠ a, set L(x) = ∞. Let T be the set

of vertices.

(2) If b ∈ T stop. L(b) is the Length of the shortest path from a to b.

(3) Get new vertex. Choose V∈T with the smallest value of L(V) set T : = T-{V}.

(4) Revise labels. For each vertex x ∈ T adjacent to v.

Set L(x) = min {L(x), L(v) + w(v, x)} Go to step 2.

Example 1

Use Dijkstra's shortest path algorithm to determine the shortest path between A

and H in the following graph.

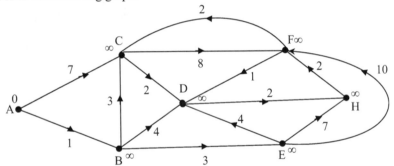

Solution

Label all vertices to ∞ except A vertex it is assigned to 0.

L(A) = 0

Consider the nearest vertices to A (i.e.) B & C.

L(B) = min (L(B), L(A) + weight (A, B)}

= min (∞, 0 + 1)   = 1

L(C) = min (∞, 0 + 7}   = 7

Here minimum is L(B) so it is selected. L(B) = 1, put the values 7 in vertex C

and 1 in vertex B.

Consider the nearest vertices for B, (i.e.) C, E and D

We know C vertex has the value 7

∴   L(C)   = min (7, 1 + 3)   =   4

       L(E)   = min (∞, 1 + 3)   =   4

       L(D)   = min (∞, 1 + 4)   =   5

∴ Here minimum is E and C select any one.

Select C,

Consider vertices near to C vertex. They are F and D.

L(F)   = min(∞, 4 + 8)   =   12

L(D)   = min(5, 4 + 2)   =   5

Select D

       H is the nearest vertex

       L(H)   = min{∞, L(D) + weight (D, H)}   = min {∞, 5 + 2} = 7

       The process terminates

       ∴ The length of the shortest path = 7 and the shortest path.

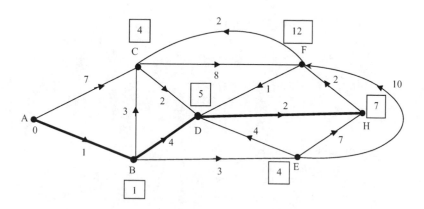

∴ The shortest path A→B→D→H

Example 2

Find the length of the shortest path from the vertex A to H by using Dijkstra's shortest

path algorithm.

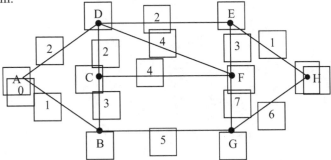

Solution

L(A) = 0, consider the nearest vertices to A (i.e.) B and D, put B = ∞ and D = ∞

L(B) = min {L(B), L(A) + weight (A, B)}

= min{∞, 0+1} = 1

L(D) = min {L(D), L(A) + weight (A, D)}

= min{∞, 0 + 2} = 2

Select B (it is minimum)

L(B) = 1

L(C) = min {L(C), L(B) + weight (B, C)}

= min{∞, 1 + 3}   = 4

L(G) = min {L(G), L(B) + weight (B, G)}

= min{∞, 1 + 5}   = 6

Here   C has got minimum value, so select C

L(F) = min {L(F), L(C) + weight (C, F)}

= min {∞, 4 + 4}   = 8

L(D) = min {L(D), L(C) + weight (C, D)}

     = min {2, 4 + 2}   = 2

Here, D has got minimum value, so select D

L(E) = min {L(E), L(D) + weight (D, E)}

       = min {∞, 2+2}   = 4

L(F) = min {L(F), L(D) + weight (D, F)}

       = min {8, 2+4}   = 6

Select E it is minimum.

L(H) = min{∞, 4+1}   = 5

L(F) = min{6, 4+3}   = 6

∴ L(H) = 5

The length of the shortest path is 5.

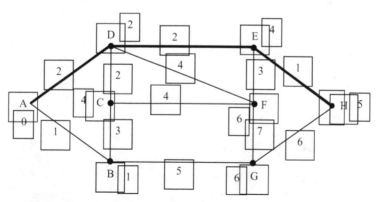

The path is A→D→E→H

Example 3

Apply Dijkastra's algorithm to the graph given below and find the shortest path from a to f.

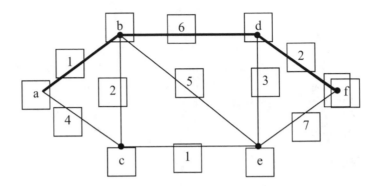

Solution

Put L(a) = 0, remaining vertices are ∞

Consider vertex a, the nearest vertices are b & c.

L(b) = min {L(b), L(a) + weight (a, b)}

    = min {∞, 0 + 1} = 1

L(c) = min {L(c), L(a) + weight (a, c)}

    = min {∞, 0+4} = 4

Here b is smallest, select b.

L(d) = min {L(d), L(b) + weight (b, d)}

    = min {∞, 1+6} = 7

L(c) = min {4, 1+2} = 3

L(e) = min{∞, 1 + 5} = 6

Here c has got minimum value, so select c.

L(e) = min {6, 3+1} = 4

L(b) = min {1, 3+2} = 1

We have already select b. So select e.

L(f) $= \min \{\infty, 4 + 7\}$ $= 11$

L(d) $= \min \{7, 4 + 3\}$ $= 7$

Select d

L(f) $= \min \{11, 7+2\}$ $= 9$

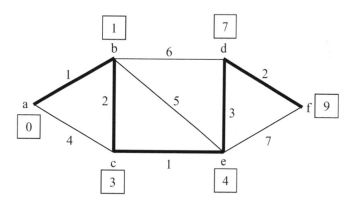

The shortest distance from a to f is 9.

The shortest path is

a→b→c→e→d→f

5.7 SHORTEST PATH IN A GRAPH WITHOUT WEIGHTS

Algorithm : Breadth First Search Algorithm (BFS)

Step 1

Label vertex S with 0, set i = 0

Step 2

Find all unlabelled vertices in G which are adjacent to vertices labelled i. There

are no such vertices then t is not connected to S. If there are such vertices label them

i + 1.

Step 3

If t is labelled go to step 4, if not increase it to i + 1 and go to step 2.

Step 4

The length of a shortest path from S to i + 1. Stop.

Once the length of the shortest path is found from the previous algorithm we use the **Back Tracking Algorithm** to find the actual shortest path from S to t. This algorithm uses the label $\lambda(V)$ which are generated in the **BFS** algorithm.

Back Tracking Algorithm for a Shortest Path

Step 1

Set $i = \lambda(t)$ and assign $v_i = t$.

Step 2

Find a vertex u adjacent to v_i and with $\lambda(u) = i - 1$. Assign $v_{i-1} = u$

Step 3

If $i = 1$, stop

If not, decrease, i to i-1 and go to step 2.

Example

Find the shortest path from vertex s to t and its length from the graph given below.

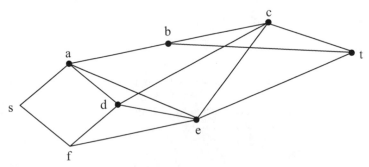

Solution

Using BFS, label s as 0. Then a and f are labelled $0 + 1 = 1$. Then b, d, e are labelled $1 + 1 = 2$. Then c and t are labelled $2 + 1 = 3$. Since t is labelled 3, the length of a shortest path from S to t is 3.

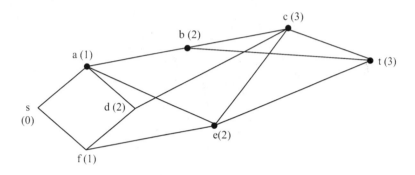

Now using second algorithm. Since $\lambda(t) = 3$, we start $i = 3$ and $v_i = t$.

We choose e (or) b adjacent to $v_3 = t$, with $\lambda(e) = 2$, and assign $v_2 = e$.

Next, we choose f adjacent to $v_2 = e$ with $\lambda(f) = 1$ and assign $v_1 = f$. Finally we take S adjacent to f with $\lambda(S) = 0$ and assign $v_0 = S$. This gives the shortest path $v_0, v_1, v_2 \ldots, v_3 = $ sfet from s to t.

Note : There could be several paths from s to t, to be precise, there are 3 (i.e) saet, sabt and sfet.

5.8 TRAVELING SALESMAN PROBLEM

Given a weighted graph the problem of finding a circuit $(e_1, e_2, ..., e_n)$ that visits every vertex exactly once and minimizes the sum of weights is called the **Traveling Sales Person Problem**.

Example 1

Solve the following Traveling Salesman Problem.

From City	To City				
	A	**B**	**C**	**D**	**E**
A	∞	13	19	16	15
B	14	∞	18	15	16
C	14	18	∞	14	13
D	13	17	16	∞	18
E	19	17	16	17	∞

Solution

First we take shortest value in from city (i.e.) D.

Start at D and go to A (13 is smallest)

Go from A to B (13 is smallest)

Go from B to E (Here A and D have already been selected. So next smallest value is E (i.e.) 16).

Since A, B & D have already been selected

Go from E to C (16 is smallest)

Go from C to D (to complete the circuit we are selecting the value D is 14)

Sum of weights   =   13 + 13 + 16 + 16 + 14   = 72

∴ The optimal route is

$$D \to A \to B \to E \to C \to D \quad = \quad 72$$

With sum of the weights as 72.

Example 2

Solve the following Travelling Salesman Problem

From City	To City				
	1	2	3	4	5
1	∞	1	7	4	3
2	2	∞	6	3	4
3	1	6	∞	2	1
4	1	5	4	∞	6
5	7	5	4	5	∞

Solution

$$3 \to 1 \to 2 \to 4 \to 5 \to 3 = 15$$

For start at 3 and go to 1   [1 is smallest]

Go from 1 to 2   [1 is smallest]

Go from 2 to 4   [since 1 is already selected next smallest value of 2 is 3]

Go from 4 to 5   [since 1, 3 and 2 are already selected. The next smallest

value of 4 is 6]

Go from 5 to 3   [To complete the circuit we are selecting the value 3, 4]

Sum of Weights

$$1 + 1 + 3 + 6 + 4 = 15$$

The optimal route is

$$3 \to 1 \to 2 \to 4 \to 5 \to 3$$

With the sum of weights as 15.

5.9 BINARY TREES

Tree

A tree is a connected graph without any **Cycles** and also it does not have **Self Loop and Parallel Edges**.

Binary Tree

If each internal vertex of a rooted tree has at most two children, then such a tree is called **Binary Tree**.

Example

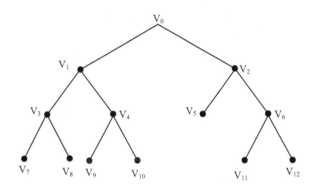

Here V_0 is the root, V_1 is the **left sub tree**, V_2 is the **right sub tree**

Here V_1 is non-empty then its root is called left-successor of the root vertex.

Here V_2 is non-empty then its root is called right-successor of the root vertex.

A vertex of degree one is called **Pendant Vertex**.

Forest

A graph with no cycle, where each node (vertex) has one or no predecessors is called **Forest**.

Example

Consider the binary tree shown above fig. Find the level and height or depth of each vertex & list the children of each vertex.

Solution

Level	0	1	2	3
Vertex	V_0	V_1, V_2	V_3, V_4, V_5, V_6	$V_7, V_8, V_9, V_{10}, V_{11}, V_{12}$

(2) Height of each vertex

Height	1	2	3	4
Vertex	V_0	V_1, V_2	V_3, V_4, V_5, V_6	$V_7, V_8, V_9, V_{10}, V_{11}, V_{12}$

(3) Children of each vertex

Level	V_0	V_1	V_2	V_3	V_4	V_6
Children	V_1, V_2	V_3, V_4	V_5, V_6	V_7, V_8	V_9, V_{10}	V_{11}, V_{12}

Tree of an Algebraic Expression

An Algebraic expression E containing operands and binary operators can be represented by using a binary tree called **Expression Binary Tree**.

Expression Tree : In expression tree we consider 3 different orders (i) Inorder, (ii) Preorder (iii) Postorder.

In Order : Left, Root, Right.

Pre Order (Prefix or Polish Form) : Root, Left, Right.

Post Order (Postfix or Reverse Polish Form) : Left, Right, Root

Example

$(a - b) * c$

5.10 TRAVERSALS OF BINARY TREES AND EXPRESSION TREES

There are 3 Traversals called Preorder Traversal.

❖ Pre Order Traversal

❖ Inorder Traversal

❖ Postorder Traversal

(1) Preorder Traversal

a. Visit the root of the tree

b. Preorder traverse the left subtree

c. Preorder traverse the right subtree

So preorder traversal is used root / left / right

Binary Tree

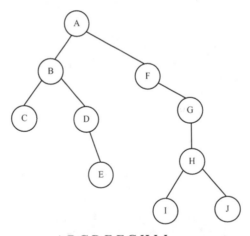

A B C D E F G H I J

Postorder Traversal

a. Postorder traverse the left sub tree.

b. Postorder traverse the right sub tree.

c. Visit the root of the tree.

The order in which the vertices of binary tree in the figure is processed if post order traversal is used : Left / Right / Root.

CEDBIJHGFA

Inorder Traversal

a. Inorder traverse the left sub tree.

b. Visit the root of the tree.

c. Inorder traverse the right sub tree.

The order in which the vertices of binary tree in the figure is processed if inorder traversal is used : Left / Root / Right.

CBDEAFIHJG

Expression Trees

The standard way of representing arithmetic expression is called the infix form of an expression

$$(a-b) * c + \frac{d}{e}$$

The variables a, b, c, d, e referred to as operands, operators are +, -, * and /.

5.11 INFIX, POSTFIX AND PREFIX EXPRESSIONS

Infix Notation

The notation used in writing the operator between operands is called **Infix Notation**.

Left root right

Postfix Notation (Reverse Polish Notation)

Prefix Notation (Polish Notation)

Infix	Prefix (Parentheses are not needed)	Postfix (Parentheses are not needed)
1) (x*y) + z	+ * xyz	xy*z+
2) ((x + y) * (z + t))	* + xy + zt	xy + zt + *
3) ((x + y * z) – (u/v + w))	-+ x*yz + /uvw	xyz*+uv/w+-

Example 1

Represent the expression as a binary tree and write the prefix and postfix forms

of the expression.

$$A * B - C^D + E/F$$

Solution

The binary tree representing the given expression is shown below.

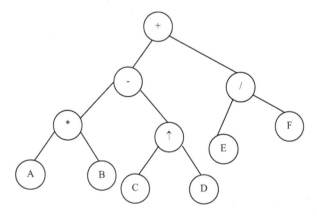

Prefix   : + - * AB ↑CD / EF

Postfix   : AB * CD ↑ - EF / +

Example 2

The binary tree representation of the expression $((a-b) * c + (\frac{d}{e}))$

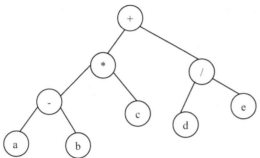

Prefix form (or) Polish Notation   : + * - abc / de

Postfix form (or) Reverse Polish Notation   : ab - c * de + /

Expression Tree

(i) (A + B) * (C + D)

Inorder	(A+B) * (C+D)	
Preorder	*+ AB + CD	
Postorder	AB + CD +*	

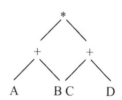

(ii) (A↑2 + B) + C

Inorder	(A↑2+B) + C
Preorder	++↑ A2 BC
Postorder	A2↑B + C +

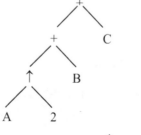

(iii) (a * (b + c)) * (e + f)

Inorder	(a*(b+c)) * (e+f)
Preorder	** a + bc + ef
Postorder	abc +* ef +*

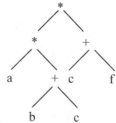

CHAPTER – VI

6. GRAMMARS AND LANGUAGE

6.1 PSG (Phrase Structure Grammar)

Definitions

A Phrase-Structure Grammar (or grammar) G is defined by $G = (V_N, V_T, S, P)$

Where

(i) V_N : a finite non-empty set of non-terminal symbols.

(ii) V_T : a finite non-empty set of terminal symbols, where $V_N \cap V_T = \phi$

(iii) S : a distinguished element of V_N called **starting symbol** or among all the non-terminals in V_N, there is a special non-terminal in V_N called the starting symbol.

(iv) P : a finite non-empty set called the set of **Productions**, each of the form $\alpha \rightarrow \beta$, where $\alpha \in (V_N \cup V_T)^+$, $\beta \in (V_N \cup V_T)^*$.

Note

In general an element (α, β) is written as $\alpha \rightarrow \beta$ and is called a **Production Rule**

(or) a Rewriting Rule.

NOTATION AND MEANING

(i) $V_T = \{a, b, c, \ldots, x, y, z, 0, 1, 2, \ldots 9, \ldots\}$ (small letters, set of terminals). Terminals symbols are used to make up the sentences in the language. **Eg.** the set {a, the dog, cat, meet, runs}

(ii) $V_N = \{A,B,C,\ldots\ldots,X,Y,X,\ldots..\}$ (capital letters, set of non-terminals). The non-terminals symbols are intermediate symbols which are used to describe the structure (syntax) of the sentences.

   Eg. {SENTENCE, NOUN, ARTICLE, VERB, ...}

(iii)   P : Set of productions. The productions are grammatical rules that specify how sentences in the (Formal) languages can be made up. A production is of the form of $\alpha \rightarrow \beta$, where $\alpha \in (V_N \cup V_T)^+$, $\beta \in (V_N \cup V_T)^*$ i.e. α must include atleast one non-terminal where as β can consists of any combination of terminals and non-terminals A production specifies that string α can be transformed into string β.

   Eg. {S→aAB, A→aB, B→b}

(iv)   S : The starting symbol is a special non-terminal that begins the generation of any sentence in the language.

   In the above example SENTENCE is the starting symbol.

Note : If G is a phrase structure grammar, L(G) is the set of strings that can be obtained by starting with S and applying the production rules a finite number of times until no non-terminal characters remain.

Example Problems

(1) The language $L(G_3) = \{a^n b^n c^n \, / \, n \geq 1\}$ is generated by the grammar

$G_3 = \{\{S,B,C\}, \{a,b,c\}, S,P\}$ where P consists of the productions

S→aSBC, S→aBC, CB→BC, aB→ab, bB→bb, bC→bc, cC→cc.

Solution

   The following is the derivative for the string $a^2 b^2 c^2$

   S $\Rightarrow$ a $\underline{S}$BC $\Rightarrow$ aaB$\underline{CB}$C $\Rightarrow$ aa$\underline{B}$BCC

$\Rightarrow$ aab<u>B</u>CC $\Rightarrow$ aabb<u>C</u>C $\Rightarrow$ aabb<u>c</u>C

$\Rightarrow$ aabbcc $\Rightarrow$ $a^2b^2c^2$

(2) Construct the grammar for the language

L(G) =   {aaaa, aabb, bbaa, bbbb}

Solution

Since L(G) has a finite number of strings, we can simply list all strings in the language. Therefore

Let V_T={a,b}, V_N={S} and S be the starting symbol, P be the set of productions.

i.e., G = (V_N,V_T, S, P) is a grammar with the set of productions

S→aaaa, S→aabb, S→bbaa, S→bbbb

(3) Construct the grammar for the language

L(G) = {a^i, b^{2i} / i ≥ 1}

Solution

Let V_T = {a,b}, V_N = {S} and S be the starting symbol, P be the set of productions given by

S→aSbb,   S→abb

For example if i = 3, then we obtain the string

aaabbbbbb   = a^3b^6 as follows

S $\Rightarrow$ a<u>S</u>bb $\Rightarrow$ aa<u>S</u>bbbb $\Rightarrow$ aaabbbbbb $\Rightarrow$ a^3b^6

G = ({a,b},{S},S,P) is the grammar for the given language.

Note : The language L(G), generated by phrase-structure grammar (PSG) is called **Phrase-Structure Language (PSL).**

6.2 TYPES OF GRAMMAR

Let V_T =   {a, b} where a, b are arbitrary

       V_N =   {A, B} where A, B are arbitrary

And α, β are arbitrary strings of terminals and non-terminals.

1. Type-0 grammar

A phrase structure grammar with no restrictions is called a type-0 grammar. A language that can be defined by a type-0 grammar is called **type-0 language**.

2. Type-1 grammar or context-sensitive grammar (CSG)

In this grammar, for every production on $\alpha \rightarrow \beta$, the length of β is larger than or equal to the length of α. i.e. $\alpha \rightarrow \beta$ with $|\alpha| \leq |\beta|$, $\alpha \, \varepsilon \, V_N$

Eg : A→ab, A→aA, aAb→aBcb

The name context sensitive refers to the fact that when we apply a rule $x\alpha y \Rightarrow x\beta y$ it means that α is replaced by β in the context of x and y.

The language that can be generated by a type-1 grammar is called a **type-1 or context-sensitive language (CSL)**.

3. Type-2 grammar or context-sensitive grammar (CFG)

In this grammar, every production is of the form A→ β. In otherwords, in any production, the left hand string is always a single non-terminal.

A language that can be generated by a type-2 grammar is called a **type-2 Language or a Context-Free Language (CFL)**.

Example

The Language $L(G) = \{a^k b^k / k \geq 1\}$ is a type-2 language, because it can specified by the type-2 grammar, $A \rightarrow aAB, A \rightarrow ab, B \rightarrow b$.

i.e.,   A $\Rightarrow$ a$\underline{A}$B   Eg : for $a^2 b^2, k = 2$

              $\Rightarrow$ aab$\underline{B}$

              $\Rightarrow$ aabb

              $\Rightarrow$ $a^2 b^2$

4. Type-3 grammar or regular grammar (RG) (or) Right-linear grammar.

A grammar is said to be a type-3 grammar if all production in the grammar of the forms.

A→a,   A→aB

In other words, in any production, the left hand string is always a single non-terminal and the right hand string is either a terminal or a terminal followed by a non-terminal.

A language that can be generated by a type-3 grammar is called a **type-3 Language or a Regular Language (RL) or a Regular set**.

Example Problems

(1) Construct the grammar for the language.

Solution

Let $V_N = \{S, B, C\}$, $V_T = \{a, b\}$ and S be the starting symbol, P be the set of productions given by

S→aS, S→aB, B→bC, C→aC, C→a.

For a^2ba^3 S $\Rightarrow a\underline{S} \Rightarrow aa\underline{B} \Rightarrow aab\underline{C}$

$\Rightarrow aaba C \Rightarrow aabaa C \Rightarrow aabaaa \Rightarrow a^2ba^3$

Clearly this grammar G = {V_N, V_T, S, P} is a Regular Grammar and the language

L(G) = {$a^n b \ a^m/n$, m ≥ 1} is a Regular Language.

(2) Construct a phrase structure grammar G such that L(G) is equal to the language L = {$x^n \ y^m/n$, n ≥ 2, m non-negative and even}

Solution

Let V_T = {x, y}, V_N = {S}, S the starting symbol and P be the set of productions given by S → Syy, S → xS, S → xx.

For example, we obtain the string x^4y^2 as follows :

S → x$\underline{S}$ $\Rightarrow$ xx$\underline{S}$ $\Rightarrow$ xx$\underline{S}$yy $\Rightarrow$ xxxx yyy = x^4y^2.

$\therefore$ G = ({x, y}, {S}, S, P) is the grammar for the given language.

(3) Define the following languages over B = {0, 1} with phrase structure grammars. Which of these languages are regular ?

(i) the string with an odd number of characters

(ii) the string of length 4 or less.

Solution

(i) Let V_T = B = {0, 1}, V_N = {S, A}, S be the starting symbol and P be the set of productions given by

S → 00S, S → 01S, S → 10S, S → 11S, S → A, A → 0, A → 1

This is a regular grammar

(ii) Let $V_T = B = \{0, 1\}$, $V_N = \{S, A, B, C\}$ S the starting symbol and P be the set of productions given by

$\quad$ $S \rightarrow 0A$, $S \rightarrow 1A$, $S \rightarrow \lambda$, $A \rightarrow 0B$, $A \rightarrow 1B$, $A \rightarrow \lambda$.

$\quad$ $B \rightarrow \lambda$, $C \rightarrow 0$, $C \rightarrow \lambda$. This is regular grammar.

(4) Define the set of string in B* for which all 0's precede all 1's with a regular grammar.

Solution

$\quad$ Let $V_T = B = \{0, 1\}$, $V_N = \{S, A\}$ S the starting symbol and P be the set of productions given by $S \rightarrow 0S$, $S \rightarrow A$, $A \rightarrow 1A$, $A \rightarrow \lambda$.

6.3 PRODUCTIONS

PROBLEMS

(1) Let $G_2 = \{\{E, F, T\}, \{a, +, *, (,)\}, E, \phi\}$ where ϕ consists of the productions.

$\quad$ $E \rightarrow \quad E + T$

$\quad$ $E \rightarrow \quad T$

$\quad$ $T \rightarrow \quad T * F$

$\quad$ $T \rightarrow \quad F$

$\quad$ $F \rightarrow \quad (E)$

$\quad$ $F \rightarrow \quad a$

$\quad$ Where the variables E, T and F represented the names "expression, term and factor". The derivation for the expression a * a + a is

Solution

$\quad$ E $\quad \rightarrow \quad$ E + T

$\quad\quad\quad \rightarrow \quad$ T + T

$\quad\quad\quad \rightarrow \quad$ T * F + T

$\quad\quad\quad \rightarrow \quad$ F * F + T $\quad \rightarrow a * F + T \Rightarrow a * a + T \Rightarrow a * a + F \Rightarrow a * a + a$

(2) Let the Language $L(G_3) = \{a^n b^n c^n \mid n \geq 1\}$ is generated by the following grammar.

$G_3 = \{\{S, B, C\}, \{a, b, c\}, S, \phi\}$

Where ϕ consists of the productions

$S \rightarrow aSBC$

$S \rightarrow aBC$

$CB \rightarrow BC$

$aB \rightarrow ab$

$bB \rightarrow bb$

$bc \rightarrow bc$

$cC \rightarrow cc$

The following is a derivation for the string $a^2 b^2 c^2$

Solution

$S \quad \Rightarrow aSBC$

$\Rightarrow aaBCBC$

$\Rightarrow aaBBCC$

$\Rightarrow aabBCC$

$\Rightarrow aabbCC$

$\Rightarrow aabbcC$

$\Rightarrow aabbcc$

$\Rightarrow a^2 b^2 c^2$

(3) Let the Language $L(G_4) = \{a^n ba^n \mid n \geq 1\}$ is generated by the following grammar.

$G_4 = \{\{S, C\}, \{a, b\}, S, \phi\}$

Where ϕ consists of the productions

$S \rightarrow aCa$

$C \rightarrow aCa$

$C \rightarrow b$

A derivation for $a^2 ba^2$ consists of the following steps

Solution

$S \Rightarrow aCa \quad \Rightarrow \quad aaCaa \quad \Rightarrow \quad aabaa \quad \Rightarrow \quad a^2 ba^2$

(4) Let the Language $L(G_5) = \{a^n ba^m \mid n. m \geq 1\}$ is generated by the following

grammar. $G_5 = \{\{S, A, B, C\}, \{a, b\}, S, \phi\}$

Where the set of production is

$S \rightarrow aS$

$S \rightarrow aB$

$B \rightarrow bC$

$C \rightarrow aC$

$C \rightarrow a$

The sentence $a^2 ba^3$ has the following derivation

$S \Rightarrow aS \quad \Rightarrow aaB \quad \Rightarrow \quad aabC \Rightarrow aabaC \quad \Rightarrow aabaaC \quad \Rightarrow aabaaa$

$\Rightarrow a^2 ba^3$

6.4 DERIVATION TREE

A derivation tree is a pictorial form of representing a derivation.

Example

1) Let G = ({S, A}, {a, b}, S, P), where P consists of the production rules.

$$S :: = \quad aAS \,|\, a$$
$$A :: = \quad SbA \,|\, SS \,|\, ba$$

The derivation for the sentential form aabbaa is

$$S \Rightarrow a\underline{A}S \Rightarrow a\underline{S}bAS \Rightarrow aab\underline{A}S \Rightarrow aabba\underline{S} \Rightarrow aabbaa$$

Let us now illustrate how to construct a derivation tree corresponding to this derivation. This process is shown as a sequence of diagram.

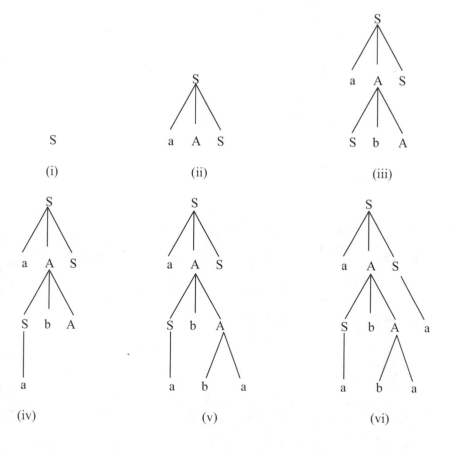

(i)   (ii)   (iii)

(iv)   (v)   (vi)

The last diagram represents the derivation tree for the given sentential form. In the derivation tree, if we read the labels of the leaves in left-to-right order. We get sentential form aabbaa. i.e., S $\overset{*}{\Rightarrow}$ aabbaa.

Now consider the subtree.

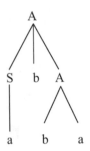

Here the label of the root of the subtree is A. So it is an "A-tree" and A $\overset{*}{\Rightarrow}$ abba. A derivation in this case is A $\Rightarrow$ $\underline{S}$ b A $\Rightarrow$ ab A $\Rightarrow$ abba.

(2) Let G={V_N, V_T, <identifier>, P} be a grammar, where V_N={<identifier>, <letter>, <digit>}. V_T = {a to z, 0 to 9} and P consists of the productions :

<identifier> : : = <letter> | <identifier> <letter> | <identifier> <digit>

      <letter> : : = a | b | c .... | x | y | z

      <digits> : : = 0 | 1 | 2 .... | 7 | 8 | 9

The two possible derivations for the sentential form a2 are

       <identifier> $\Rightarrow$ <identifier> <digit> $\Rightarrow$ <letter> <digit>

                     $\Rightarrow$ a <digit> $\Rightarrow$ a2

and   <identifier> $\Rightarrow$ <identifier> <digit>

                     $\Rightarrow$ <identifier> 2 $\Rightarrow$ <letter> 2 $\Rightarrow$ a2

Both of these derivations have the same derivation tree

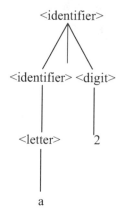

Therefore, for each derivation tree there exists atleast one derivation and in general any sentential form can have a derivation tree. The leaf nodes in such a tree can designate terminal and non-terminal symbols.

Note : A sentential form may have more than one derivation tree.

(3) For the grammar G defined by : S→AB, B→a, A→Aa, A→bB, B→Sb. Give derivation trees for the following sentential forms (i) baSb (ii) baabaab (iii) bBABb.

Solution

(i) The derivation for the sentential form baSb is

$S \Rightarrow \underline{A}B \Rightarrow b\underline{B}B \Rightarrow ba\underline{B} \Rightarrow ba\,Sb$

The corresponding derivation tree is

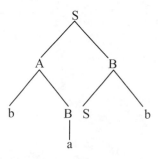

(ii) The derivation for the sentential form baabaab is

S ⇒ A̲B ⇒ A̲a B ⇒ b B̲aB ⇒ baa B̲ ⇒ baa S̲ b

⇒ baa A̲ B b ⇒ baab B̲ B b ⇒ baaba B̲ b ⇒ baabaab

The corresponding derivation tree is

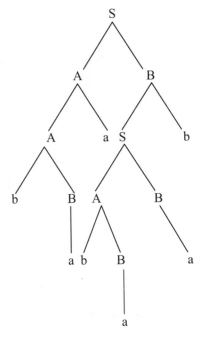

(iii) The derivation for the sentential form bBABb is

S ⇒ A̲B ⇒ b B B̲ ⇒ b BS̲b ⇒ bB A B b

The corresponding derivation tree is

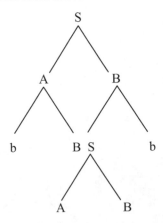

(iv) Consider the derivation tree of a sentential form α in the language L of a context-free grammar G. (i) Find α (ii) Which terminal, non terminals and productions must lie in G ?

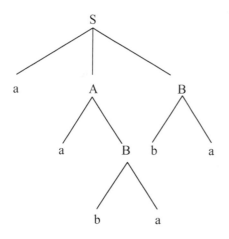

Solution

(i) Reading the labels of the leaves from left to right yields α = aababa.

(ii) G must contain V_T={a,b}, V_N={S,A,B} and the productions S→aAB, A→aB, B→ba.

6.5 LEFT MOST AND RIGHT MOST DERIVATIONS

Definition

Given a grammar G={V_N,V_T,S,P}. If at each step in a derivation a production is applied to the left most non terminal symbol, then the derivation is said to be a **Leftmost Derivation**.

Similarly, a derivation in which the rightmost non terminal symbol is replaced at each step is said to be a **Rightmost Derivation**.

A sentential form have several leftmost or rightmost derivations.

Ambiguity in a programming languages is to be avoided. Hence the study of ambiguity and how to construct unambiguous grammars is important.

Definition

A grammar G is said to be **ambiguous** if there is some word in L(G) generated by more than one leftmost derivation or rightmost derivation. (or) A grammar G is said to be **ambiguous** if there is some word in L(G) has atleast two derivation trees.

A grammar which is not ambiguous is said to be **unambiguous** (or) A grammar is said to be **unambiguous** if every word generated by it has a unique derivation tree.

Definition

A **language** is said to be **unambiguous** if there is atleast one unambiguous grammar generating it and **inherently ambiguous** if there is no unambiguous grammar generating it.

Example

Let G = {V_N, V_T, P, S} where V_N ={S, A} V_T = {a, b} and P consists of the production rules.

S : : = aAb | abSb | a, A :: = bS | aAAb.

The word abab $\in$ L(G) has two leftmost derivations, namely,

S $\Rightarrow$ abSb $\Rightarrow$ abab

and S $\Rightarrow$ aAb $\Rightarrow$ abSb $\Rightarrow$ abab

Thus abab is ambiguously derivable in G. Hence the grammar G is ambiguous.

Note that the derivation trees corresponding to the two left most derivation of abab are given by

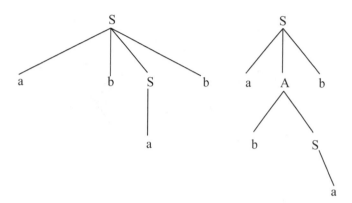

It is clear that the two derivation trees are different. That is we have two distinct derivation trees for the sentence abab generated by the grammar G. Hence the grammar G is ambiguous.

Example

Let G = {V_N, V_T, P, S} where V_N ={S, A} V_T = {a, b, c} and P consists of the production.

S : : = a^2Sa | aSa | | aS | λ

Consider a word aaa ∈ L(G). We shall derive this word by using leftmost derivations.

S ⇒ a^2Sa ⇒ a^2λa ⇒ a^3 = aaa and S ⇒ a S a ⇒ aa S a ⇒ aa λ a ⇒ aaa

i.e., the word **aaa** ∈ L(G) has more than one leftmost derivation. Thus G is ambiguous,

Note that the derivation trees corresponding to the two leftmost derivations of **aaa** are.

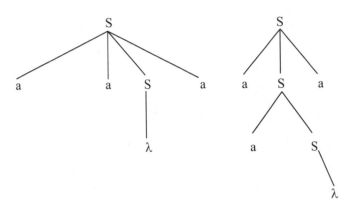

That is the word **aaa** has more than one derivation tree. Hence G is ambiguous.

Example

      Consider a grammar G for arithmetic expressions consisting of the operations +

and * with single letter variables :

<expression> : : = i | <expression> + <expression> | <expression> *

                  <expression>

For the sentence i * i + 1, the two possible leftmost derivations are

<expression> $\Rightarrow$ <expression> * <expression> $\Rightarrow$ i * <expression>

        $\Rightarrow$ i * <expression> + <expression> $\Rightarrow$ i * i + <expression>

        $\Rightarrow$ i * i + i

and <expression> $\Rightarrow$ <expression> + <expression>

          $\Rightarrow$ <expression> * <expression> + <expression>

          $\Rightarrow$ i * <expression> + <expression>

          $\Rightarrow$ i * i + <expression> $\Rightarrow$ i * i + i

Their corresponding derivation trees are given by

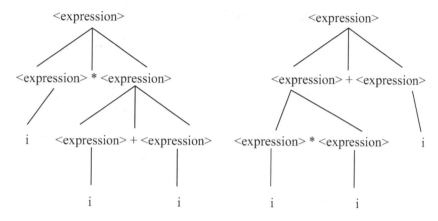

Since there are two distinct derivation trees for the sentences i * i + i, the grammar G is ambiguous. This is because it is not known whether to evaluate * before + or + before *.

Example

Let $G = (V_N, V_T, P, S)$, where $V_N = \{S\}$, $V_T = \{a\}$ an P consists of the productions $S \rightarrow a S$, $S \rightarrow a$.

Consider the language $L(G) = \{a^n \mid n \geq 1\}$

$$S \Rightarrow aS \qquad \Rightarrow aaS \Rightarrow a^3 = a^2 S$$

$$\overset{*}{\Rightarrow} a^{n-1} S \Rightarrow a^n$$

Also this is the only leftmost derivation of a^n in G. Thus the grammar G is unambiguous. Since the language L(G) is generated by the unambiguous grammar, L(G) is an unambiguous language.

6.6 FINITE STATE AUTOMATA

A class of machine which accept exactly the regular language (RL) or type-3 language (Regular set) is called as **Finite State Automata (FSA) or (Finite Automation (FA) or Finite State Machine (FSM).**

Functioning of FSA

The FSA consists of a finite number of **states** and a finite number of **input symbols**. There is a **start state** and designated set of **final states** (accepting states). The moves of the FSA are determined by a finite set of mappings.

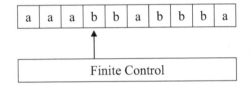

The set of states consists of the states of the finite control. There is a linear input tape containing the input symbols. Initially the finite controls is in the start state and is reading the left most symbol of the input tape. The input symbols are read one at a time, sequentially, from left to right. For every move there is change of state in the finite control. A string of input symbols ifs accepted when the finite control reads the input tape, symbol by symbol and enters a final state, after reading the right most input symbol.

6.7 DETERMINISTIC FINITE AUTOMATA (DFA)

Formal Definition (1) : (DFA)

A finite state automata M consist of

1. I : a finite non-empty set of input symbols.

2. S : a finite non-empty set of states.

3. $f : S X I \rightarrow S$, the next state function or state transition function defined by $f(x, s_i)$

   $= g_x(s_i)$

4. $s_i \subseteq S$ of accepting states (or) set of final states.

5. The initial state s_0 of S. i.e. $M = (S, I, f, s_i, s_0)$

Notation and Meaning

1. The meaning of $f(s_0, a) = s_1$ is that, when M is in state s_0, reading the input symbol a, it can move one cell to right and go to state s_1.

2. The meaning of $f(s_0, \lambda) = s_0$ is that, when no input symbol is read, the machine does not change its state.

3. The interpretation of $f(s_i, x) = s_j$ is that the machine starting from state s_i, reads the strings x on the input tape from left to right and reaches the state s_j.

Definition 2

A word (or string or sentence or tape) is said to be **accepted** if the automata starts from the initial state and enters a final state after reading the word one letter at a time from left to right. The set of strings accepted by the automata is called the language accepted or recognized by the automata.

Definition 3

Let $M = (M = (S, I, f, s_i, s_0)$ be a finite state automata. A non-null string $a = x_1 x_2 \ldots x_n$ is said to be accepted by M if

(i) s_0 is the initial state,   (ii) $f(s_{i-1}, x) = s_i$, $i = 1, 2, \ldots, n$

(iii) s_n be an accepting state.

Definition 4

The set of all strings x accepted by M is denoted by $T(M) = \{x/f(s_0, x)\ \varepsilon\ S_i$, $x\ \varepsilon\ I^*\}$. It is called the language **Accepted or Recognized** by M, and this set of strings x is called a **Finite State Language or A Regular Set**.

State Diagram or Transition Diagram

The pictorial method of specifying the finite state machine is called the **state diagram or the transition diagram.**

Formal Definition 5

Let $M = (S, I, f, s_i, s_0)$ be a finite state automata. The state diagram of M is a digraph G whose vertices are the members of S. An arrow designates the initial state s_0. A directed edge (s_1, s_2) exists in G if there exists an input i with $f(s_1, i) = s_2$. Accepting states (Final States) are marked by double circle.

Example 1

$$M = \{S, I, f, S_0, A\}$$

Where $S = \{S_0, S_1\}$

$$I = \{a, b\}$$

f is defined by

$$f(S_0, a) = S_1, \quad f(S_0, b) = S_1$$

$f(S_!, a) = S_0, \quad f(S_1, b) = S_1$

It is given in M.

Solution

Here initial state is S_0, final (or) accepting state A.

$\therefore A = \{S_1\}$ is a finite-state automation.

The state table (or) transition table for this automation is shown in table.

S \ I	f	
	a	b
S_0	S_1	S_1
S_1	S_0	S_1

Here

$S \rightarrow$ States, $I \rightarrow$ Input Symbol

Here

$S = \{S_0, S_1\}, \ I = \{a, b\}$

The transition diagram (or) state diagram for this automation is

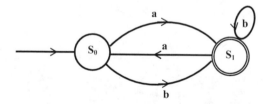

The accepting state S_1 is indicated by using double circles.

Example 2

Some times are FSA is denoted as

$M = \{S, I, O, f, g, S_0\}$ where the letters

S   → Consists of finite set of states

I   → Finite set of input symbols

O   → Finite set of output symbols

f   → A transition function f that assign a newstate to every pair of state and input

g   → An output function g that assign an output to every pair of state and

input and an initial state S_0.

Here $O = \{0, 1\}$, O consists of only two output symbols 0 and 1.

Here all the incoming edges for which have the same output label 1 is taken as

an accepting state.

Here

$\qquad M = \{S, I, O, f, g, S_0\}$

Where

$\qquad S = \{S_0, S_1\}, \qquad I = \{a, b\}, \qquad O = \{0, 1\}$

f is defined by $f(S_0, a) = S_1, f(S_0, b) = S_1$

$\qquad\qquad\qquad f(S_1, a) = S_0, f(S_1, b) = S_1$

$\qquad\qquad\qquad g(S_0, a) = 1, g(S_0, b) = 1$

$\qquad\qquad\qquad g(S_1, a) = 0, g(S_1, b) = 1$

Solution

State Table

S \ I	f		g	
	a	b	a	b
S_0	S_1	S_1	1	1
S_1	S_0	S_1	0	1

Consider f $S_0 \xrightarrow{a} \left(S_1 \right)$

Consider g $S_0 \xrightarrow{a}$ goes to S_1. So 1 is labeled near a.

The State Diagram

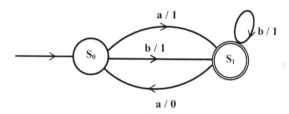

Here all the incoming edges for the states S_1 have the same output label 1 it is an accepting state and hence it is enclosed by double circles.

Note : If we want to check whether an input tape is accepted by the FSA we must start at the initial state and find out whether by traveling along the directed edges we reach a final state and on the way accepted the input, symbol by symbol.

Definition 6

Let $\alpha = x_1 x_2 \ldots\ldots x_n$ be a non-null string. Define the states $s_0, s_1, \ldots.., s_n$ (s_0 : initial, s_n : accepting state).

We call the (directed) path ($s_0, s_1, \ldots, s_n$), the path representing α in M.

An Important Note : If the path P represents the string α in a finite state automata M, then M accepts α if and only if P ends at an accepting state.

LANGUAGE ACCEPTED BY FSA

The string is said to be **recognized or accepted** by M (or) **rejected** by M.

The set of all strings that are accepted by M is called the Language **accepted or recognized** by M. Two finite state automata are said to be equivalent if they accept the same language.

Example 1

The string abbab is accepted by FSA. The string ababa is rejected by FSA (Finite State Automata).

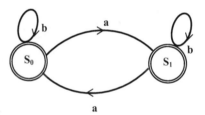

Note

abbab

From left to right process read one symbol at a time.

Solution

The sequential arrow diagram corresponding to the string abbab.

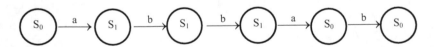

The last state is S_0 in the above diagram. The accepting state is S_0. So FSA accepts the string.

The sequential arrow diagram for ababa

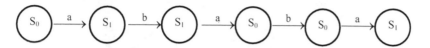

The last state in this diagram is not the accepting state in the state diagram given above. So it is rejected by FSA.

Example 2

Is the string abaa accepted by the finite state automata.

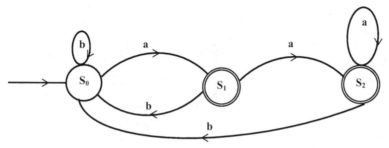

Solution

We begin at s_0. When **a** is input, we move to state s_1. When **b** is input, we move to state s_0, when **a** is input, we move to state s_1. Finally, when the last symbol **a** is input we move to state s_2.

The given string abaa

The path $(s_0, s_1, s_0, s_1, s_2)$ represents the string **abaa**. Since the final state s_2 is an accepting state, the string **abaa** is accepted by the finite state automata.

Example 3

Is the string α = abbabba accepted by the finite state automata.

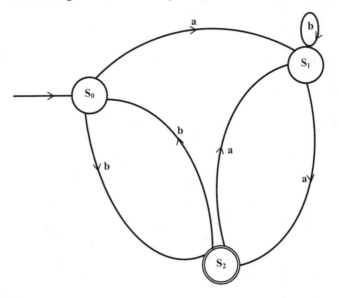

Solution

We start at s_0. When **a** is input, we move to state s_1. When **b** is input, we move to s_1, when **b** is input, we move to state s_1. When **a** is input, we move to state s_2 when **b** is input, we move to state s_0. When **b** is input, we move to state s_2. Finally, when the 1st symbol **a** is input, we move to state s_1.

The given string α = abbabba

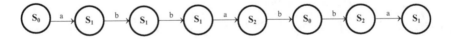

The path (s_0, s_1, s_1, s_1, s_2, s_0, s_2, s_1) represents the string α = abbabba. Since the final state is not an accepting state, the string α = abbabba is not accepted by the Finite State Automata.

Example 4

Design a finite state automata that accepts precisely those non-null strings over {a, b} that contain no a's.

Solution

Let us assume that the state s_0 : An a was found and s_1 : No a's were found.

Here s_0 is the initial state and the only accepting state. The finite state automata is defined by

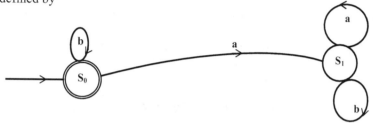

Example 5

Design a finite, state automata that accepts precisely those strings over {a, b} that contain an odd number of a's.

Solution

Let us assume that the state s_0 : An even number of a's was found, and s_1 : An odd number of a's was found. Here s_0 is the initial state and s_1 is the accepting state. We obtain the transition diagram as

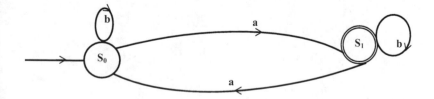

Definition 7

If $w = x_1, x_2, \ldots, x_n \in I^*$, we let $f_w = f_{x_n} \circ f_{x_{n-1}} \circ \ldots \circ f_{x_1}$ the composition of the

functions $f_{x_n}, f_{x_{n-1}}, \ldots f_{x_1}$. Also define $f_\lambda(s) = 1_s(s) = s$, for all s is S. In this way we

assign an element f_w of S^s to each element w of I^*. If we think of each f_x as the "effect"

of the input x on the states of the machine M, then f_w represents the combined effect of

all the input letters in the word w, received in the sequence specified by w. We call f_w

the **state transition function corresponding to w.**

PROBLEMS FOR DETERMINISTIC FINITE AUTOMATON

Example Problems

(1) Let M = (S, I, f, S_i, s_0) be a finite state machine, where S = {s_0, s_1, s_2}, I = {0, 1}

and f is given by the following state transition table

	0	1
s_0	s_0	s_1
s_1	s_2	s_2
s_2	s_1	s_0

Let   w   = $011 \in I^*$.

Solution

i.e., $f(0, s_0) = s_0 = f_0(s_0) = s_0$

$f(1, s_0) = s_1 = f_1(s_0) = s_1$

$f(0, s_1) = s_2 = f_0(s_1) = s_2$

$f(1, s_1) = s_2 = f_1(s_1) = s_2$

$f(0, s_2) = s_1 = f_0(s_2) = s_1$

$f(1, s_2) = s_0 = f_1(s_2) = s_0$

Here $f_w \rightarrow$ state transition function corresponding to w.

Then

$$f_w(s_0) \quad = \quad f_{011}(s_0)$$

Reverse 011, then we get 110

$$= \quad (f_1 \circ f_1 \circ f_0)\,(s_0)$$

$$= \quad (f_1 \circ f_1 \circ f_0\,(s_0))$$

$$= \quad (f_1 \circ f_1 \circ (s_0))$$

$$= \quad f_1(s_1) \qquad\qquad = \quad s_2$$

Similarly

$$f_w(s_1) \quad = \quad (f_1 \circ f_1 \circ f_0(s_1))$$

$$= \quad (f_1 \circ f_1 \circ (s_2))$$

$$= \quad (f_1(s_0)) \qquad\qquad = \quad s_1$$

and $f_w(s_2) \quad = \quad (f_1 \circ f_1 \circ f_0(s_2))$

$$= \quad (f_1 \circ f_1 \circ (s_1))$$

$$= \quad (f_1\,(s_2)) \qquad\qquad\qquad = \quad s_0$$

Result:

$$f_{011}(s_0) = s_2$$

$$f_{011}(s_1) = s_1$$

$$f_{011}(s_2) = s_0$$

(2) Let $M = (S, I, f, S_i, s_0)$ be a finite state machine whose transition or state diagram is given by

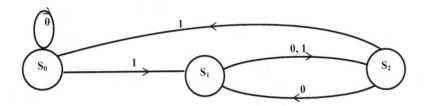

Let us compute f_w where $w = 01011$

Solution

The successive transitions of s_0 are

$$S_0 \xrightarrow{0} \boxed{S_0} \xrightarrow{1} \boxed{S_1} \xrightarrow{0} \boxed{S_2} \xrightarrow{1} \boxed{S_0} \xrightarrow{1} \boxed{S_1}$$

Here start at S_0, first input is 0, it goes to S_0, the 2nd input is 1, it goes to S_1 and so on.

$\therefore f_w(s_0) = f_{01011}(s_0) = s_1$

Similarly, the successive transitions of s_1 are (input 01011)

$$S_1 \xrightarrow{0} \boxed{S_2} \xrightarrow{1} \boxed{S_0} \xrightarrow{0} \boxed{S_0} \xrightarrow{1} \boxed{S_1} \xrightarrow{1} \boxed{S_2}$$

$\therefore f_w(s_1) = s_2$ and the successive transitions of S_2 are (input is 01011)

$$S_2 \xrightarrow{0} \boxed{S_1} \xrightarrow{1} \boxed{S_2} \xrightarrow{0} \boxed{S_1} \xrightarrow{1} \boxed{S_2} \xrightarrow{1} \boxed{S_0}$$

$f_w(s_2) = s_0$

(3) $M = (\{q_0, q_1, q_2\}, \{a, b\}, \delta, q_0, \{q_2\})$ is a finite automaton δ is given by

$\delta(q_0, a) = q_1$ $\delta(q_0, b) = q_2$

$\delta(q_1, a) = q_1$ $\delta(q_1, b) = q_2$

$\delta(q_2, a) = q_1$ $\delta(q_0, b) = q_0$

Here

$\{q_0, q_1, q_2\} \rightarrow$ Set of States

$\{a, b\}$ Input symbols

$\delta \rightarrow$ Next state function

$q_0 \rightarrow$ Initial State

$q_2 \rightarrow$ Accepting State

Construct the table & state transition diagram for the automaton.

Solution

Table

	a	b
q_0	q_1	q_2
q_1	q_1	q_2
q_2	q_1	q_0

State Transition Diagram

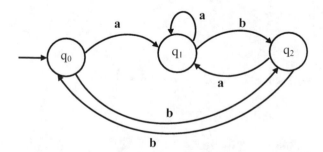

(4) $M = (\{q_0, q_1, q_2\}, \{a, b\}, \delta, q_0, \{q_2\})$ is a finite automaton δ is given by

i q	a	b
q_0	q_1	q_2
q_1	q_1	q_2
q_2	q_1	q_0

Find $\delta(q_0, abab)$, $\delta(q_2, bbab)$

Solution

From transition table

$\delta[q_0, a] = q_1$ $\delta(q_1, a) = q_1$ $\delta[q_2, a] = q_1$

$\delta[q_0, b] = q_2$ $\delta[q_1, b] = q_2$ $\delta[q_2, b] = q_0$

(i) $\delta[q_0, abab]$

     $= \delta(q_0, a)\, bab$ here $\delta(q_0, a) = q_1$

     $= \delta[q_1, bab]$ here $\delta(q_1, b) = q_2$

     $= \delta[q_2, ab]$ here $\delta(q_2, a) = q_1$

     $= \delta[q1, b]$ $= q_2$

(ii) $\delta[q_2, bbab]$

     $= \delta[q_0, bab]$ here $\delta(q_0, b) = q_2$

     $= \delta[q_2, ab]$ here $\delta(q_2, a) = q_1$

     $= \delta[q_1, b]$ $= q_2$

(iii) $\delta(q_1, \in)$ $= q_1$

(5) Let $M = \{\{q_0, q_1, q_2, q_3\}, \{a, b\}, \delta, q_0, \{q\}\}$ where δ is given by

     $\delta(q_0, a) = q_1$ $\delta(q_0, b) = q_2$

     $\delta(q_1, a) = q_3$ $\delta(q_1, b) = q_0$

$$\delta(q_2, a) = q_2 \qquad\qquad \delta(q_2, b) = q_2$$

$$\delta(q_3, a) = q_2 \qquad\qquad \delta(q_3, b) = q_2$$

(a) Represent M by its state table.

(b) Represent M by its state diagram.

(c) Which of the following strings are accepted by M ?

(i) ababa   (ii) aabba   (iii) aaaab   (iv) bbbaa

Solution

a) The state table (or) transition table

State	Inputs	
	a	b
q_0	q_1	q_2
q_1	q_3	q_0
q_2	q_2	q_2
q_3	q_2	q_2

In the given problem M = {{q_0, q_1, q_2, q_3}, {a, b}}

(b) State Diagram

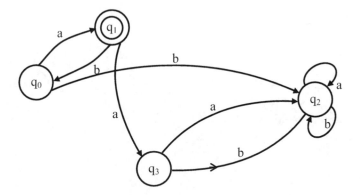

(c) Which of the following strings are accepted by M ?

(i) ababa

$$\delta (q_0, ababa) = \delta (q_1, ababa)$$

$$= \delta (q_0, aba)$$

$$= \delta (q_1, ba)$$

$$= \delta (q_0, a) = q_1$$

Here q is the finite state. In the transition diagram q_1 is the finite state. Hence ababa is accepted by M. Since q_1 is finite state.

(ii) $\delta (q_0, aabba)$

$$= \delta (q_1, abba) = \delta (q_3, bba), \delta (q_2, ba)$$

$$= \delta (q_2, a) = q_2$$

As q_2 is not a finite state aabba is not accepted by M.

(iii) $\delta (q_0, aaaab)$

$$= \delta (q_1, aaab) = \delta (q_3, aab) = \delta (q_2, ab)$$

$$= \delta (q_2, b) = q_2$$

is not accepted by M.

(iv) $\delta (q_0, bbbaa) = q_2$, so bbbaa

is not accepted by M.

Example

Let $M = (S, I, f, S_i, s_0)$ be a finite state machine, where $S = \{s_0, s_1, s_2\}$, $I = \{0, 1\}$ and f is given by the following state transition table

	0	1
s_0	s_0	s_1
s_1	s_2	s_2
s_2	s_1	s_0

Let $\qquad$ w $\qquad = \qquad 011 \in I^*$.

Solution

i.e., $f(0, s_0) = s_0 = f_0(s_0) = s_0$

$\qquad f(1, s_0) = s_1 = f_1(s_0) = s_1$

$\qquad f(0, s_1) = s_2 = f_0(s_1) = s_2$

$\qquad f(1, s_1) = s_2 = f_1(s_1) = s_2$

$\qquad f(0, s_2) = s_1 = f_0(s_2) = s_1$

$\qquad f(1, s_2) = s_0 = f_1(s_2) = s_0$

Here $f_w \rightarrow$ State Transition Function Corresponding to w.

Then

$$f_w(s_0) = \qquad f_{011}(s_0)$$

Reverse 011, then we get 110

$$= \qquad (f_1 \circ f_1 \circ f_0)(s_0)$$

$$= \qquad (f_1 \circ f_1 \circ f_0(s_0))$$

$$= \qquad f_1 \circ f_1 \circ s_0$$

$$= \qquad f_1(s_1) \qquad \qquad = \qquad s_2$$

Similarly

$$f_w(s_1) = (f_1 \circ f_1 \circ f_0(s_1))$$

$$= (f_1 \circ f_1(s_2))$$

$$= (f_1(s_0)) \qquad = \qquad s_1$$

and $\quad f_w(s_2) = (f_1 \circ f_1 \circ f_0(s_2))$

$$= (f_1° f_1(s_1))$$

$$= (f_1(s_2)) \qquad = \qquad s_0$$

Answer

$$f_{011}(s_0) = s_2$$

$$f_{011}(s_1) = s_1$$

$$f_{011}(s_2) = s_0$$

(2) Let $M = (S, I, f, S_i, s_0)$ be a finite state machine whose transition or state diagram is given by

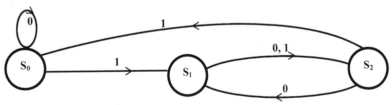

Let us compute f_w where $w = 01011$

Solution

The successive transitions of s_0 are

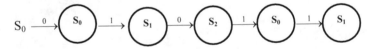

Here start at S_0, first input is 0, it goes to S_0, the second input is 1, it goes to S_1 and so on.

$$\therefore f_w(s_0) = f_{01011}(s_0) = s_1$$

Similarly, the successive transitions of s_1 are (input 01011)

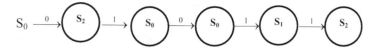

$\therefore f_w(s_1) = s_2$ and the successive transitions of S_2 are (input is 01011)

$$S_2 \xrightarrow{0} S_1 \xrightarrow{1} S_2 \xrightarrow{0} S_1 \xrightarrow{1} S_2 \xrightarrow{1} S_0$$

$f_w(s_2) = s_0$

6.8 NON-DETERMINISTIC FINITE-STATE AUTOMATA

A generalization of DFA called a **Non-Deterministic Finite-State Automata (NFA)**, which despite its reputation for supernatural behaviour, also proves to be a valuable tool for pattern recoginition. A NFA is usually much easier to design then the corresponding DFA. In NFA, one state is distinguished as an initial state, one or more are distinguished as accepting states, and there are labeled, directed edges, connecting the states.

A string is accepted by the NFA if and only if there is path from the initial state to one to the accepting states, such that the edge labels on the path generate the string.

Definition

A non-deterministic finite-state automata (NFA) M is $M = (S, I, A, f, s_0)$ or

$M = (Q, \Sigma, F, \delta, q_0)$

where

    (i)   Q (or) S : a finite non-empty set of states.

    (ii) Σ (or) I : a finite non-empty set of input symbols.

(iii) F (or) A : a subset of S of accepting states.

(iv) δ (or) f : a mapping from SXI to the finite subsets of S.

(v) q_0 (or) s_0 : the initial state and s_0 ε S.

Note : The main difference between the DFA and NFA is that in the DFA, $f(s_i, a)$ is a single state, while in a NFA, $f(s_i, a)$ may consists of a set of (possibly empty) states, i.e., $f(s_i, a) = \{s_1, s_2, \ldots, s_k\}$ means that when M is in the state s_i, reading the input 'a' on the input tape, it can move to any one of the states $s_1, s_2, \ldots, s_k$ as the next state and start reading the input symbol to the right of 'a'.

Example Problem

(1) Let $M = (S, I, A, f, s_0)$ be a NFA where $S = \{s_0, s_1, s_2\}$, $I = \{a, b\}$ and s_0 is the initial state, f is defined by

$$f(s_0, a) = \{s_0, s_1\}, \ f(s_1, a) = \phi, f(s_1, b) = \{s_2\}$$

$$f(s_2, a) = \phi, f(s_2, b) = \{s_2\}, f(s_0, b) = \phi \text{ and } A = \{s_2\},$$

here A is a final state.

(i) Draw a transition diagram and check whether it is DFA or NFA

Solution

Construct Transition Table

	a	b
s_0	s_0, s_1	ϕ
s_1	ϕ	s_2
s_2	ϕ	s_2

ϕ means empty values (or) null

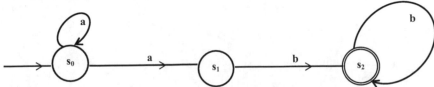

This is a NFA, because $f(s_0, a)$ can be either s_0 or s_1.

Note : DFA and NFA represented the type-3 or Regular Language.

Difference between Deterministic FSA and Nondeterministic FSA

If, in a finite state automaton the transition function assigns a unique next state to every pair of state and input, then the FSA is called a deterministic finite state automation (DFA).

On the other hand if the transition function assigns several next states to every pair of state and input, the FSA is called a non deterministic finite state automaton (NFA).

1) State table for NFA is given

S \ I	F	
	a	**b**
S_0	$\{S_1, S_2\}$	ϕ
S_1	$\{S_1\}$	$\{S_0, S_2\}$
S_2	ϕ	ϕ

Initial state is S_0. Accepting states are S_1 and S_2

For $(S_0, b) = \phi$

$(S_2, a) = \phi$ and $(S_2, b) = \phi$ combinations, there is no output. These are not marked by edges in the diagram. The state diagram for NFA is

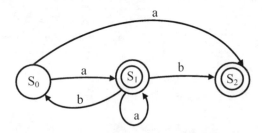

Language Accepted by NFA

A non null string α is accepted by an NFA. The set of all strings accepted by an NFA is called the language accepted by the NFA.

For Example

aab, aaba are accepted or rejected by NFA.

Problems

(1) Draw the transition diagram of the NFA, M = {S, I, A, F, S_0}, where I = {a, b}, S = {S_0, S_1, S_2}, A = {S_1, S_2} with initial state S_0 and next state function.

S / I	a	b
S_0	{S_0, S_1}	{S_2}
S_1	ϕ	{S_1}
S_2	{S_1, S_2}	ϕ

(ii) Is the string α = aabaabb accepted by the NFA (i)

Solution

Here S_0 is the initial state and S_1, S_2 are accepting states. The transition diagram is

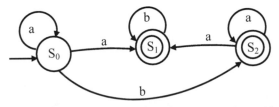

(ii) Given α = aabaabbb

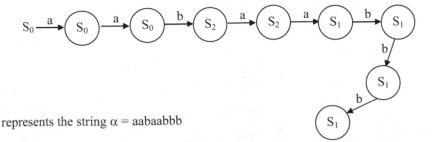

represents the string α = aabaabbb

Here final state is S_1 is an accepting state, the string α is accepted by the above NFA.

The path $(S_0, S_0, S_0, S_2, S_2, S_1, S_1, S_1, S_1)$.

(2) Consider a regular grammar $G=\{V_T, V_N, S, P\}$ where $V_N=\{S, A\}$, $V_T=\{a, b\}=I$ and the set of productions $P = \{S \rightarrow aA, A \rightarrow aA, A \rightarrow bS, A \rightarrow a\}$.

The corresponding automata is $M = (S, I, A, f, s_0)$ where $S = \{s_0, A, B)$, f is defined as follows :

$$f(s_0, a) = A, f(A, a) = \{A, B\}, f(A, b) = s_0$$

The corresponding transition diagram is

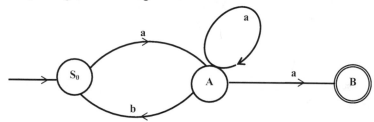

Clearly M is NFA (Non-deterministic Finite-state automata) and its accepting state is B.

$$L(G) = T(M).$$

Note

Two automatas M, M' are said to be equal if $T(M) = T(M')$, i.e., if they accept exactly the same language.

Example

(i) Draw the transition diagram of the NFA, $M = (S, I, A, f, s_0)$, where

$$I = \{a, b\}, S = \{s_0, s_1, s_2\}, A = \{s_1, s_2)$$

With initial state s_0 and next state function

I \\ S	a	b
s_0	$\{s_0, s_1\}$	$\{s_2\}$
s_1	ϕ	$\{s_1\}$
s_2	(s_1, s_2)	ϕ

(ii) Is the string α = aabaabbb accepted by the NFA (i).

Solution

(i) Here s_0 is the initial state and s_1, s_2 are accepting states. The transition diagram is

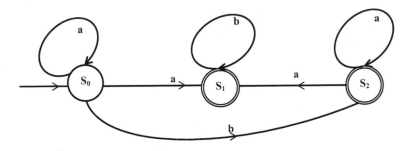

(ii) Given α = aabaabbb

The path $\{s_0, s_0, s_0, s_2, s_2, s_1, s_1, s_1, s_1\}$ represents the string a = aabaabbb. Since the final state s_1 is an accepting state, the string α is accepted by the above NFA.

6.9 PROCEDURE FOR CONVERTING NON-DETERMINISTIC FINITE STATE AUTOMATA (NFA) TO DETERMINISTIC FINITE STATE AUTOMATA (DFA).

Given a NFA, M = (S, I, A, f, s_0), where

I : a set of input symbols, S : a finite set of states,

A : a subset of S, consisting the accepting states,

s_0 : initial state, f : the next state function.

Construct the corresponding deterministic finite state automata (DFA),

$M' = (S', I, A', f', s_0')$

(i) Here the input I is unchanged

(ii) The states S' consisting of all subsets of the original set S, i.e., $S' = (P(S) = Power$ set of S).

(iii) The initial state is s_0'.

(iv) The accepting (A') states are all subset of A that contain an accepting state of the original

i.e., $A' = \{X \subseteq A / X \cap A \neq \phi\}$

(v) The next state function f' is defined by

$$f'(X, x) = \begin{cases} \phi, \text{ if } X = \phi \\ \underset{s \in X}{\cup} f(s,x) \text{ if } X \neq \phi \end{cases}$$

(vi) Draw the transition diagram of M' and by deleting states which can never be reached, we can obtain the simplified DFA (M') equivalent to the given NFA.

Example Problem

(1) Construct a deterministic finite state automata (DFA) equivalent to a given Non-deterministic finite state automata (NFA).

Let $\qquad M = (S, I, A, f, s_0)$ is a NFA,

Where $\qquad S = \{s_0, s_1, s_2\}$, $I = \{a, b\}$, s_0 is the initial state and s_2 is the accepting state. The next state function f is defined by

f	a	b
s_0	$\{s_0, s_1\}$	ϕ
s_1	ϕ	$\{s_2\}$
s_2	ϕ	$\{s_2\}$

and its transition diagram is given by

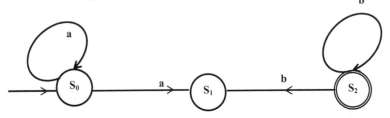

Solution

Consider a deterministic finite state automata (DFA),

M' $= (S', I, A', f, s_0')$ where

S' $= \{\{s_0\}, \{s_1\}, \{s_2\}, \{s_0, s_1\}, \{s_0, s_2\}, \{s_1, s_2\}, \{s_0, s_1, s_2\}, \phi\}$

       $=$ collection of all subsets of S.

Here S' $=$ Consisting of all subsets of original set S

            (i.e.) $S' = P(S) =$ Power Set of S

Note :

Power Set : A collection of family of all subsets of S is called power set of S.

It is denoted as $P(S)$.

Example

If $A = \{x, y\}$, $P(A) = \{\{x\}, \{y\}, \{x, y\}, \{\ \}\}$

$nP(A) = 2^m$

Here $m = n(A)$

I $= \{a, b\}$, $s_0' = \{s_0\}$

A' $= \{\{s_2\}, \{s_0, s_2\}, \{s_1, s_2\}, \{s_0, s_1, s_2\}\}$

= collection of subsets of A that contain an accepting state of

the original NFA.

The next state function f' is defined by

f'	A	b
$\{s_0\}$	$\{s_0, s_1\}$	ϕ
$\{s_1\}$	ϕ	$\{s_2\}$
$\{s_2\}$	ϕ	$\{s_2\}$
$\{s_0, s_1\}$	$\{s_0, s_1\}$	$\{s_2\}$
$\{s_0, s_2\}$	$\{s_0, s_1\}$	$\{s_2\}$
$\{s_1, s_2\}$	ϕ	$\{s_2\}$
$\{s_0, s_1, s_2\}$	$\{s_0, s_1\}$	$\{s_2\}$
ϕ	ϕ	ϕ

i.e. $$f'(X, x) = \begin{cases} \phi, & \text{if } X = \phi \\ \bigcup_{s \in X} f(s,x) & \text{if } X \neq \phi \end{cases}$$

Consider Transition Diagram

Here we start from S_0, a goes to S0 again it also goes to S_1, so we get

$S_0\{S_0, S_1\}$.

From S_0 there is no output of b.

So ϕ (null set) no output.

$\{S_1\} \rightarrow$ a $\rightarrow \{\phi\}$

$\{S_1\} \rightarrow$ b $\rightarrow \{S_2\}$

$\{S_2\} \rightarrow$ a $\rightarrow \{\phi\}$

$\{S_2\} \rightarrow$ b $\rightarrow \{S_2\}$

$\{S_0, S_1\} \rightarrow S_0 \xrightarrow{a} \{S_0, S_1\}$, similarly $S_1 \xrightarrow{a} \{\phi\}$

Now the transition diagram is given by

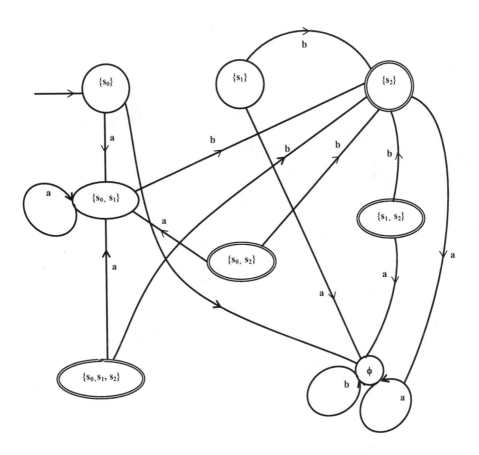

Here the states $\{s_0, s_2\}$, $\{s_1, s_2\}$, $\{s_0, s_1, s_2\}$, $\{s_1\}$ which can never be reached can be deleted (except the initial state). Thus we obtain the simplified, equivalent deterministic finite state automata (DFA) M′ corresponding to the given Non-deterministic finite state automata (NFA).

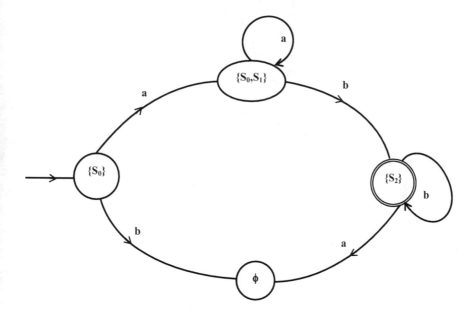